Is Goodness without God Good Enough?

Is Goodness without God Good Enough?

A Debate on Faith, Secularism, and Ethics

Edited by
Robert K. Garcia and Nathan L. King

ROWMAN & LITTLEFIELD PUBLISHERS, INC.
Lanham • Boulder • New York • Toronto • Plymouth, UK

ROWMAN & LITTLEFIELD PUBLISHERS, INC.

Published in the United States of America
by Rowman & Littlefield Publishers, Inc.
A wholly owned subsidiary of The Rowman & Littlefield Publishing Group, Inc.
4501 Forbes Boulevard, Suite 200, Lanham, Maryland 20706
www.rowmanlittlefield.com

Estover Road, Plymouth PL6 7PY, United Kingdom

British Library Cataloguing in Publication Information Available

Library of Congress Cataloging-in-Publication Data

Is goodness without God good enough? : a debate on faith, secularism, and ethics /
edited by Robert K. Garcia and Nathan L. King.
    p.   cm.
Includes bibliographical references.
ISBN-13: 978-0-7425-5170-1 (hardcover : alk. paper)
ISBN-10: 0-7425-5170-9 (hardcover : alk. paper)
ISBN-13: 978-0-7425-5171-8 (pbk. : alk. paper)
ISBN-10: 0-7425-5171-7 (pbk. : alk. paper)
ISBN-13: 978-0-7425-6389-6 (electronic)
ISBN-10: 0-7425-6389-8 (electronic)
1. Religion and ethics. I. Garcia, Robert K., 1970– II. King, Nathan L., 1976–
BJ47.I84 2009
205—dc22   2008012542

Printed in the United States of America

♾^{TM} The paper used in this publication meets the minimum requirements of American
National Standard for Information Sciences—Permanence of Paper for Printed Library
Materials, ANSI/NISO Z39.48-1992.

Contents

Preface

Professors Paul Kurtz and William Lane Craig came to Franklin and Marshall College in October of 2001 to debate the question that serves as this book's title: Is goodness without God good enough? Kurtz argued for the affirmative position and Craig the negative. After opening statements, they engaged in two rounds of rebuttal, followed by closing statements.

Months later, Kurtz and Craig agreed to publish the debate alongside a collection of new essays on the topic. The editors were fortunate to secure contributions from prominent scholars who represent a wide range of views about the relationship (if any) between God and ethics. These resulting essays both comment on the Kurtz/Craig debate and advance the discussion of the many important issues that arise therein. The volume closes with a pair of essays containing final reflections from Craig and Kurtz.

Some of our authors argue for a tight connection between God (or belief in God) and ethics. William Lane Craig argues that theism, and only theism, can serve as a metaphysical foundation for objective moral values, duty, and accountability. John Hare argues that the rational status of morality is undermined, absent belief in God. C. Stephen Layman argues that certain plausible and traditional claims about morality support the claim that God exists. Other authors (Paul Kurtz, Louise Antony, Donald Hubin, and Walter Sinnott-Armstrong) argue that a wide range of traditional ethical beliefs fit comfortably within a secular worldview. Moreover, they add, such beliefs cannot gain support from theism. Still other authors (Mark Murphy and Richard Swinburne) argue for positions that in important respects lie between the views mentioned above. The overall result is a multifaceted discussion among first-rate scholars, all of whom take morality seriously. We the editors hope that the discussions in this book will benefit students, scholars, and laypersons who wish to think more carefully about religion and morality.

We have a long list of people to thank for helping us bring this project to completion. We would first like to thank Franklin and Marshall College for sponsoring the debate that was the genesis of this volume. Thanks to Michael Murray, who organized the debate on behalf of the Bonchek Institute for Rational Thought and Inquiry at Franklin and Marshall (now known as Bonchek Institute for Reason and Science in a Liberal Democracy). We are especially grateful to Mike for encouraging us to take on this project and for providing invaluable advice throughout the editorial process. Mike's wisdom and encouragement were simply essential to this book's success. Thanks also to Suzanne Campbell (Suzanne Farmer at the time) for her tireless efforts on behalf of the Institute and the event. Our teachers David Solomon and Jim Sterba provided generous and helpful advice at crucial points in the development of this project, including our preparation of the introduction. Likewise, William Lane Craig, Paul Kurtz, and Mark Murphy read various drafts of the introduction and provided many helpful suggestions. Others to whom appreciation is owed include Louise Antony, Robert Audi, Terrence Cuneo, C. Stephen Evans, Doug Geivett, John Hare, Donald Hubin, Steve Layman, Michael Loux, Walter Sinnott-Armstrong, and Fritz Warfield. We also thank Ross Miller, Ruth Gilbert, and Janice Braunstein of Rowman & Littlefield Publishers for their abundant good advice and considerable patience in working with a pair of rookie editors.

We are grateful to C. Malcolm Powers for generously allowing us to use a photo of his bronze sculpture, *Moses Breaking the Tablets of the Law*, as our cover image, and to Kurt Hillig for the photo itself. Thanks also to Marion Powers for arranging the photo shoot of Malcolm's work. More of Malcolm's work can be viewed at http://www.cmalcolmpowers.com.

We are grateful to our parents, Joe and Evelyn Garcia and Jim and Dede King, for many more acts of kindness and support than we could possibly recount. Thanks to (one-year-old) Joel Garcia, for reminding us that life's most important lessons aren't always learned from books. Finally, we thank our wives, Amy Garcia and Kristie King, who provided a great deal of encouragement and tolerated frequent absences while we carried out this project. We gratefully dedicate this volume to them, without pretending that we have thereby begun to repay their loving support.

Introduction

Robert K. Garcia and Nathan L. King

[T]he lesson of today's terrorism is that if God exists, then everything, including blowing up thousands of innocent bystanders, is permitted—at least to those who claim to act directly on behalf of God, since, clearly, a direct link to God justifies the violation of any merely human constraints and considerations.

—Slavoj Žižek, "Defenders of the Faith," *New York Times*, March 12, 2006

[T]hose are not to be tolerated who deny the being of a God. Promises, covenants, and oaths, which are the bonds of human society, can have no hold upon an atheist. The taking away of God, though but even in thought, dissolves all.

—John Locke, *A Letter concerning Toleration*

Dostoyevsky is reported to have written, "If God does not exist, then everything is permitted." This claim expresses a belief that has been widely held throughout the history of Western culture. The belief is that unless God exists, ethics is in serious trouble. This idea has seemed so obvious to some that it has been deployed as a premise in so-called moral arguments for the existence of God. In general, moral arguments have the following form:

1. If God does not exist, then some apparent and important feature F of ethics or the ethical life is illusory.
2. The apparent feature F of ethics or the ethical life is not illusory.
3. Thus, God exists.

Arguments of this form can be grouped into families in terms of the different features of morality for which God is alleged to be necessary. Some moral arguments, for instance, aim to show that the apparent *objectivity* of ethical

1

claims requires a theistic foundation. Other arguments focus on the apparent fact that moral reasons for action *override* all other kinds of reasons, and argue that there is no such fact if God does not exist. And, according to a third kind of moral argument, God's existence is needed to ground the apparent fact that the moral life is not futile. Many other kinds of moral arguments can be found in the literature.[1]

Moral arguments have occupied a relatively prominent place in the history of Western philosophy. Such arguments are part of a larger project—often called "natural theology"—that aims to support theistic belief by appeal to premises that are knowable by human reason or observation (and independent of special revelation from God). This project involves the articulation and defense of various arguments for the existence of God, such as design arguments, cosmological arguments, ontological arguments, and moral arguments. Natural theology was widely regarded as an intellectually viable project prior to the Enlightenment, and the arguments for God's existence are currently a topic of much discussion.[2]

The popularity of moral arguments, in particular, has likely been due to a widespread assumption that morality depends upon God. In keeping with this assumption, some have thought that nonbelievers cannot be trusted to act morally. The following comment by John Locke (1632–1704) is typical:

> [T]hose are not to be tolerated who deny the being of a God. Promises, covenants, and oaths, which are the bonds of human society, can have no hold upon an atheist. The taking away of God, though but even in thought, dissolves all.[3]

As we can see, Locke was suspicious about the moral trustworthiness of atheists. Although this suspicion may have been historically popular, it seems to be rejected by most contemporary philosophers. Indeed, each contributor to this volume rejects Locke's view on the matter. According to some, moreover, the widespread acceptance of a God-based morality has actually *impeded* moral and philosophical progress. When such a moral theory is firmly in place, one might find little incentive to search for a nontheistic foundation for ethics. Thus Derek Parfit writes, "Belief in God, or in many gods, prevented the free development of moral reasoning."[4]

During the Enlightenment, belief in God waned while moral reasoning flourished. Moreover, the idea that God plays an essential role in ethics was subjected to serious critique. It is fair to say that in the wake of the Enlightenment, belief in God was widely taken to be unsupportable by reason. Theism was defrocked, in no small part, by numerous published critiques of the traditional arguments for the existence of God; the impact of such objections is still with us.[5] As a result, many thinkers have concluded that God is either unreal or unknowable—and in either case, unavailable to play a role in an ethical theory.

In view of this, many Enlightenment and post-Enlightenment thinkers took themselves to have two options: either find a suitably adequate alternative to God, or deem certain apparent features of ethics illusory. Those whom we might call *pessimists* picked the latter option. They accepted the premise—that is, premise (1)—according to which, without God, ethics is in serious trouble. But they also took the Enlightenment critique of theism to provide sufficient reason to think that God is, in some way or another, no longer available to play a role in an ethical theory. And since by accepting (1) they in effect accepted the claim that nothing else can play that role, they drew the conclusion that ethics is in trouble. The following remark by the atheist-existentialist Jean-Paul Sartre is representative:

> Existentialists find it extremely disturbing that God no longer exists, for along with his disappearance goes the possibility of finding values in an intelligible heaven. There could no longer be any a priori good, since there would be no infinite and perfect consciousness to conceive of it. Nowhere is it written that good exists, that we must be honest or must not lie, since we are on a plane shared only by men. Dostoyevsky once wrote: "If God does not exist, everything is permissible." . . . Indeed, everything is permissible if God does not exist, and man is consequently abandoned, for he cannot find anything to rely on—neither within nor without.[6]

Referring back to our syllogism, pessimists like Sartre took (1) to be true and (3) to be false; they thus inferred the falsity of (2).[7]

Other philosophers—call them *optimists*—took (2) to be true but (3) to be false. They accordingly inferred the falsity of (1)—that is, the claim that ethics depends upon God. Thus, the optimists bore the burden of finding a nontheological foundation for ethics. We may better understand the optimists' project by contrasting it with the Ancient and Medieval ethical theories that preceded it. A crucial feature of these theories is the notion of a *telos*, an ultimate end, purpose, or goal, which is essential to and shared by all things of a certain kind. In the Ancient and Medieval view, a thing's *telos* determines what it is to be a good thing of that sort. For example, the purpose of a knife is to cut things, and a knife can cut well only if it is sharp. Thus, a knife fulfills its *telos* only if (and to the extent that) it is sharp.

For much of the history of Western thought, it was believed that not only artifacts, but also living things, have a *telos* in the sense described above. In particular, such important thinkers as Plato, Aristotle, Augustine, and Aquinas unite in claiming that human beings have a *telos*. The latter two thinkers believe that humans have the *telos* they do in virtue of God's having created human beings and given their lives a specific purpose—chiefly, to know God himself. On some interpretations, the Platonic and Aristotelian accounts of human teleology, though perhaps not fully theistic, are nevertheless theological in the sense that they link the human *telos* to the divine in substantive ways (for more on these theories, see John Hare's chapter in this volume). In any case, the notion of a human *telos* plays a crucial role in all four thinkers' ethical theories.

On Alasdair MacIntyre's influential account, these theories are structured by a three-part conceptual scheme consisting of (i) human nature as it is, (ii) moral precepts (i.e., principles for moral action), and (iii) human nature as-it-could-be-if-it-realized-its-*telos*. Very roughly, a crucial purpose of moral precepts (second component) is to tutor untrained human nature (first component) in such a way as to move it closer to its *telos* (third component).[8] On MacIntyre's view, the concepts comprising this structure are mutually inter-dependent—each concept is intelligible only when taken together with the other two. Thus, cutting out one part of this conceptual structure renders the remaining parts unintelligible conceptual fragments.[9]

So, ethical theorizing in the Ancient and Medieval periods was substantially teleological. Moreover, as we saw above, some important philosophers during these periods considered teleology to be essentially bound up with theological premises. With the advent of the Scientific Revolution, however, the teleological view of the world was called into question. This trend unfolded first in the downfall of Aristotle's physics and biology, and gradually found its way into thinking about human nature. Physicists began to center their attention on *efficient* or *push causes* instead of *final causes*. (To see the difference between efficient and final causes, consider a billiards player hitting the cue ball so as to send the eight ball into the corner pocket. The collisions between the cue stick and the cue ball, and the cue ball with the eight ball, are examples of efficient causation. The player's intention of landing the eight ball in the corner pocket fixes the final cause of his action, namely, the ball landing in the pocket.) Purpose-oriented, teleological explanations of physical phenomena became less and less prominent in physical theories; similar developments in biology led many to expunge even the notion of a human *telos*. These trends, coupled with the above-mentioned crisis in theology, led many traditional ethicists to seek an ethical theory that was both nontheological and nonteleological.[10] This search has been called the "Enlightenment Project,"[11] and its proponents include those we have dubbed optimists above.

Both Modern and contemporary attempts to carry out the Enlightenment Project divide into several branches, resulting in numerous competing ethical theories.[12] Some of these account for moral norms in terms of rational norms—on such views, to be immoral is, at root, to be irrational. Others account for the moral status of an action in terms of its empirical consequences. Utilitarianism, for example, says that an action is immoral if, relative to other possible acts, it produces an overall disfavorable proportion of pain to pleasure in society as a whole. Still other prominent accounts could be mentioned. What is notable, however, is the widespread disagreement as to which account, if any, provides an adequate nontheological and nonteleological account of ethics. Nor, on the other hand, is there agreement as to whether an updated theological and/or teleological account would be adequate.

Not surprisingly, some have declared that we have a crisis on our hands. This crisis, moreover, is no longer quarantined inside the academy walls. According to John Rist,

> The *effects* of this crisis in ethical theory are already visible in the world outside the universities as well as inside: in reassessments of our responsibility for the poor in Western states (not to speak of those in the Third World), in arguments over the "ethics" of the market economy or of modern warfare or arms trading, in debates about what, if any, public policies should be adopted to control research in genetics and about the increasing number of "quality of life" issues which arise in the practice of medicine.[13]

It seems, then, that Western culture is to a significant extent confused about the structure and content of morality, even as lively discussion of these issues continues.

Concurrent with the crisis in ethics has been a series of interesting developments in the philosophy of religion. By the middle of the twentieth century, much of Western culture remained under Judeo-Christian influence. The same was not true of philosophy as an academic discipline. To be sure, there were many theistic philosophers about in those days, particularly at Catholic universities. But philosophy as practiced in the world's most prestigious departments was markedly nontheistic.

Nontheistic philosophers typically fell into one of two groups. In the first group were those who claimed that there is no God—that is, who claimed that the statement "God exists" is *false*. Prominent among those belonging to the first group were the philosophical descendents of Marx, Freud, and Nietzsche. The latter's (1882) declaration "God is dead" had already gained widespread influence by mid-century.[14] The second group consisted of those who believed that such statements are neither true nor false, but rather, *meaningless*.[15] Belonging to the second group were the proponents of *logical positivism* and its infamous *verifiability criterion* of meaning. According to an important version of this criterion, a statement is cognitively meaningful if, and only if, it is either empirically verifiable or true by definition. And, so it went, because statements about God are neither empirically verifiable nor true by definition, such statements fail to carry cognitive meaning. This is not to say that religious statements are unimportant. Perhaps such statements can be used to express deep emotions or commend certain attitudes or behaviors.

Rather, the point is that religious claims are just not the *kind of thing* that can be true or false. And if not—if talk about God is meaningless in this sense—then questions about his existence and nature are nonstarters.[16]

Theism floundered in philosophical exile for much of the 1950s and 1960s. News of the exile began to appear in popular culture. More accurately, the news was not so much of theism's exile as of its *death*. A 1966 cover story in *Time* magazine asked, "Is God Dead?" and reported an affirmative answer, at least as far as many philosophers and theologians were concerned.[17]

But things change. In an ironic twist, the very next year confirmed the death, not of theism, but of logical positivism. The verifiability criterion of meaning was now widely thought to be self-defeating.[18] Thus, in 1967 John Passmore announced that "Logical positivism . . . is dead, or as dead as a philosophical movement ever becomes."[19] While Passmore rightly went on to note that logical positivism had left a philosophical legacy, the demise of the view nevertheless made room for serious philosophical discussions of theism. Talk of God was not at this point in the philosophical mainstream, but it was no longer regarded as *meaningless*.

In the same year that Passmore wrote his obituary for logical positivism, Alvin Plantinga published the book *God and Other Minds*, a carefully argued work advancing the claim that design arguments for God's existence are as strong as arguments for the claim that other minds exist.[20] This work marked the beginning of an unexpected renaissance in the philosophical treatment of several important religious topics. In the decades that followed, theistic philosophers used the most powerful conceptual tools available to revamp the traditional arguments for God's existence and to develop sophisticated treatments of the rationality of religious belief, religious experience, religious diversity, the problem of evil, immortality, and the relationship between God and ethics.[21] These developments were of such significance that they were soon detected outside of academic culture. In 1980 a follow-up article in *Time* reported:

> In a quiet revolution in thought and argument that hardly anyone could have foreseen only two decades ago, God is making a comeback. Most intriguingly, this is happening not among theologians or ordinary believers—most of whom never accepted for a moment that he was in any serious trouble—but in the crisp, intellectual circles of academic philosophers, where the consensus had long banished the Almighty from fruitful discourse. Now it is more respectable among philosophers than it has been for a generation to talk about the possibility of God's existence.[22]

The resurgence of theism was further evidenced by the founding of several professional organizations devoted to the philosophy of religion, including the Society of Christian Philosophers and the Evangelical Philosophical Society, along with their respective flagship journals, *Faith and Philosophy* and

Philosophia Christi. In an article detailing the recent history of the philosophy of religion, atheist Quentin Smith laments that during much of the late twentieth century,

> [n]aturalists passively watched as realist versions of theism, most influenced by Plantinga's writings, began to sweep through the philosophical community, until today perhaps one-quarter or one-third of philosophy professors are theists, with most being orthodox Christians. . . . God is not "dead" in academia; he returned to life in the late 1960s and is now alive and well in his last academic stronghold, philosophy departments.[23]

While Smith's numerical estimate may be a bit generous, it does speak to the felt impact of theism's return to the academic scene.

The point of the above story is *not* that the theists are "winning" the debate. Despite recent trends, naturalism remains the dominant view. On this score, a notable counterpart to the resurgence of philosophical interest in theism is the institution of *Philo*, a professional journal founded by Paul Kurtz in 1998 and published by the recently established Society of Humanist Philosophers. The express purpose of the journal is to define and defend philosophical naturalism and secular humanism (more on secular humanism below). The real point of the above story is that, regardless of whether they have religious commitments, many contemporary philosophers treat questions about God and religion with great seriousness. This is a good thing—such questions are too important to pass over. And if this is the case for questions about *God*, then it is more obviously the case for questions about *God and ethics*.

[An important aside here: One can ask important questions about "God and ethics" *without assuming that God exists*. We can appreciate this point by considering the sorts of questions that bear on the relationship between God and ethics. In rough and ready form, here are some of those questions:

- If God were to exist, would morality depend—whether completely or in part—upon God's commands or nature?
- If God exists and morality depends upon God, can a nonbeliever live a life that is genuinely morally praiseworthy?
- If God exists and morality depends upon God, do we have to consult a sacred text in order to know our moral obligations? And if so, how do we decide *which* sacred text to consult?
- If God exists and morality depends upon God, is the separation of church and state inadvisable?
- If God exists and one believes in God, can one do what is morally right for its own sake, rather than for the sake of reward or out of fear of punishment?

- If there is no God, is morality groundless, arbitrary, relative, or even illusory?
- If there is no God, do we lack a sufficient reason to do what is morally right, especially when doing so is not in our own self-interest?
- If there is no God, does it follow that morality is merely a human convention or by-product of natural selection? Would that implication be problematic?

Notice that all of the above questions are *hypothetical* in nature. Their conditional (if-then) form provides us with an invitation to suppose, *for the sake of argument*, that God exists (or does not exist), and to consider what follows from such suppositions. Many of the questions discussed in this volume are of just this sort. And as the essays in this volume make clear, "yes" and "no" answers to such questions do not always divide along the line between theists and nontheists.]

The main point at present is that answers to questions about God and ethics impact our lives in ways that our answers to other philosophical questions may not. For some of these questions, one's answers will naturally affect one's daily decisions, one's vote, and one's pocketbook. Thus, news headlines during recent elections have been abuzz with talk of "religion and morality," "faith-based initiatives," and "the separation of church and state" (where the latter is often glossed as "the separation of religion and law"). The outcomes of these elections have been largely shaped by the substantial views lying behind such buzzwords. Moreover, a glut of best-selling books has ensured that these terms and the discussions that attend them will remain in the popular consciousness for the foreseeable future.[24]

It should therefore be clear that we cannot address properly the great issues of our day without careful reflection on the connections, if any, between God and ethics. It was the importance of such reflection, together with the resurgence of theism and the continued prominence of secular humanism, that prompted this book. Created for the benefit of students, laypersons, and professionals, the book has three parts. Part I contains the edited version of a debate on the topic between Paul Kurtz and William Lane Craig. Part II contains seven new essays in which prominent philosophers comment on the debate and provide their own perspectives on the issue. In Part III, Craig and Kurtz respond to the essays in the second part of the book. In what remains of this introduction, we sketch some of the main arguments that occur in Parts I and II, presenting several important concepts along the way. Though our remarks are nowhere near comprehensive, they provide a map of the material in these parts of the book. The professional scholar may wish to skip these summaries, but may also find them useful in planning research, or in determining the order in which students should read.

SUMMARIES

The touchstone for the debate is the question "Is goodness without God good enough?" This question can be interpreted in several ways. Interpreting the question as pertaining primarily to human behavior, Kurtz argues for the affirmative position. One of his central claims is that belief in God is not a necessary condition for morally good behavior or character. On the contrary, many morally exemplary men and women throughout history have been non-believers. Moreover, religious belief often *impedes* moral progress and reasoning. This is evidenced both by the historical pervasiveness of evils committed in the name of religion and by the conflicting moral imperatives issued by competing religious traditions. Against Craig, Kurtz argues that morality requires no ontological foundation—and, indeed, putative reference to such a foundation is of no help in solving concrete moral problems. Kurtz therefore proposes to replace religion-based views of morality with what he calls *secular humanism*:

> What do I mean by secular humanism? I submit that first of all it expresses a set of ethical values and virtues. Humanists wish to enhance the intrinsic qualities of joyful and creative experiences, and to realize some measure of happiness in this life. . . . Humanists focus on temporal and secular values. They believe that their primary ethical obligation is to enrich life for ourselves and others. . . . Humanist ethical principles are autonomous, in the sense that they do not derive from theological or metaphysical premises.[25]

Particularly important for ethical decisions, Kurtz says, is reflection upon the consequences of one's actions. The good for mankind is "happiness in the here and now," and morally correct actions are those whose consequences promote this good. Finally, Kurtz notes, secular humanists acting in accordance with this ethic have produced much good in Western culture.

In contrast to Kurtz, Craig takes the debate's key question to concern moral *ontology* rather than moral behavior, psychology, or epistemology. For Craig, the relevant question is not whether one can behave morally without *belief* in God. Rather, the question is whether there would *be* objective moral values, duties, or accountability in an atheistic world. Craig aims to establish two conditional theses. First, if theism is true, then we have a solid foundation for morality. Second, if theism is false, then we do not have a solid foundation for morality. With respect to the first thesis, Craig argues that God's holy and loving nature grounds objective moral values, while God's commands constitute our moral duties. Likewise, God's providential justice guarantees moral accountability—God ensures that, ultimately, evil persons will be punished and that righteous persons will be vindicated. As to the second thesis, Craig argues that the atheistic view cannot account for objective moral values or duties, or for moral accountability. Though he refrains from arguing for God's existence directly, Craig does claim that if his second thesis is correct, then the atheistic position leads not to humanism, but to nihilism. In other words, given Craig's second thesis, the consistent atheist is forced toward the view that moral values are ultimately illusory—thus, goodness without God is not good enough. In Craig's view, the atheist must therefore either embrace nihilism or find a way to undermine his second thesis.

In the volume's first chapter after the debate, C. Stephen Layman offers a moral argument for the existence of God. Layman does not affirm Craig's claim that if theism is false, then there are no objective moral truths. In this respect, Layman stops short of fully endorsing Craig's position. In another respect, however, Layman goes *beyond* Craig's conditional claims in arguing that certain commonly held beliefs about morality support the claim that God exists. A central feature of morality, Layman says, is that whenever moral requirements are concerned, moral reasons for action always override other reasons. For example, an action might be morally required but performing it might be very unpleasant for the agent (think of protesting an injustice). Nevertheless, whenever moral duty is concerned, the moral reasons to perform the act outweigh or override any reasons one might have not to perform it. Our common moral beliefs, then, support the following thesis:

• Overriding Reasons Thesis (ORT): The overriding (or strongest) reasons always favor doing what is morally required.

ORT is widely accepted by both theists and nontheists. However, Layman argues, ORT is not a necessary truth. Indeed, ORT is true only if either God exists or there is life after death (or both). This latter claim is equivalent to the following thesis:

• Conditional Thesis (CT): If there is no God and no life after death, then the Overriding Reasons Thesis is not true.

Layman argues that certain thought experiments provide CT with significant intuitive support. And when conjoined with ORT, CT entails that either God exists or there is a life after death in which virtue will be rewarded (or both). This claim leaves open the possibility that there is no God, but there is nevertheless a life after death in which virtue is rewarded. However, Layman argues, the notion of a life after death in which virtue is rewarded is itself most plausibly accommodated by theism.

In her chapter "Atheism as Perfect Piety," Louise Antony agrees with Kurtz that belief in God is not necessary for living a moral life. She takes this a step further, however, by arguing that one can achieve perfect contrition for one's moral failings only if one does *not* believe in God. The reason is that a person who *does* believe in God will find it difficult, if not impossible, to remove thoughts of God's recompense from his or her contrition. Central to this line of thought is the principle that an all-good God who loves what is good will be more pleased with creatures who do what is good *because it is good* than with creatures who do what is good *in order to curry God's favor or avoid God's wrath*. According to Antony, this principle implies that God cares more about our doing what is right than our doing what is in accord with his will. As she puts it, "It's the right and wrong he cares about, not that he said do it or don't" (70). But this difference in what God cares about only makes sense if *that which is right* isn't simply constituted by *that which God commands*. In other words, it makes sense only if, contrary to what Craig thinks, morality isn't dependent upon God's commands.

Antony finds support for this line of thought in a famous dilemma found in Plato's *Euthyphro*.[26] The dilemma presents the theist with two options. Either (A) God commands us to do *x* because *x* is morally right, or (B) *x* is morally right because God commands us to do *x*. If (A) is the case, then *x* is morally right independent of what God commands, which suggests that morality isn't dependent upon God. Thus, for example, God commands us not to rape because rape is—independently of and prior to his command—morally wrong. Antony calls a theory that adopts (A) a divine independence theory (DIT). If (B) is the case, then an act *x*'s moral status depends upon God's will: *x* is wrong if and only if (and because) God commands us not to do *x*; *x* is permissible if and only if (and because) God does not command us not to do *x*; and, *x* is obligatory if and only if (and because) God commands us to do *x*. Thus, if God commands us not to rape, then rape is wrong; and if God commands us to rape, then rape is obligatory. A theory that adopts (B) is called a divine command theory (DCT). On Antony's view, the trouble with DCT is twofold. First, DCT implies that is it *possible* for any kind of action, such as rape, to not be wrong. But it seems intuitively impossible for rape not to be wrong. So, DCT is at odds with our commonsense intuitions about rape. And second, it suggests that the moral status of an action (such as rape) is arbitrary—merely due to what God happens to command. Given these objections to DCT, Antony argues that a theist should adopt DIT. But DIT is directly at odds with Craig's contention that moral values are dependent upon God.

Antony goes on to argue that many theists evince a rejection of DCT in their interpretive approach to certain biblical passages. The passages Antony has in mind are those that appear to represent God as commanding an act that

we ordinarily would take to be immoral. A standard example is 1 Samuel
15:1–3, where God commands an action that we would normally call genocide. As Antony notes, the interpretive principle that theists typically *don't*
use is "God commanded it, so it's good!" Instead, the theist usually looks for
an interpretation that is both adequate to the passage and consistent with both
(i) the fact, known independently of the passage, that genocide is wrong and
(ii) the doctrine of God's goodness. The soundness of this interpretive strategy aside, Antony's claim is that this pervasive strategy is incompatible with
DCT. As she says, if DCT is correct, that is, "if there is nothing more to moral
goodness than God's preferences, then there can be no rationale for seeking
alternative readings of morally troubling texts" (75).

In his contribution to the volume, John Hare addresses an important question that also serves as his title: "Is Moral Goodness without Belief in God
Rationally Stable?" In the first half of the chapter, Hare identifies two fundamental commitments of traditional morality that, in his view, cannot be defended adequately without appeal to theological premises. Hare devotes the
second half of the chapter to cataloguing the crucial role theological claims
have played in historically prominent ethical theories.

An important premise in Hare's argument is the so-called Ought Implies
Can principle (OIC). This principle is widely accepted in ethical theorizing
and is roughly the idea that if I cannot possibly do something, then the question whether I ought to do it does not in normal circumstances arise. More
simply: if I *ought* to do *x*, then I *can* do *x*. With OIC in hand, Hare draws our
attention to two fundamental moral principles, both of which state that we
ought to do something. For the sake of convenience, we have labeled these
"Ought1" and "Ought2," respectively:

(Ought1) We ought to be good in a way that is consistent with our own and
others' happiness.
(Ought2) We ought to become good *internally*.

Given OIC, from (Ought1) and (Ought2) we can infer the following claims
about what is *possible* for us:

(Can1) It is possible for us to be good in a way that is consistent with our own
and others' happiness.
(Can2) It is possible for us to become good *internally*.

Crucial to Hare's argument, then, is the claim that we are rational in accepting Ought1 (or Ought2) only if we are rational in accepting Can1 (or Can2).
According to Hare, a person is rationally unstable if he or she accepts Ought1
without good grounds for accepting Can1. The same goes for Ought2.

But what, precisely, are the claims that Can1 and Can2 express? And what grounds do we have for believing these claims? On Hare's reading, Can1 says that there is no fundamental incompatibility between our own happiness and that of others—the universe is the sort of place in which it is possible for us to pursue our own happiness without precluding others' well-being. But how is this possible? What reason do we have for thinking that the universe is this sort of place? Hare argues that the theist can defend his belief in this possibility via appeal to "the agency of Providence." The atheist, on the other hand, does not (*qua* atheist) have a good reason for thinking that this alignment of justice and personal advantage is possible. Because belief in this possibility is a fundamental commitment of morality, the atheist who is also a traditional moralist occupies a rationally unstable position.

Whereas Can1 concerns the coordination of one's own (morally permissible) ends with the (morally permissible) ends of others, Can2 expresses a commitment to the possibility of "achieving a morally good ranking of ends within oneself"—chiefly, to ranking our affection for our own advantage *under* our affection for what is good in itself, independent of its relation to our advantage (88). However, says Hare, this sort of ranking does not come naturally for us. There is a "moral gap" between our actual (and preferred) ways of acting and those that morality requires. The traditional religious solution to this problem is that God can close this gap through regeneration—that is, through reordering our desires. Hare explores a handful of nontheistic attempts to explain how the gap might be filled (or to explain away the gap itself). If all such attempts fail and no others are forthcoming, he suggests, then we are left with a choice: either abandon Can2 and traditional morality along with it, or accept the theistic solution to the problem of the moral gap.

In the second part of the chapter, Hare examines the three predominant moral theories in the teaching of ethics in Western universities—virtue theory, duty theory, and utilitarianism. He argues that the original versions of these theories were structurally dependent on theism, so that theological claims played a crucial role in the theories. For example, in Platonic and Aristotelian versions of virtue theory, the character traits most worthy of pursuit are those of divine beings. In Kantian duty theory, the supposition of God's existence is required to ensure the possibility that human virtue and happiness align. Similarly, in Mill's utilitarian theory, the hope that morality and happiness (pleasure) will coincide cannot be grounded apart from hope in divine providence and man's destiny after death. Thus, philosophers who advance versions of these theories that delete their theistic elements must consider whether something besides God can play the relevant conceptual role. If no such substitute can be found, then the resulting theories will be incoherent.

In "Why Traditional Theism Cannot Provide an Adequate Foundation for Morality," Walter Sinnott-Armstrong raises a number of objections against

Craig. We will mention only a few of these. Sinnott-Armstrong argues that the traditional theistic doctrine of God's transcendence undermines Craig's thesis that God's nature can supply an absolute standard for moral judgments. He argues as follows: In the course of making moral judgments, we clearly use *something* as a standard. But if something transcends our cognitive grasp, then we cannot use it as a standard. According to traditional theism, however, both God and his nature transcend our cognitive grasp. Thus, if traditional theism is true, then although God exists, we can use neither God nor his nature as a moral standard. But, again, we are using *something* as a standard in our moral judgments. So whatever it is that we are using as a standard, it cannot be God or his nature. On this point, Sinnott-Armstrong is in agreement with Kurtz that belief in God is not necessary for making moral judgments.

With respect to objective moral duties, Sinnott-Armstrong argues that Craig fails to explain how we have anything more than *prudential* reasons for obeying God's commands. Why, in other words, are we *morally* obligated to obey God's commands? Sinnott-Armstrong also challenges Craig's resolution of the *Euthyphro* dilemma. To avoid the charge that God's commands are arbitrary, Craig claims that such commands "flow from his nature." God's command to not rape, for example, is grounded in God's essential goodness. In response, Sinnott-Armstrong argues that this grounding holds *only* on the assumption that rape is morally wrong on independent grounds—i.e., grounds that are independent of God and/or his nature. But if rape is wrong on independent grounds, then the command not to rape is superfluous. Sinnott-Armstrong concludes that the moral status of rape (or anything else) cannot be constituted by God's commands. Instead, Sinnott-Armstrong suggests that a harm-based morality—one that is free of reference to God—can suffice to provide reasons for acting morally. On this score, he is in agreement with Kurtz that there are sufficient nontheistic reasons for living a moral life.

Finally, Sinnott-Armstrong considers Craig's claim that theism can provide a basis for moral accountability. Mere theism—simply the existence of an all-good, all-powerful, all-knowing God—does not entail that wrongdoers ultimately will be punished, since mere theism is consistent with God simply *forgiving* people for some or all of their sins. Mere theism is consistent, for instance, with the nonexistence of hell. And, while there *is* a hell on traditional Christian theism, not *all* wrongdoers are ultimately held accountable, since some wrongdoers (those who turn to Christ) have their sins forgiven and are thus not punished for their sins. Thus, mere theism isn't *sufficient* for ultimate accountability and Christian theism denies the *universality* of ultimate accountability.

In "Theism, Atheism, and the Explanation of Moral Value," Mark Murphy begins by noting that nobody except a "few cranks" would disagree with

Kurtz's thesis that atheists can live morally admirable lives. The more interesting question—one not discussed by Kurtz—is this: Can atheists live *fully* admirable lives? According to Murphy, it is not obvious that Craig and Kurtz would agree on the answer to *this* question.

Murphy sets this question aside and devotes the bulk of his chapter to evaluating Craig's arguments for the claims that theism can ground moral values, duties, and obligations, and atheism cannot. To this end, Murphy attempts to clarify two key notions operative in Craig's arguments—the notion of a *grounding* or *foundation*, and the notion of *morality* itself. Let us take these in turn.

Murphy notes that the sort of grounding Craig has in mind is *ontological*. In other words, Craig is addressing questions of the following sort: What kinds of things exist? And in what ways are these things related to one another? Murphy construes Craig's account of grounding as follows: To show that some entity *x* is grounded in some other entity *y* is to say that *y* is a more basic feature of reality than is *x*, and that *y* explains *x*'s existence. In Craig's view, then, God is more ontologically basic than moral values, and God's existence explains the existence of those values. Moreover, for Craig, *only* God can ground moral values in this way.

On Murphy's reading, Craig's account of morality consists of four features. Morality is (i) *universal* (it applies to everyone), (ii) *objective* (moral facts do not depend upon what we think), (iii) *normative* (moral values provide reasons for action), and (iv) *other-directed* (at least some morally valuable actions or states of affairs concern persons other than the agent).

Given these accounts of grounding and morality, Murphy sets out to evaluate Craig's arguments. Recall Craig's argument for the claim that atheism cannot ground morality. A chief shortcoming of this argument, Murphy says, is that Craig fails to exclude the possibility that in an atheistic universe, moral values can be grounded in prudential values. *Prudential value*, roughly, is what is *good for* a subject. Murphy thinks that this sort of value can be objective, universal, and normative, even in an atheistic universe—and he thinks that Craig will agree. Prudential value, then, shares features (i) to (iii) of Craig's account of moral value. The sticking point is over whether prudential value is sufficient to ground the fourth feature of Craig's account: the other-directedness of morality. Here Murphy offers the atheist the idea that we should care about the well-being of others because we possess *reflective* and *objectivizing* intelligence, a faculty that enables its possessor to call his or her inclinations into question, and to see himself or herself "as one person among others" (125). If Craig's argument is to succeed, he must show not only that this faculty (taken together with prudential value) is insufficient to ground morality's other-directedness, but also that Craig's own theistic account is sufficient on those points where the nontheistic account falls short.

Toward the end of his chapter, Murphy draws on recent work by Robert Adams in developing an argument that is more amenable to Craig's position. He argues that, plausibly, theism and only theism can ground moral *obligations*. On Adams's view, all obligations (moral and otherwise) have a feature that goes *beyond* Craig's (i) to (iv)—namely, an "irreducible social element, involving actually made demands by one party in the social relationship on another" (128). Morally obligatory actions are those actions such that if one fails to perform them, one properly incurs guilt. But at least one feature of one's being in a state of guilt is that one has damaged one's relationship(s) with some other person(s). Thus, morally obligatory actions are those actions such that, by failing to perform them, one puts oneself at odds with others, and renders oneself properly subject to punishment, rebuke, censure, or ill thought on the part of the offended party. But to account for this social element of obligation, "we need to know who it is that has the power to hold humans (universally!) subject to censure for failing to perform their moral obligations" (129). Plausibly, God is the only good candidate for such a being. If so, then it appears that at least one moral phenomenon—moral obligation—requires a theistic explanation. However, Murphy adds, such a conclusion needn't serve as an insurmountable obstacle to those who wish to build a secular ethic. For, such ethicists can simply develop an ethical system that does not include the notion of moral obligation. If Murphy's earlier arguments are correct, secular ethicists can still talk about morally good states of affairs, morally good persons, moral reasons for action, and even obligations of a nonmoral sort.

In his chapter "Empty and Ultimately Meaningless Gestures?" Donald C. Hubin raises an objection to Craig's views about the ethics of self-sacrifice. One of Craig's central theses is that there is moral accountability if and only if God exists. According to Hubin, if Craig is right about this, then the existence of God entails the thesis of "eschatological moral compensation" (EMC). According to EMC, in the afterlife God will ensure that each person is perfectly and justly compensated for his or her deeds. As Craig says, "evil and wrong will be punished; righteousness will be vindicated. Despite the inequalities of this life, in the end the scales of God's justice will be balanced" (31, 133). The lesson Craig draws is that if God does not exist, then acts of genuine self-sacrifice are "empty and ultimately meaningless gestures." In response, Hubin argues not only that Craig is mistaken about this implication, but also that if God exists then it is *impossible* for any action to count as an act of morally laudable, altruistic, genuine self-sacrifice. As Hubin says, "[s]uch acts are possible only if righteous self-sacrifices sometimes go unrewarded" (134). Hubin is thus in agreement with Kurtz's claim that altruistic behavior is consistent with naturalism.

According to Hubin, EMC also calls into question the traditional ethic of self-sacrifice, which is arguably a prominent part of theistic ethics. If a theist is "clear-headed" enough to recognize that theism implies EMC and that EMC precludes the possibility of any actions counting as genuinely self-sacrificial, then he or she will be unable to *intend* to engage in such an action (on the assumption that an agent cannot intend to do what he or she believes to be impossible). Thus, an ethic of self-sacrifice will impose an impossible requirement upon the clear-headed theist.

Hubin concludes by considering Craig's claim that if God does not exist, then acts of self-sacrifice are "stupid." He notes that there must be a normative principle that warrants the judgment that such acts are "stupid." Since such acts are not stupid if EMC is true, Hubin suggests that the principle Craig is assuming must be the principle that a sacrificial action that isn't compensated in this world makes sense only if it is compensated in the next world. But Hubin finds this principle to be "morally troubling": it implies that one would be stupid to act for the *well-being* of another without a good reason for thinking that one's act would be fully rewarded. But this implication undermines the virtue of altruism itself. After all, "there is manifestly no stupidity in [a father] sacrificing his worldly well-being for that of his children, even in the full expectation that this will result in a long-run, net harm to himself" (147). Indeed, Hubin insists, the praiseworthiness of self-sacrificial actions is *precisely* due to the fact that there is no guarantee that those making such sacrifices will receive perfect compensation.

In "What Difference Does God Make to Morality?" Richard Swinburne argues against *both* Craig and Kurtz. Against Craig, Swinburne argues that there are moral truths even if God does not exist. And against Kurtz, Swinburne argues "that the existence and actions of God make a great difference to the content of morality, the seriousness of morality, and our knowledge of morality" (151).

Swinburne argues that some (but not all) moral claims are necessarily true, in that those claims are true in every possible world (where a "possible world" is a possible set of circumstances). Thus, such claims are true even in worlds in which God does not exist and regardless of what God commands in worlds in which he does exist. The fact that certain moral claims are necessarily true is based on the so-called logical supervenience of moral properties on nonmoral properties. Nonmoral properties are purely descriptive ones; examples include *being a killing, being an act of self-defense, being premeditated, being nonconsensual, being an act of sexual intercourse, being painful, being in such-and-such circumstances*, and so on. Moral properties are normative; examples include *being wrong, being obligatory, being permissible, being supererogatory*, and so forth.

Thus, when Swinburne says that a moral property of an action logically supervenes on the act's nonmoral properties, he is claiming that the type of

moral property that an action has is *wholly determined* by the nonmoral properties of the act in question. Why, for instance, does what we call "rape" have
the property of *being morally wrong*? Because it is an act that has the nonmoral properties of *being an act of sexual intercourse*, *being against the will
of one of the participants*, *being painful*, and so forth.[27] The action's moral
status is determined by its nonmoral properties.

This determination, Swinburne argues, holds in *every* possible world. In
other words, consider two different worlds, W1 and W2, and suppose that action *x* occurs in W1 and action *y* occurs in W2. Swinburne's thesis is that if *x*
and *y* have exactly the same nonmoral properties, then it is impossible for them
to have different moral properties. For example, acts of sexual intercourse in
which one party overrides the will of the other are morally wrong in every
world in which they occur. Philosophers often express this by saying that it is a
necessary truth that such an act is wrong. The important implication is that such
an act is wrong even in worlds in which there is no God (on the assumption that
there are such worlds). In affirming this, Swinburne rejects Craig's contention
that in a Godless world, there wouldn't be such a thing as a morally wrong act.

Nevertheless, Swinburne argues, the existence of God in a world does make
a significant difference as to the nonmoral properties that obtain in that world.
According to Swinburne, it is a necessary truth that it is "obligatory to thank and
please benefactors" (155). In worlds in which God exists, God is our benefactor.
Thus, if God exists it is obligatory to thank and please Him. In this way, the existence of God has crucial implications for the *content* of morality. Similarly, it
is necessarily true that if there is an (all-good) God, then whatever he commands
is obligatory. Thus, if God exists and issues commands, then we have obligations
we wouldn't have in a world in which God didn't exist.

NOTES

1. A useful distinction may be drawn between those moral arguments which focus
on a *formal* or *general* feature of ethics and those which focus on the *content* of ethics.
An argument of the former sort draws our attention to a feature apparently shared by
all or most ethical claims, such as *overridingness* or *objectivity*, and tries to show that
if God does not exist, then this feature is illusory. An argument of the latter sort draws
our attention to a more specific concept, such as *intrinsic value*, *human dignity*, *equality*, and so on, and tries to show that such concepts are inapplicable if there is no God.

For those interested in gaining greater facility with the literature on moral arguments,
or the relationship between God and ethics in general, we recommend the important and
recent books listed on the "Further Reading" pages at the end of this volume.

2. Some recent works advancing natural theology are the following: C. Stephen
Layman, *Letters to Doubting Thomas: A Case for the Existence of God* (New York:

Oxford University Press, 2007); James F. Sennett and Douglas Groothuis, eds., *In Defense of Natural Theology: A Post-Humean Assessment* (Downers Grove, Ill.: Intervarsity Press, 2005); Richard Swinburne, *The Existence of God*, 2nd ed. (New York: Oxford University Press, 2004); Michael Murray, ed., *Reason for the Hope Within* (Grand Rapids, Mich.: Eerdmans, 1999); and William Lane Craig, *Reasonable Faith: Christian Truth and Apologetics*, 3rd ed. (Wheaton, Ill.: Crossway Books, 2008).

For a good overview of the literature on natural theology see William Lane Craig and J. P. Moreland, eds., *A Companion to Natural Theology* (Malden, Mass.: Blackwell, forthcoming).

Recent works criticizing natural theology include the following: J. L. Mackie, *The Miracle of Theism: Arguments for and against the Existence of God* (New York: Oxford University Press, 1982); Nicholas Everitt, *The Non-Existence of God* (New York: Routledge, 2004); Jordan Howard Sobel, *Logic and Theism: Arguments for and against Belief in God* (New York: Cambridge University Press, 2004); and Graham Oppy, *Arguing about Gods* (New York: Cambridge University Press, 2006).

For a popular-level debate, see William Lane Craig and Walter Sinnott-Armstrong, *God? A Debate between a Christian and an Atheist* (New York: Oxford University Press, 2004).

3. Ironically enough, Locke says this in his *A Letter concerning Toleration*, 2nd ed. (1689; repr., Indianapolis: Bobbs-Merrill, 1955), 52.

4. Derek Parfit, *Reasons and Persons* (New York: Oxford University Press, 1986), 454.

5. Some of the most important and influential of these objections were articulated by David Hume and Immanuel Kant. For a helpful discussion of the impact of these objections on contemporary theology, see Thomas V. Morris, "Philosophers and Theologians at Odds," *Asbury Theological Journal* 44 (Fall 1989): 31–41. It is important to note that Kant did not think that *all* the traditional theistic arguments failed; in fact, he is famous for defending his own version of a moral argument.

6. Jean-Paul Sartre, *Existentialism Is a Humanism* (New Haven, Conn.: Yale University Press, 2007), 28–29.

7. We are choosing ease of expression over precision here. To be precise, we should speak of "a substitution instance of the form expressed in (1)" being true (or false) and "a substitution instance of the form expressed in (2)" being true (or false).

8. Such tutoring is not, on MacIntyre's view, the *only* purpose of the precepts. Rather, the precepts are themselves partly constitutive of the life of the virtues. Thanks to Mark Murphy for this point.

9. See Alasdair MacIntyre, *After Virtue*, 3rd ed. (Notre Dame, Ind.: University of Notre Dame Press, 2007).

10. There is potential for confusion here, given that utilitarian ethical theories are often referred to as "teleological" theories. While we lack the space to develop the point in detail, it should be noted that the concept of teleology that is deployed in utilitarian theories is different from the Aristotelian concept of teleology. In briefest outline: while both theories construe the human end as *happiness*, one paradigmatic sort of utilitarian thinks of happiness as pleasure (and the absence of pain). The Aristotelian concept of happiness includes the goods of pleasure and the absence

of pain, but adds much else besides. Happiness, for the Aristotelian, requires the ho-
listic *flourishing* of the moral agent, where this includes the actualization and proper
orientation of his or her physical, affective, and rational capacities. Of course, some
philosophers question whether the utilitarian concept of happiness differs significantly from that of the Aristotelian. John Stuart Mill, for instance, famously distinguished between higher pleasures (e.g., as experienced by the philosopher while
thinking) and lower pleasures such as those enjoyed in food and sex. We cannot here
address the extent to which this distinction brings Mill's concept of happiness closer
to Aristotle's.

11. See chapters 1–6 of *After Virtue* for MacIntyre's explication and critique of the
Enlightenment Project.

12. For a helpful survey of contemporary ethical theories along with a rigorous but
accessible attempt to come to terms with moral diversity, see Robert Audi, *Moral
Value and Human Diversity* (New York: Oxford University Press, 2007). For an ex-
cellent historical survey of ethical theories, see Alasdair MacIntyre, *A Short History
of Ethics* (New York: Routledge, 2006).

13. John M. Rist, *Real Ethics: Reconsidering the Foundations of Morality* (Cambridge: Cambridge University Press, 2002), 1.

14. Nietzsche makes this pronouncement in *The Gay Science* (1882; New York:
Random House, 1974), 181.

Nietzsche's name is often mentioned in discussions of God and ethics. Thus, we can
imagine someone asking, "Was *Nietzsche* an optimist or a pessimist?" (in the senses of
those terms described above). We cannot address this question in detail here, but note
the following salient points, which accord with fairly standard readings of Nietzsche.
First, Nietzsche did not endorse the claim that if God does not exist, then everything is
permissible—for Nietzsche did not think that morality depends upon God. (However,
he was keenly aware that many of his contemporaries believed that morality *does* depend on God.) Second, Nietzsche disliked many features of traditional morality (in
particular, what he perceived to be its overemphasis on moral prohibitions). Thus, he
does not seem to fit neatly into the optimist-pessimist schema. Recall: optimists seek
a nontheistic account of traditional morality; pessimists mourn the fall of traditional
morality, which they take to be a logical implication of atheism. Nietzsche does not
meet either description. Third, it is not the case that in rejecting traditional morality,
Nietzsche thereby thought that it does not matter how one lives. Nor did he think that
all ways of living are equally good. Indeed, he advocated the replacement of traditional
morality by what he viewed as a superior, more life-affirming alternative.

For an accessible introduction to Nietzsche's thought, see Robert C. Solomon and
Kathleen M. Higgins, *What Nietzsche Really Said* (New York: Schocken Books, 2000).

15. We say that nontheists only *typically* fell into one of these groups in order to
make room for *agnostic* nontheists, who denied neither God's existence nor the cognitive meaningfulness of religious language, but who also did not affirm theism. T. H.
Huxley famously advocated a kind of agnosticism in the nineteenth century, and there
were doubtless many agnostics among twentieth-century philosophers. But there was,
during this time, no agnostic movement comparable in prominence to the atheistic
and positivistic movements.

16. It is worth noting that several prominent philosophers during this period also took the view that *ethical* statements are cognitively meaningless. See, for example, A. J. Ayer, *Language, Truth, and Logic* (New York: Dover Publications, 1946), chap. 6.

17. "Toward a Hidden God," *Time*, 8 April 1966.

18. Roughly, the main problem is that the verifiability criterion is itself neither empirically verifiable nor true by definition. Thus, the criterion rules itself out as cognitively meaningless. Of course, this characterization of the problem is overly simple. For a more detailed account see Scott Soames, *Philosophical Analysis in the Twentieth Century*, vol. 1, *The Dawn of Analysis* (Princeton, N.J.: Princeton University Press, 2003), chap. 13.

19. John Passmore, "Logical Positivism," in *The Encyclopedia of Philosophy*, ed. Paul Edwards (New York: Macmillan, 1967), 5:52–57. Our friend David Solomon reminds us that Passmore's announcement was old news by the time it hit the press — logical positivism had been dead for well over a decade prior to Passmore's writing.

20. Alvin Plantinga, *God and Other Minds* (Ithaca, N.Y.: Cornell University Press, 1967).

21. For a helpful topical introduction to this body of work, see Michael J. Murray and Michael C. Rea, *An Introduction to the Philosophy of Religion* (New York: Cambridge University Press, 2008). See also Philip Quinn and Charles Taliaferro, eds., *A Companion to Philosophy of Religion* (Malden, Mass.: Blackwell, 1997).

For a historical treatment of the resurgence in the philosophy of religion, see Alvin Plantinga, "Christian Philosophy at the End of the Twentieth Century," in *The Analytic Theist: An Alvin Plantinga Reader*, ed. James F. Sennett (Grand Rapids, Mich.: Eerdmans, 1998); see also Charles Taliaferro, "One Hundred Years with the Gods and Giants: Christians and Twentieth-Century Philosophy," *Christian Scholars Review* 29, no. 4 (Summer 2000): 695–712.

There are also several good anthologies that contain important recent contributions to the field. Among these are Louis Pojman and Michael Rea, eds., *Philosophy of Religion: An Anthology* (Belmont, Calif.: Wadsworth, 2007); William Lane Craig, ed., *Philosophy of Religion: A Reader and Guide* (New Brunswick, N.J.: Rutgers University Press, 2002); Michael Peterson, William Hasker, Bruce Reichenbach, and David Basinger, eds., *Philosophy of Religion: Selected Readings* (New York: Oxford University Press, 2001); and Eleonore Stump and Michael J. Murray, eds., *Philosophy of Religion: The Big Questions* (Malden, Mass.: Blackwell, 1999).

22. "Modernizing the Case for God," *Time*, 7 April 1980.

23. Quentin Smith, "The Metaphilosophy of Naturalism," *Philo* 4, no. 2 (2001): 3–4. This paper is available online at www.philoonline.org.

24. See, for example, Sam Harris, *Letter to a Christian Nation* (New York: Knopf, 2006) and Jim Wallis, *God's Politics: Why the Right Gets It Wrong and the Left Doesn't Get It* (New York: HarperCollins, 2005).

25. Paul Kurtz, *Skepticism and Humanism: The New Paradigm* (New Brunswick, N.J.: Transaction, 2001), 145.

26. John Cooper, ed., *Plato: Complete Works* (Indianapolis, Ind.: Hackett, 1997).

27. This example is the editors'. However, we take the example to illustrate accurately the supervenience claim that Swinburne advocates.

Part I

THE DEBATE

Chapter One

The Kurtz/Craig Debate: Is Goodness without God Good Enough?

Paul Kurtz and William Lane Craig

What follows is the edited version of a debate between Paul Kurtz and William Lane Craig that took place in October of 2001 on the campus of Franklin and Marshall College. The main question of the debate was, Is goodness without God good enough? Kurtz argued for the affirmative position and Craig the negative. Professors Kurtz and Craig wish to thank the Bonchek Institute for Rational Thought and Inquiry, the Center for the Liberal Arts and Society, and Franklin and Marshall College, for their respective roles in sponsoring and organizing the debate.

OPENING STATEMENT BY PAUL KURTZ

The topic resolved for this debate is "Goodness without God is good enough." Indeed, for many individuals, goodness without God is better. I wish to interpret this question in *concrete behavioral* terms to mean that a person can be moral without a belief in God. Moreover, belief in God is not sufficient to guarantee morality. Morality and moral behavior do not depend on divine commandments but on the development of an internal moral sense and, particularly in the young, the growth of moral character, and the capacity for moral reasoning.

Millions of people do not believe in a personal God. Many of them do not practice a religion or, at most, they are only nominal members of a particular denomination. They may be agnostics, skeptics, secular humanists, atheists, or just plain "backsliders." But they do believe very deeply in morality. Indeed, to tell them that without God their morality makes no sense strikes them as repressive cant.

These folks are the last repressed minority in America. They need to come out of the closet and be appreciated, for they have much to offer to society. Many of these nonbelievers trace their lineage back through the history of thought: from Greece and Rome through the Renaissance, the birth of modern science, the Enlightenment, to the democratic revolutions of our time. These freethinkers represent many of the heroes and heroines of human civilization. Many of them are precursors of modern secular humanism: Socrates, the Epicureans and skeptics, Hume, Kant, Darwin, and Freud. Among their numbers, we can also count the founders of the American republic: Madison, Franklin, Jefferson, and Paine. (Contrary to popular belief, the founders of our nation were deists, not theists.) And this lineage continues through today with well-known men and women of thought and action, including John Dewey, Bertrand Russell, Marie Curie, Elizabeth Cady Stanton, Margaret Sanger, Mark Twain, Robert Ingersoll, Thomas Edison, Francis Crick, Isaac Asimov, Sidney Hook, W. V. Quine, and Carl Sagan. The list is very long indeed.

Many of these individuals have led exemplary lives of nobility and excellence, and they have contributed greatly to the social good. They were (or are) kind, considerate, altruistic, caring, and interested in improving the human condition. They have a deep sense of responsibility and good will. They live creatively as scientists, philosophers, poets, artists, or as ordinary men and women. They have been able to exercise self-discipline, exemplify self-respect, and act through noble motives. They are self-actualizers.

Indeed, it may be a surprise to many to learn that, according to a recent poll, 60 percent of American scientists are unbelievers. Likewise, 92 percent of the members of the National Academy of Sciences, made up of the most prestigious scientists in the United States and many Nobel Prize winners, are also unbelievers.[1] Even outside of the halls of academia, we discover that twenty-nine million Americans in answer to a recent poll said that they have no religion.[2]

All of this is drowned out today by propagandists for religion who maintain that a person cannot be moral unless he or she believes in a personal God. If we look at the fruits of modern society, democracy, science, and technology, we find that many achievements have resulted from the work of these freethinkers, who believe deeply in aiding humanity. The best illustration is surely to be found in the helping professions, such as modern medical science, which has improved the human condition and human health, reduced suffering and pain, and contributed enormously to human happiness.

America is an anomaly. For when you travel around the world as I do, you see that Americans appear to be an excessively religious people. This is in stark contrast to many nations of Europe and other democracies as well. According to a recent poll, 31.7 percent of people in Great Britain do not believe in God. The same is true for 41.7 percent in Norway, 48.2 percent in France, 53.9 percent in Sweden, and 57.5 percent in Japan. Indeed, in many of these countries, less than 10 percent of the population attend religious prayer meetings or are active in their churches, synagogues, mosques, or temples. Moreover, according to this recent poll, when asked the question "Do you agree or disagree with the following: 'To me, life is meaningful only because God exists,'" 61.8 percent in France, 57.7 percent in Britain, 59.1 percent in West Germany, 68.1 percent in Japan, and 73.7 percent in Sweden replied, "No."[3]

Thus, nonreligious people have contributed enormously to the modern world and they constitute hundreds of millions of people worldwide. It is interesting to note, as well, that many of these democratic countries have a high quality of life, less crime, and less violence than the United States.

Indeed one can even argue that religion is often an impediment to morality. Now I do recognize, of course, that religions do yield some positive values, and they may—indeed they do—give consolation and hope to people. Furthermore, religions can and do arouse charitable impulses. But, on the other hand, religion often has negative consequences. We are all familiar with many famous examples of immorality committed in the name of God.

Many theists maintain that if you do not believe in God—or have God as your premise—then you cannot be good. But what do these people mean by "God"? Their definitions differ. And even when the definitions are the same, irreconcilable moral quandaries still arise. From the fatherhood of God one can deduce contradictory moral imperatives. For example, are you in favor of monogamy? Catholics favor monogamy and ban divorce. Protestants and Jews favor monogamy and permit divorce. Are you in favor of polygamy? Muslims (and some Mormons) are for polygamy. Yet all of these religious traditions claim to believe in God.

Do you believe in capital punishment? The Catholic Bishops of the United States and many Protestant theologians have condemned capital punishment. Virtually all of the Western democracies are against it. However, Protestant fundamentalists, President George W. Bush, and Muslims are strongly in favor of the death penalty.

And so you can go down the list. Do you believe in birth control, contraception, abortion, stem-cell research, or euthanasia? Do you believe in equality for women and gays? On each of these key issues, you will find that the major religious traditions disagree in fundamental ways. Thus there is no necessary deductive relationship between God and moral commandments—given the contradictory moral imperatives that have been drawn from him.

But if you are without God, Dr. Craig asks, where does morality "come from"? If you find yourself rejecting commandments from God as a basis for morality, where do you turn? Ever since the Renaissance, humanism has been developing answers to the questions of morality. Humanists believe that happiness here and now is our basic good—not salvation in the afterlife. This life is not simply a preparation for some future eternal state. It is intrinsically *good in itself*. And as a result, we should strive for creative joy, actualizing our potentialities, realizing excellence.

"What is the meaning of life," ask the theists such as Dr. Craig, "if there is no God?" For secular humanists, life is meaningful on its own terms. Life presents us with manifold opportunities. The meaning of life is to be found in the things we pursue, our plans and projects, ideals and aspirations. We are to some extent in control of our own destinies. Each person has the ability to determine his or her own meaning fully. Fulfilling a person's life goals is very important for humanist ethics. There is thus a kind of autonomy of moral choice. It is "life, liberty, and the pursuit of happiness" that we seek—not only for every person taken singly, but also for the social good. Humanists believe that social responsibility is vitally important. Our obligation to others is genuine. Secular humanists are keenly aware of their responsibilities to their children and relatives, friends and colleagues, members of their community, their country, the world community, and indeed, also, the planetary habitat.

I submit that human beings are *potentially* moral: that is, that the nature of humanity is such that each person is capable of making moral choices and of behaving morally. Whether this happens depends, in part, upon social conditions, including social justice. It also depends upon moral education. It is, therefore, very important that we nourish in our young the capacity and passion for morality. Under such conditions, it is possible to develop character, a sense of empathy, and caring sentiments for other human beings.

As we live our lives, we find that we often face moral dilemmas, and that these dilemmas show us that we cannot depend on simple abstract principles that, according to many religions, are inviolable and unchangeable. Although there are general moral principles drawn from experience, what we do is related to the context in which we make our choices. What we ought to do depends upon an examination of alternatives, and the wisest and most effective decision is best made in light of considering the consequences of our choices.

Young children learn what they ought and ought not do from education and experience. Adults likewise learn from experience. It is through such learning that we are able to cultivate our moral sensibilities. These do not depend simply upon the commandment of religious authority. Rather, such sensibilities permit us to frame decisions in the light of rational inquiry. Often our decisions are difficult to make. Often we face moral quandaries where there is a choice not between good and bad or right and wrong, but between incompatible goods or the lesser of two evils. The frequency of such circumstances points to the fact that some morality inquiry is basic to the human condition. A morally developed person needs to be sensitive to the nuances inherent in the problems that he or she may face. His or her moral choices may ultimately emerge from a process of wrestling with conflicting values.

It is hazardous to rest our moral reasoning upon absolute principles handed down from on high. Instead we must rest, in the last analysis, upon the development of reflective intelligence. We learn by living and we can change in the light of experience. This is particularly true in the modern world where social change is so rapid—where often there is a clash of competing cultures, where different religious traditions are at odds with each other, and where there are no easy solutions.

What better process than that of rational ethical inquiry, when we weigh alternatives in the balance? What better method than a method of negotiation and compromise where we attempt to understand the point of view of other persons and where we try to work out, as best we can, meliorative principles that are adequate within the situation? I submit that we cannot look back to ancient documents—the Bible or the Qur'an—for simple moral recipes. We cannot look back to our nomadic and rural forebears, who wrote those documents. However eloquent, they expressed the experience of their own age—the rudimentary scientific, literary, and moral outlook of ancient times. We have to draw upon wisdom that is relevant to the modern world, and we need to look ahead to the world of the future. Our postindustrial information and global culture presents us with new challenges unlike any that we have seen before.

Accordingly, I submit that the best method for solving moral problems is the method of ethical intelligence. We need to learn to reason together and find common moral principles, particularly within the present epoch in human history. We need to look beyond the intransigent, intolerant attitudes of the past and develop a new global humanism that transcends the ancient dogmas that divide people. Can we find such common ground? Is it possible to formulate ethical principles upon which we can agree? This, of course, is the great question of our time. It seems to me that people of good will and rationality, dedicated to realizing the best of which we are capable, need to work together to achieve this.

OPENING STATEMENT BY WILLIAM LANE CRAIG

Let me just say at the outset, as clearly as I can, that I agree that a person can be moral without having a belief in God, but that is not the topic under debate. We are not talking about goodness without *belief in God,* but rather goodness without *God*. When Professor Kurtz says, "Goodness without God is good enough," he's raising in a provocative way the question of the *basis* of moral values. In a recent book he helpfully distinguishes *three* views in answer to this question.[4] *Theism* maintains that moral values are grounded in God. *Humanism* maintains that moral values are grounded in human beings. And *nihilism* maintains that moral values have no ground at all and are therefore ultimately illusory and nonbinding.

This analysis is instructive because it helps us to see that Dr. Kurtz is engaged in a struggle on two fronts: on the one side against the theist and on the other side against the nihilist. This is important because it helps us to see that humanism is *not* a default position. That is to say, if the theist is wrong, that does *not* mean that the humanist is right. For if God does not exist, maybe it's the nihilist who is right. In order to carry his case, Dr. Kurtz must defeat both the theist and the nihilist. In particular, he must show that in the absence of God, nihilism would not be true.

With that in mind, I'm going to defend two basic contentions in this debate:

I. If theism is true, we have a sound foundation for morality.
II. If theism is false, we do not have a sound foundation for morality.

Let's look at that first contention together: *If theism is true, we have a sound foundation for morality.* Here I wish to make three subpoints.

First, if theism is true, we have a sound basis for *objective moral values*. To say that there are *objective* moral values is to say that something is good or evil independently of whether anybody believes it to be so. It is to say, for example, that the Holocaust was morally evil even though the Nazis who carried out the Holocaust thought that it was good.

On the theistic view, objective moral values are rooted in God. He is the locus and source of moral value. God's own holy and loving nature supplies the absolute standard against which all actions are measured. He is by nature loving, generous, just, faithful, kind, and so forth. Thus if God exists, objective moral values exist.

Second, *if theism is true, we have a sound basis for objective moral duties.* To say that we have *objective* moral duties is to say that we have certain moral obligations regardless of whether we *think* so or not.

On the theistic view, God's moral nature is expressed toward us in the form of divine commands that constitute our moral duties. Far from being arbitrary, these commands flow necessarily from his moral nature. On this foundation we can affirm the objective goodness and rightness of love, generosity, self-sacrifice, and equality, and condemn as objectively evil and wrong selfishness, hatred, abuse, discrimination, and oppression.

Third, *if theism is true, we have a sound basis for moral accountability.* On the theistic view, God holds all persons morally accountable for their actions. Evil and wrong will be punished; righteousness will be vindicated. Despite the inequities of this life, in the end the scales of God's justice will be balanced. We can even undertake acts of extreme self-sacrifice that run contrary to our self-interest, knowing that such acts are not empty and ultimately meaningless gestures. Thus, the moral choices we make in this life are infused with an eternal significance.

So I think it's evident that if God exists, the objectivity of moral values, moral duties, and moral accountability is secured. Theism therefore provides a sound foundation for morality.

That brings us to my second contention: *If theism is false, we do not have a sound foundation for morality.* Here again, let me make three subpoints.

First, *if theism is false, why think that human beings are the basis of objective moral values?* Dr. Kurtz thinks that human flourishing is "the be-all and end-all" of human life.[5] But if there is no God, what reason is there to regard human flourishing as in any way significant? After all, on the atheistic view, there's nothing special about human beings. They're just accidental by-products of nature that have evolved relatively recently on an infinitesimal speck of dust called the planet Earth, lost somewhere in a hostile and mindless universe and doomed to perish individually and collectively in a relatively short time. As Dr. Kurtz himself has written, "The human species is only one among many life forms that have emerged on Earth . . . . The discoveries of Copernicus and Darwin . . . have [undermined] the belief that we are fundamentally different from all other species."[6]

He muses that "[m]any [people] still refuse to accept the full implications of these discoveries."[7] They "still seek to find a special place for the human species in the scheme of things."[8] Ironically, however, it is precisely *humanists themselves* who seek to find a special place for the human species in the scheme of things, who refuse to accept the full implications of reducing human beings to just another animal species. For humanists continue to treat human beings as *morally* special in contrast to other species.

What justification is there for this differential treatment? On an atheistic view, moral values are just by-products of sociobiological evolution. Just as a troop of baboons exhibits cooperative behavior and even altruistic, sacrificial behavior because evolution has determined it to be advantageous in the struggle for survival, so their primate cousins *Homo sapiens* exhibit similar behavior for the same reason. As Michael Ruse, a philosopher of science, explains,

> The position of the modern evolutionist . . . is that humans have an awareness of morality . . . because such an awareness is of biological worth. Morality is a

biological adaptation no less than are hands and feet and teeth. . . . Considered as a rationally justifiable set of claims about an objective something, ethics is illusory. I appreciate that when somebody says "Love thy neighbor as thyself," they think they are referring above and beyond themselves. . . . Nevertheless, . . . such reference is truly without foundation. Morality is just an aid to survival and reproduction, . . . and any deeper meaning is illusory.[9]

As a result of sociobiological pressures, there has evolved among *Homo sapiens* a sort of "herd morality" that functions well in the perpetuation of our species in the struggle for survival. But on the atheistic view there doesn't seem to be anything about *Homo sapiens* that makes this morality objectively true. To think that human beings are special is to be guilty of speciesism, an unjustified bias toward one's own species.

Thus, if there is no God, then any basis for regarding the herd morality evolved by *Homo sapiens* as objectively true seems to have been removed. Some action—say, rape—may not be biologically or socially advantageous and so in the course of human evolution has become taboo; but on the atheistic view there's nothing really *wrong* about raping someone. Such behavior goes on all the time in the animal kingdom. If, as Dr. Kurtz states, "The moral principles that govern our behavior are rooted in habit and custom, feeling and fashion,"[10] then the rapist who chooses to flout the herd morality is doing nothing more serious than acting unfashionably.

So if theism is false, it's hard to see what basis remains for the affirmation of objective moral values and, in particular, of the special value of human beings. It's not at all clear to me why, if theism were false, humanism would be true rather than nihilism.

Second, *if theism is false, then what is the basis for objective moral duties?* On the atheistic view, human beings are just animals, and animals have no moral obligations to one another. The ethicist Richard Taylor illustrates the point. He invites us to imagine human beings living in a state of nature without any customs or laws. Suppose one of them kills another one and takes his goods. Taylor reflects,

> Such actions, though injurious to their victims, are no more unjust or immoral than they would be if done by one animal to another. A hawk that seizes a fish from the sea *kills* it, but does not *murder* it; and another hawk that seizes the fish from the talons of the first *takes* it, but does not *steal* it—for none of these things is forbidden. And exactly the same considerations apply to the people we are imagining.[11]

Why think that if God does not exist, we would have any moral obligations to do anything? Who or what imposes these moral duties upon us? As Taylor says, "The concept of moral obligation [is] unintelligible apart from the idea of God. The words remain, but their meaning is gone."[12]

Thus, if atheism is true, it becomes impossible to condemn war, oppression, or crime as evil. Nor can one praise brotherhood, equality, or love as good. It doesn't matter *what* you do—for there is no right and wrong; good and evil do not exist.

So if theism is false, it's very hard to understand what basis remains for objective moral duties. Why wouldn't nihilism, which holds that there is no right and wrong, be true rather than humanism?

Finally, *if theism is false, what is the basis of moral accountability*? Even if there were objective moral values and duties under atheism, they seem to be irrelevant because there's no moral accountability. As Dr. Kurtz writes, "There is no cosmic Prospect for the human species. . . . There is no metaphysical basis for hope."[13] But if life ends at the grave, it makes no difference whether one lives as a Stalin or as a saint. As the Russian writer Fyodor Dostoyevsky rightly said, "If there is no immortality, then all things are permitted."[14] Given the finality of death, it really does not matter how you live.

Acts of self-sacrifice become particularly inept on an atheistic worldview. Such altruistic behavior is merely the result of evolutionary conditioning that helps to perpetuate the species. A firefighter rushing into a burning building to rescue people in danger or a policeman who sacrifices his life to save those of his comrades does nothing more praiseworthy, morally speaking, than an ant that sacrifices itself for the sake of the ant heap. On an atheistic view this is just stupid. We should resist the sociobiological pressures to such self-destructive activity and choose instead to act in our own self-interest. The absence of moral accountability from the philosophy of atheism thus makes an ethic of compassion and self-sacrifice a hollow abstraction. R. Z. Friedman, a philosopher at the University of Toronto, concludes, "Without religion the coherence of an ethic of compassion cannot be established. The principle of respect for persons and the principle of the survival of the fittest are mutually exclusive."[15]

In summary, Professor Kurtz has not, I think, shown that theological foundations are dispensable when it comes to morality. We've seen that if theism is true, then we have a sound foundation for objective moral values, moral duties, and moral accountability. On the other hand, if theism is false, then it's very hard to see what basis remains for the affirmation of objective moral values, moral duties, and moral accountability. In short, it's hard to see why nihilism would not be true. In that case, goodness without God is not good enough.

FIRST REBUTTAL BY PAUL KURTZ

Thank you very much, Professor Craig—you have conceded my first and main point. You admitted that people can be moral without belief in God. If God is essential, then how is it possible that millions of people who do not believe in

God, nonetheless behave morally? On your view, they should not. And so, your God is not essential for the moral life, but a mere ontological abstraction. Second, the alternatives do not reduce to three either/or positions as you suggest—theism, humanism, or nihilism. There have been many other available philosophical and ethical alternatives in life (e.g., Buddhism, Epicureanism, Confucianism, Marxism, etc.). Third, many people have been optimistic about life; they have lived a full life without benefit of clergy or theology, and have found life exhilarating, immensely satisfying, and richly significant. Nor do they wring their hands about whether or not there is an afterlife. It's living life here and now that counts. Thus if you reject theism and are a skeptic about religious claims, I submit, you can still lead the good life fully, without in any way falling into pessimistic despair. Indeed, I have found that it is theists, not nontheists, who often have an exacerbated sense of sin and guilt that causes many religious people to be fearful of death and divine punishment.

I like to tell the humorous story of Woody Allen, who lay awake nights worrying about whether or not the sun would burn out in five billion years, thus eliminating the possibility of all human life on the planet Earth. The secular humanist contends that one can live a full life even in the face of such prospects, a life of prosperity and actualization, of love and exuberance, of moral concern and empathy for others. The intensity of living can be so pregnant with interesting adventures and excitement that there is no need to fall into the abyss of nihilistic angst.

Dr. Craig did not respond in his remarks to the basic challenge that I have posed: The theist faces the significant problem of deciding which of the many different Gods—and there are radically different religious traditions—should command our ultimate allegiance. He says that he is a theist and that he believes in God—but which God? And what does his God command? The Islamic martyrs slammed their planes into the World Trade towers on September 11, 2001, proclaiming "Allahu Akhbar!" as they died for belief in their God. And many religious folk in America responded "God bless America," supplicating the blessings of a Judaic-Christian God. The German army went to war singing "*Gott mit uns*" and the French army proclaiming "*Dieu avec nous*," believing, apparently, in the same God, but attributing to that God quite incompatible allegiances! The bloody American Civil War pitted the North against the South, with Christians on both sides quoting the Bible to justify their contending views of slavery.

So appealing to God doesn't solve the matter. Even if everyone believed in God (as prevailed for long periods of cultural history), there still are powerful moral disagreements and irresolvable disputes.

Now Dr. Craig maintains that God is the only objective basis for morality, and that this all-good and loving God manifests his justice and righteousness in his creation. But is this so? How do you explain the dying of 3,000 innocent people at the World Trade towers? How and why did a loving God permit that to happen? For the humanist, the universe is as we find it; we try to live the best life we can, and we try to use our intelligence and good will to resolve our problems in order to live together in peace and harmony. But to postulate an all-loving, omniscient, and just God who nonetheless allows evil to exist, is the Achilles heel of the classical notion of an omnipotent and beneficent God. Thus, Craig's ontological postulate is riddled with contradictions.

Professor Craig asks why humanists favor the human species. This, he contends, is just human speciesism. Yes, it is indeed. We *are* human, and as such we love, live, and work together with other human beings. Our whole life is tied up with our relationships to our fellow humans. We are aware of our relationships to others and the claims made upon us, and it is in terms of these that we are willing to fulfill our duties and obligations, and also to be held accountable for our deeds. Humanists and others who do not accept Dr. Craig's Christian theism are willing to make sacrifices; they are willing to die for others; they are empathetic and caring of the needs of their children, parents, friends, colleagues, and other human beings. It seems to me that some form of altruism is basic to the human species—and to our compassionate nature. We can and should be sensitive to the pain and suffering of other sentient organisms and species on the planet, but perhaps not to the extent that we are sensitive to the human species. Why this moral concern? Because it is deeply rooted in our very nature. We do not have to say, and we surely cannot say, that if God did not exist then we would be moral despots. We cannot say that whatever a Cesare Borgia or Hitler might do makes no moral difference and that we cannot distinguish between a morally beneficent person and a moral transgressor. Humans do abhor degradation, injustice, and inhumanity, whether or not God exists. (Incidentally, Dr. Craig's quotations from my book *Forbidden Fruit* were made out of context, since I argue that we can distinguish between a moral despot such as Stalin and a moral saint.)

It is not a question of mere taste and subjectivity. There are objective standards that we can use. But these standards are, of course, relative to human interests and needs, and they change over time. There is an evolution within human history and civilization and a corresponding development of basic moral principles, and these are often won only after arduous struggles, as in the battles against slavery and racism and for the rights of women.

Thus, the humanist can and does have a good deal to say about the origin, ground, and legitimacy of morality. In fact, let me turn the tables and let me submit to Dr. Craig the proposition that, if the reason that the theist is moral is because of a belief in God, then the theist has not developed the full dimensions of moral personality. I hold that there are fundamental human tendencies and potentialities for developing a moral appreciation for others, and for realizing genuine moral virtues. It is of course absent in some individuals—sociopaths and psychopaths. Here we have civil laws to regulate conduct and ensure human accountability, applicable to both religious and nonreligious individuals. But these laws are no substitute for morality itself. If the theist claims that these moral sensibilities would not exist absent a law-giving God, then the theist's moral capacities are deficient. Moral development is autonomous; moral principles are a part of who and what we are. They define us as human beings. And therefore, for Dr. Craig to imply that those who do not accept his particular dogma of religious theism are immoral nihilists, is patently false, libelous, and immoral.

FIRST REBUTTAL BY WILLIAM LANE CRAIG

We have agreed in this debate that a belief in God is not essential to living a moral life. But my argument is that without the existence of God there would not be moral values, moral duties, or moral accountability in any objective sense. Dr. Kurtz asks, "Well, if you can live a moral life without *belief* in God, then how is God essential?" Well, very simply, without God there is no foundation, as I believe and have argued, for objective values, duties, and accountability.

Dr. Kurtz himself writes in his book *Forbidden Fruit*, "The central question about moral and ethical principles concerns their ontological foundation"—that is to say, their basis in reality. "If they are neither derived from God nor anchored in some transcendent ground, are they purely ephemeral?"[16] That is the question that is before us, and Dr. Kurtz must show that in the absence of God, human beings would, in fact, have intrinsic moral value and moral duties, and he must supply some sort of moral accountability. And I don't think that he can do that. That is why God is essential for providing a foundation or a basis for the affirmation of these elements of the moral life.

Why is this important? Well, because it is not obvious to me that if God doesn't exist, then humanism would be true. On the contrary, it seems very plausible to think that if God doesn't exist, nihilism would be true. This is important because Dr. Kurtz admits in his book that nihilism is not enough for the foundation of the moral life. He writes, "No one can consistently live his or her life under the domination of such an attitude" as nihilism.[17] So it is impossible to live the individual moral life from a nihilistic view. Also, it undermines the moral fabric of society. He writes, "Common moral decencies . . . lay down moral imperatives necessary for group cohesion and survival."[18] So if nihilism is true, we lack those moral principles that are necessary for the moral fabric of society. Thus I think it is critical in this debate that Dr. Kurtz address the question, "Why, if there is no God, wouldn't nihilism be true?"

Now I argued two things in my opening remarks. First, if theism is true, we have a sound foundation for morality. Dr. Kurtz didn't dispute my claim that if theism is true, there would be objective moral values, objective moral duties, and objective moral accountability. But he did bring in several red herrings to distract us from this central issue.

He asked, for example, why is there so much evil and suffering in the world? Notice, this is a question about the *existence* of God, and we are not arguing about that in this debate. This is not a debate about the existence of God. My claim is a conditional one. *If* theism is true, *then* we have a sound foundation for morality. So even if he is right, that wouldn't prove that God would not be a sound foundation for morality if theism were true. Second, in addition to that, I would simply say that God has morally sufficient reasons for permitting the evil and suffering in the world, and then it's going to be Dr. Kurtz who bears the burden of proof to show that this is either impossible or improbable. Still, I don't think that the problem of evil is at the heart of the present debate; it is a red herring.

Similarly, it is also a red herring to say, "Well, which God exists and what does he command?" These are questions of moral epistemology, not moral ontology. That is to say, these are questions about how we know the good or how we discover God's commands, but they are not about what is the basis, the ontological foundation, for moral values, duties, and so forth. Indeed, I would say that once we have arrived at the conclusion that if theism is true, there is an objective basis for morality, then it's very important to find out which God exists because as Dr. Kurtz said, "Not all Gods are the same." There are some religions in the world that have very vicious concepts of God, and so it's important for us to discover which theism is true. But that is a secondary question to the one that faces us in this debate. So I don't think that Dr. Kurtz has said anything to refute my first contention that if theism is true, then we have a sound foundation for objective moral value, duties, and moral accountability.

Now what about my second contention, that if theism is false, there is no sound foundation for morality? I asked Professor Kurtz, "What is the basis of objective moral values if there is no God?" Human beings are just like other animal species. He says, "Well, that doesn't mean that if God doesn't exist, we would all be despots. There can be standards that can be relative to human needs and desires." Right, there can be standards that are relative to human needs and desires, but they are then not unconditional, objective, categorical moral principles or standards. There is thus no more reason to think that this herd morality, evolved by *Homo sapiens* as a result of the evolutionary process, is objectively true than to think that guinea pig morality or horse morality, which is relative to the needs and values of those species, would be objectively true. The question is: "Why think that human beings and their values are special on an atheistic view?" I don't think Professor Kurtz has been able to give us an answer.

Peter Haas, in his book *Morality after Auschwitz,* uses Nazi Germany as an illustration of the problem we face. He points out that

> far from being contemptuous of ethics, the perpetrators [of the Holocaust] acted in strict conformity with an ethic which held that, however difficult or unpleasant the task might have been, the mass extermination of the Jews and Gypsies was entirely justified. The Holocaust was possible only because a new ethic was in place that did not define the arrest and deportation of Jews as wrong and in fact defined it as ethically tolerable and even good.[19]

Moreover, Haas points out that because of its internal consistency and coherence, the Nazi ethic couldn't be discredited from within. It could only be pronounced false by way of some transcendent vantage point from which you can rise above sociocultural relativism and say that this society's values are wrong, that they are objectively wrong. But for the humanist, there isn't any basis for that because moral values are simply the by-product of sociocultural evolution, and there is no way to judge if one is objectively right and one is objectively wrong.

Similarly, without God there are no *objective* moral duties. Animals don't have moral obligations to one another. Massimo Pigliucci, a biologist, writes, "What we call homicide or rape or . . . even infanticide is very, very common among different types of animals. Lions, for example, commit infanticide on a regular basis. . . . Now are these kind of acts to be condoned?" He answers, "I don't even know what that means, because the lion doesn't understand what morality is. Morality is an invention of human beings."[20] There is no such thing, he says, as objective morality. So, if morality is simply an invention of human beings rooted in sociobiological evolution, there is no reason to think that we are obligated to follow it.

Similarly, there is no basis for moral accountability on atheism. The thing that is important about moral accountability is that it makes our moral choices significant. In the absence of moral accountability, our choices become trivialized because they make no ultimate contribution to either the betterment of the universe or to the moral good in general because everyone ends up the same. Death is the great leveler.

So it seems to me that Dr. Kurtz still faces this crucial challenge to show us why, if there is no God, humanism would be true rather than nihilism.

SECOND REBUTTAL BY PAUL KURTZ

I think that there has been a long battle in the modern world to separate science from religion. Science could only proceed when we abandoned the quest for occult explanations and when scientific theories were freed from theological censorship. Galileo is the great symbol of free inquiry in the history of science. Similarly, the battle between religion and politics is historic. Democracies could best develop where there was a separation of the established church and the state and when political judgments could be made independent of religious constraints. We face another battleground today in our society, and that is to see whether religion and morality can be distinguished and whether or not we can make moral judgments independent of religious foundations.

I submit that we can and do. Indeed, there is a historic tradition in Western philosophy, tracing from Aristotle through Kant down to present philosophers, in which it is clear that there is an autonomy of moral judgments, and that individuals can and do make moral choices quite independently of religious considerations. There is a kind of practical moral wisdom that persons of various backgrounds can share; we can learn how to make wise decisions in concrete situations. A person does not have to refer to God to resolve most moral dilemmas.

For example, if Johnny hits Mary and Johnny's mother says, "Don't hit Mary," we may ask, why should he not hit Mary—is it because God exists? No, says mother—"If you hit Mary she will hit you back, she won't like you, and you won't have any friends if you continue this." In other words, a child needs reasons for his or her moral behavior, and we need to point to consequences of different courses of conduct; this is related to who and what we are as moral beings. The point is, we are moral agents, capable of framing moral judgments, and that is the basis of social transactions. To say that in order to solve a moral dilemma or to teach moral virtue you need to believe in or presuppose a theistic god simply is untrue, especially in concrete cases. If I borrow ten dollars from someone and promise to pay him back tomorrow, I have an obligation to do so whether I am an atheist or Jehovah's Witness, an American or Russian, Hindu or Muslim.

Dr. Craig declares that theism is the only adequate foundation for such moral standards, but he has not answered my question, Whose theism? Religious beliefs vary from culture to culture. If you look at the history of human civilization—the Crusades, the Inquisition, the jihad, the conflicts today in Northern Ireland, Bosnia, the Middle East, Kashmir, and all over the world—we find continuing conflicts of people who claim to believe in God; and yet their belief in God does not enable them to resolve moral disagreements. "I believe in God!" asserts the true believer. "Yes, and so we will kill you in the name of

God!" This is the basic problem: The belief in God does not provide an adequate foundation for moral choices. The demand for an ontological ground can indeed be a trap that leads to endless disputes of authority and legitimation.

In any case, I hold that questions of moral epistemology precede those of moral ontology. If you are going to deal with moral choices, you have to deal with concrete human moral experience. You need to test your principles by their consequences. You need to evaluate alternatives by balancing competing demands and claims, goods and bads, rights and wrongs. You need to examine the means available to achieve your goals. You need to confront conflicting values and rights, and try to settle moral disputes by negotiation and compromise. In the present multicultural world, we need to resolve our differences and to develop a common set of principles and values that will enable us to live together. Surely, moral agreement does not depend on prior religious conversion. Morality is rooted in human experience.

Dr. Craig asks, "Why should humanists prefer the human species over and above other species?" I reply, because we are humans and because we love and appreciate the needs of other humans. This is necessary if we are to balance our different interests and live together in harmony. Morality, like politics, is thoroughly *human*. Humanism does not mean that we are insensitive to animals or the need to protect the survival of other species on the planet. Dr. Craig insists that humanist morality is created in the image of man and that this is insufficient. On the contrary, I submit that it is theism that is created in the image of man and is anthropomorphic, and that it is human beings who have created gods. "If lions had gods they would be lion-like in character," said Xenophon. Religions are relative to social conditions and historical epochs. Merely to say that a theistic ontology will ground morality provides no answer to our moral dilemmas.

To claim that we need a doctrine of salvation in order to judge the meaning of this life is equally specious. I find insufficient evidence for salvation, or for the hope that after the death of the body the soul will live on to be rewarded or punished by God at Judgment Day. This is simply an article of faith. Indeed, the basic premise of Dr. Craig's morality in the last analysis is based upon his religious convictions. It seems to me that it is important that we go beyond faith and that we try to resolve our moral differences on rational grounds. And it is reason, not faith, that is a more reliable method by which our moral differences can be resolved, if they can be resolved at all.

SECOND REBUTTAL BY WILLIAM LANE CRAIG

Well, of course, my appeal in this debate has been precisely to reason and not to faith!

I have argued two things: First, if theism is true, we have a sound foundation for morality. We have objective moral values, objective moral duties in the divine commands, and moral accountability. Dr. Kurtz hasn't disputed any of those points. Instead, what he has done is brought up red herrings.

For example, he said, "We can make moral judgments in the absence of or independent of religion." Of course, we can. I agree with that. You don't need to believe in God in order to recognize that you ought to love your children rather than torture them. But the question is, what is the ontological foundation of that objective moral duty that we often sense? And that is, as he said, the central ethical question that needs to be addressed.

He also says again, "Well, what if Johnny hits Mary? What happens then?" The point is, Why is it *wrong* for Johnny to hit Mary? This sort of thing goes on all the time in the animal kingdom. Remember, we saw that even infanticide goes on—lions and other animals eat their offspring. So why is it that it is objectively morally wrong for *Homo sapiens* to behave in these ugly ways toward one another? On an atheistic view, we are just primates, and I can't see anything wrong with primates doing these things to one another, given atheism.

Again, Dr. Kurtz asks, "Whose theism?" That is not the question in this debate. That is a secondary question. If we do see that there is not an adequate foundation for morality in the absence of God, *then* we need to ask the question, Which God exists? Now I am a Christian theist, so let me lay down Christian theism as my foundation for morality, and Dr. Kurtz can tell us then what is wrong with Christian theism in terms of objective moral values, moral duties, and moral accountability.

So I don't think he has said anything to show that theism is inadequate as a foundation for morality.

Now my second contention—the more important, I think—is that if theism is false, I don't see any foundation for morality on Dr. Kurtz's view. What is the basis on atheism for objective moral value? He says, "It is just because we are human." Yes, but why think that human beings are special? Why is just *this* primate species special instead of chimpanzees or bonobos? Imagine that an extraterrestrial race came from another planet, who was as superior to us in intelligence as we are to pigs and cows, and that they began to farm the earth and began using us as food and laboring animals. What could the atheist say to show them that human beings have intrinsic moral value? That they ought not do this to *human beings*? They would say, "Your values and principles are just the blind by-products of the evolutionary process that spawned you. No objectivity, no binding force is upon us!" So I can't see any reason to think that this prejudice in favor of the human species is justified on atheism.

Dr. Kurtz then tries to turn the tables by saying, "But I say theism is just created!" Maybe it is; that is not the topic of this debate. Remember, my claim is a conditional claim: *If* theism is true, *then* we have a sound foundation for morality. I'd be happy to come back to Franklin and Marshall again for another debate on the question of the existence of God and present good reasons to believe that theism is true. But for the present debate, it is sufficient to defend that conditional claim that if theism is true, we have a sound foundation for morality.

On the other hand, if theism is false, there isn't any foundation for the affirmation of objective moral values, for the existence of moral duties—where did those come from on atheism?—or for moral accountability and acts of self-sacrifice.

In short, I personally think that humanism is utterly intellectually bankrupt. It has no basis for the affirmation of the moral values that I think we all sense are true, that are the right values. We all believe in the intrinsic value of human beings, and in love for one another, and cooperative behavior. But what the theist can offer the humanist is a secure foundation for the affirmation of those values that we all hold dear and want to cling to. Therefore, I would like to challenge Professor Kurtz to consider becoming a believer in God. I think that if he will believe in God and put God into his metaphysics, into his ontology, it will give him a foundation for those very humanistic values that he wants to affirm and that we, as Christian theists, also affirm.

CLOSING STATEMENT BY PAUL KURTZ

This has been an interesting debate and Mr. Craig says that he doesn't want to debate the existence of God. But he spends all of his time attacking atheism and I've been arguing that you can be good without belief in God, and I've defined that as humanistic good, and he has not really dealt with humanism.

Humanism is a noble ethic that developed during the Renaissance period, a period during which human beings became secularized. They looked at the world in the here and now. They were not concerned about other-worldly values. They aimed to improve the human condition on the planet Earth, and they worked hard and struggled together to reform society in order to do just that. But Professor Craig bypassed that entirely. He said, over and over again, that human beings are just apes. We *are* human apes, a product of evolution undoubtedly, but we also have evolved civilization—the arts, sciences, morality, law—and all these things are oriented toward the human good.

Religion has a role to play in human life, but to allow religion to dominate morality and to say that morality depends upon religion is contrary to our understanding of the modern world. The modern world says that human beings are independent, they can determine their own fate, they can develop science and technology, they can cultivate social institutions that stand to improve the human condition, here and now.

Now what is humanist morality concerned with? It is concerned with basic moral decency, with moral principles that have evolved over a period of time and are universally recognized within civilized society. It is concerned with developing the excellences of the good life, with answering the questions of how I can achieve the good life and how I can achieve happiness, in the here and now. The love of God is the love of a transcendent being, which Professor Craig holds to exist on the basis of faith. But the love of men and women, a human love that represents the effort of each individual to achieve a creative, exuberant, exciting life, is very basic. In living your life here and now, you treat life as a work of art—a work of art that you can successfully complete. You can achieve a significant, meaningful life without belief in God, even though when life is over, it is over. Nonetheless, human life can be full and meaningful, and that is what is crucially important.

What permeates human morality and humanism is our sense of responsibility to human beings and our effort to develop human institutions that will enhance and improve the human life, the human species. At the dawn of the twenty-first century, we can use our best talents to create a better global civilization. We can transcend the ancient animosities and hatred, we can work to create new international institutions, we can use technology, the information revolution, and biogenetics to improve the human condition. And these ends are in the power of human beings, and they can and ought to be secured.

But if they are to be secured, they presuppose a prior commitment to critical inquiry. Reason—not faith in an ancient God, not belief in private religion—but critical intelligence, the use of inquiry, in all areas of human life, this is what provides the promise and the opportunity. Franklin and Marshall College is based upon such inquiry, and indeed the whole of the modern world is based upon such inquiry. And it seems to me we need further inquiry to develop new values and to develop our most noble abilities, our intelligence, and our good will to move ahead.

Now I said at the very beginning that there are millions of Americans who are skeptical of religious beliefs and yet believe deeply in morality. Professor Craig conceded my point when he acknowledged that one can be good and virtuous without belief in God. This point must be emphasized in America today. And we call upon our fellow citizens in America to tolerate the nonbelievers in our midst: the scientists and poets, artists and architects, and ordinary men and women who want to live a full life, who love their families, who love their spouses, who are good citizens, and who believe that they can live as such. It seems prejudiced and unfair to claim that unless one believes in God as the ontological foundation for morality, whatever that means (and I have taught metaphysics), one cannot be good. Your neighbor, your daughter, your son, your friend, your colleague—there are millions of us out there who want to affirm the ethics of humanism. We are skeptical of religion, yet we think we have a voice in America. And I thank the Bonchek Institute for allowing me to express this voice in this debate.

CLOSING STATEMENT BY WILLIAM LANE CRAIG

I trust that you have been able to see that this debate has not been about belief in God as a necessity for the moral life. Nor has it really been about theism. If you have been perceptive, you have seen that the debate has really been about nihilism. This is the unseen guest that Dr. Kurtz has to ward off and that he doesn't want to talk about. The problem the humanist confronts is this: If theism is false, humanism doesn't win by default. If theism is false, you've got to ask yourself, Why wouldn't nihilism be true? What proof do you have that nihilism is not the correct remaining alternative?

I argued, first of all, that if theism is true, you have a sound foundation for morality—for moral values, moral duties, and moral accountability. Dr. Kurtz has not disputed a single one of those points. All he has tried to do is introduce red herrings about the ethics of Muhammad, about religious diversity, about questions of moral epistemology—all of which are secondary.

I said that I am willing to stake my claim on Christian theism. If Christian theism is true, then you have objective moral values, duties, and accountability. I'll be very happy, another time, to talk about whether or not there are good reasons to think that Christian theism is true rather than, say, Islam. I think that there are very good reasons to think that.

In addition and more importantly, if theism is false, we've been shown no sound foundation for morality. What is the basis of objective moral value, moral duty, and moral accountability without theism? Professor Kurtz tries to say that I am depreciating human beings, when in fact it is he who is depreciating the value of human beings. It is atheism that regards human beings as mere animals and cannot provide a basis for moral obligations among these animals. So all of my statements about human beings' lacking intrinsic value are conditional statements, affirming that *if* atheism is true, *then* these conclusions follow. Dr. Kurtz has done nothing to refute those conclusions.

In a recent address to the American Academy for the Advancement of Science, Dr. L. D. Rue, confronted with the nihilism of modern man, boldly advocated that we deceive ourselves by means of some Noble Lie into thinking that we and the universe still have value.[21] He claims that the lesson of the past two centuries is that intellectual and moral relativism is profoundly the case. The result of such a realization, he says, is that the quest for personal fulfillment and the quest for social coherence fall apart. This is because in the absence of God-given values, each person must create his own set of values, thereby undermining the moral cohesiveness of society.

So what can you do in such a predicament? Well, if we are to avoid what Rue calls the "Madhouse Option," where everyone simply pursues self-fulfillment without regard to social coherence, and if we are to avoid the totalitarian option, where social coherence is imposed by the state at the expense of personal fulfillment, then, he says, we have no choice but to embrace some Noble Lie that will inspire us to live beyond selfish interests and so voluntarily achieve social coherence. A Noble Lie, he says, is one that deceives us, tricks us, compels us beyond self-interest, beyond ego, beyond family, nation, and race. It is a lie, he says, because it tells us that life is infused with value (which is a great fiction), and because it tells us that we should not live for our own best self-interest (which is manifestly false). But without such lies, Rue concludes, we cannot live.

Humanism is a Noble Lie; it is what Professor Kurtz has called a "delusional system," a way of kidding yourself in the face of unbearable consequences.[22] Unable to stare the nihilistic consequences of atheism squarely in the face, humanism looks the other way, pretending not to notice the darkness, not to feel the impending chaos, hoping that everything can go on as it was before. But the specter of nihilism still haunts us; it will not let us go. Having once let go of God, we can no longer fool oursleves by a cheery and baseless humanism. If God is dead, man is dead, too.

NOTES

1. See Edward J. Larson and Larry Witham, "Leading Scientists Still Reject God," *Nature*, 23 July 1998, 313.

2. American Religious Identification Survey: 2001. Graduate Center of the City University of New York. Available online at www.gc.cuny.edu/faculty/research_briefs/aris/key_findings.htm.

3. International Social Survey Program: Religion II, ICPSR, Ann Arbor, Michigan, 1998. Available online at www.prod.library.utoronto.ca:8090/datalib/codebooks/icpsr/3065/cb3065.pdf.

4. Paul Kurtz, *The Courage to Become* (Westport, Conn.: Praeger, 1997).

5. Kurtz, *Courage to Become*, 125.

6. Kurtz, *Courage to Become*, 5–6.

7. Kurtz, *Courage to Become*, 6.

8. Kurtz, *Courage to Become*, 53.

9. Michael Ruse, "Evolutionary Theory and Christian Ethics," in *The Darwinian Paradigm* (London: Routledge, 1989), 262, 268–69.

10. Paul Kurtz, *Forbidden Fruit* (Buffalo, N.Y.: Prometheus Books, 1988), 73.

11. Richard Taylor, *Ethics, Faith, and Reason* (Englewood Cliffs, N.J.: Prentice-Hall, 1985), 14.

12. Taylor, *Ethics, Faith, and Reason*, 83–84.

13. Kurtz, *Courage to Become*, 27–28.

14. Fyodor Dostoyevsky, *The Brothers Karamazov*, trans. C. Garnett (New York: Signet Classics, 1957), bk. 2, chap. 6; bk. 5, chap. 4; bk. 1, chap. 8.

15. R. Z. Friedman, "Does the 'Death of God' Really Matter?" *International Philosophical Quarterly* 23 (1983): 322.

16. Kurtz, *Forbidden Fruit*, 65.

17. Kurtz, *Courage to Become*, 17.

18. Kurtz, *Forbidden Fruit*, 80.

19. Critical notice of Peter Haas, *Morality after Auschwitz: The Radical Challenge of the Nazi Ethic* (Philadelphia: Fortress Press, 1988), by R. L. Rubenstein, *Journal of the American Academy of Religion* 60 (Spring 1992): 158.

20. Massimo Pigliucci, "Does the Christian God Exist?" debate with William Lane Craig, University of Georgia, 22 March 2001. Professor Pigliucci now says, "If you are going to quote me—I wouldn't say that morality is 'an invention' of human beings, rather that it is a biological phenomenon that applies only to sentient social animals, such as human beings" (personal correspondence, 1 June 2007).

21. Loyal D. Rue, "The Saving Grace of Noble Lies," address to the American Academy for the Advancement of Science, February 1991.

22. Kurtz, *Courage to Become*, 15.

Part II

NEW ESSAYS

Chapter Two

A Moral Argument for the Existence of God

C. Stephen Layman

Dr. Craig defends two conditional theses concerning God and morality: (1) if theism is true, we have a sound foundation for morality; and (2) if theism is false, we do not have a sound foundation for morality. He is right, of course, in observing that such conditional theses can be true even if their if-clauses are false. But I want to ask the further question whether our common beliefs about morality actually do provide any support for theism. I will argue that they do; that is, I will offer a moral argument for the existence of God.

Before I set forth my argument, a series of preliminary comments is in order. First, in my opinion, only a cumulative-case approach to the issue of God's existence has a chance of providing solid grounds for believing that God exists. No single argument, such as a cosmological argument, a design argument, or a moral argument, can by itself justify theistic belief.[1] Thus, anyone who criticizes my argument by pointing out that, by itself, it doesn't justify theistic belief, is saying something that is true (in my opinion), but beside the point. The question is rather whether the argument can contribute positively to a larger, cumulative case for God's existence.

Second, many people seem to think that they've made an important objection to a theistic argument if they can rightly point out that not everyone accepts the premises. In fact, this objection can be made to virtually every philosophical argument on virtually any issue of significance. As Marilyn Adams has observed, the "defense of any well-formulated philosophical position will eventually involve premises that are fundamentally controversial and so unable to command the assent of all reasonable persons."[2] So, to criticize my argument effectively, one must do more than simply point out that not everyone accepts the premises. One must make a case that those who reject the premises have solid arguments for doing so—with premises *at least* as plausible as mine.

Third, I want to make a comment about philosophical method. Descartes famously urged his method of doubt—that is, withdrawing assent from anything one can doubt. And Descartes found that he could doubt just about everything, but he couldn't doubt that he doubted; and since doubting is a form of thinking, that left him with the premise "I think," from which he inferred "I am." So far, so good; but Descartes tried to move logically from this miniscule foundation of beliefs to the belief that material objects exist. The judgment of the past 350 years of philosophy is that Descartes' method, if followed honestly, will leave a person with almost no beliefs at all. In other words, in spite of Descartes' good intentions, his method leads to radical skepticism. Even the belief that *physical objects exist* is unjustified, let alone beliefs about more controversial subjects.

I shall employ a philosophical method that contrasts sharply with Descartes'. This alternative method, or something similar to it, has often been employed by philosophers. I think Aristotle typically employs it, so I'll call it the Aristotelian method. This method gives the benefit of the doubt to enduring, widely held beliefs. It assumes that such beliefs are apt to have "something going for them." They should be rejected if they prove to be sufficiently problematic, but are not to be jettisoned simply because they can be doubted. Nor should they be rejected simply because they cannot be proved. (Note that even the natural sciences presuppose some beliefs of this type—among them, the belief that the five senses are reliable.[3]) Of course, under scrutiny, it might turn out that some enduring, widely held beliefs conflict logically with others, or with propositions that are firmly established even if not (or not yet) widely held (such as some well-established scientific theories). Then we will need to make adjustments in our belief system.[4]

I make this comment about philosophical method primarily because, in my judgment, a confused or arbitrary application of Descartes' method bedevils many philosophical discussions. For example, suppose a discussion has been proceeding in Aristotelian fashion, when suddenly one participant or another realizes that his views are under threat, and so he begins to demand proofs for enduring, widely held beliefs. These kinds of shifts in method are understandable and tempting for us all, of course, but I think they hinder progress. Unless we are willing to be radical skeptics, we must not adopt Descartes' method.[5]

Fourth, although my argument doesn't absolutely depend on this, I think it will be helpful for me to say something about how I'm inclined to approach the topic of moral knowledge. I think that certain claims about the virtues are a good place to start in forming a systematic understanding of morality. For example, I think it is fairly clear that love is good. Love is a virtue and not a vice. Justice also is good; it is a virtue and not a vice. The same goes for wisdom, courage, moderation, and honesty. I am not claiming that the concepts of love, justice, wisdom, and so on, are easy to analyze with great precision. But I think we have a significant grasp of these concepts. Furthermore, I think ordinary humans (without the aid of any special divine revelation) can see that these are good character traits, not bad ones.[6]

Fifth, for present purposes, I'm going to make a simplifying assumption regarding metaphysics. I'm going to assume that one of two views is true:

a. There is a unique Deity who is almighty and perfectly morally good. (I'll call this *theism*, for short.)
b. There is no God; ultimate reality is physical and it is self-organizing—that is, it is not organized by anything distinct from it (such as a god)—and with the possible exception of such abstract entities as numbers, all entities are physical. (I'll call this *naturalism*, for short.)

I do in fact think that these two views are the most important, large-scale, metaphysical views on the market. I recognize that, as Dr. Kurtz points out, there are alternative versions of theism; there are also alternative versions of naturalism. I have discussed many of the relevant alternatives elsewhere, but lack the space to take them up here.[7] Nevertheless, if there is a good argument that favors (a) over (b), then surely that argument is philosophically quite significant.

Sixth, I want to identify a well-known moral argument that I am not advancing, and to indicate (very briefly) why I am not advancing it:

1. If God does not exist, then there are no objective moral truths. (An *objective truth* is one that holds whether or not we humans believe it holds. A *moral truth* is a truth about right and wrong, or about good and evil.)
2. At least some moral truths are objective.
3. So, God exists.

I fully accept premise 2 of this argument. And although I don't have space to argue the point here, I think philosophical views contrary to premise 2 are highly problematic.[8] Thus, I will simply assume premise 2 in the discussion below. But I will not assume that premise 1 is true, primarily because it presupposes the falsehood of a number of metaethical theories, among the most plausible of which, to my way of thinking, is *moral Platonism*. By "moral Platonism" I mean the view that certain moral truths are necessary (whether or not God exists).[9] A *necessary truth* is one that cannot be false under any possible circumstances. Most philosophers think that mathematical truths, among others, are necessary. And even if there were no God, I assume mathematical truths would still hold—for example, $1 + 1 = 2$, $8 < 9$, and no circle is a square. This being so, might it be that "Unjustified killing is wrong" or "If there are people, then it is wrong to torture them just for fun" are necessary moral truths? This type of view has considerable plausibility, in my view; accordingly, I will concede at the outset that there can be objective moral truth even if there is no God.[10]

I will now state my moral argument for the existence of God.[11]

THE MORAL ARGUMENT: STAGE I

It is generally agreed by moral theorists that moral reasons are overriding. Let me state this thesis more precisely and give it a name: *The Overriding Reasons Thesis (ORT): The overriding (or strongest) reasons always favor doing what is morally required.* A series of clarifying comments is in order.

First, in this context, *refraining* from doing something (for example, refraining from lying) counts as "doing something." With this in mind, let me illustrate ORT. Suppose you arrive for work quite late one day. Your boss confronts you. Now, let's suppose your boss is a good person and a reasonable one, not a tyrant or a mere stickler for the rules. Furthermore, let's suppose that you don't have a good reason for being late. However, a plausible lie pops into your head, and you know your boss will believe you if you tell the lie; he or she will believe you and you'll be off the hook. It's that simple, except for one "little" detail: You know that lying would be morally wrong in this situation. Now, in this case, you have a reason to lie. Lying will get you off the hook; it will enable you to avoid your boss's (reasonable) reprimand. But you also have a reason to avoid lying, a moral reason, for it's your moral duty not to lie (in this case). Now, which of the reasons is stronger or overriding? According to ORT, the *moral* reason is—it overrides your self-interested desire to avoid your boss's reprimand.

Second, let me note that ORT is not the claim that a person always acts in accord with moral reasons when those reasons conflict with other types of reasons, such as merely self-interested ones. Suppose it is Bob's moral duty not to spend his entire monthly salary placing bets at the racetrack—as the father of three dependent children, gambling away his salary is morally wrong. Nevertheless, Bob may blow his salary at the racetrack simply for the *pleasure* he gets from gambling. And if Bob squanders his salary for this reason, then, from the standpoint of ORT, Bob acts on a reason that is weaker than the applicable moral reason (namely, it's *wrong* for Bob to gamble in this way). ORT does not say that immoral behavior never occurs; it merely says that when people do something that is *genuinely* morally wrong, they always have a weightier or stronger reason to refrain.

Third, for present purposes, I am concerned only with moral duties, obligations, or requirements. I am purposefully leaving aside what ethical theorists call supererogatory acts, which are "beyond the call of duty" (and so not *required*).[12] And if one is morally required to do something, then it is morally *wrong* for one not to do it. Furthermore, when I speak of moral requirements, duties, or obligations, I am not speaking of what moral theorists call prima facie duties, which may be overridden by other moral considerations; rather, I am speaking about what one is morally required to do, *all things considered.* For example, if I say that one is morally required not to steal in a certain situation, I do not mean simply that there are some moral reasons not to steal that may be overridden by other moral considerations in favor of stealing; I mean that, in the final analysis (taking all morally relevant reasons into account), one is required not to steal in that situation.

Fourth, you might have various kinds of reasons to do something. An act might be in your self-interest. It might be fun. It might produce something beautiful. It might be proper from the standpoint of etiquette. It might be approved of by your peer group. It might be your moral duty. And in a given case there may be no conflict between these various types of reasons; they might all back the same act. But plainly there are cases in life when matters aren't that simple, when some of these reasons point one way and some another. *ORT tells you that if you do your moral duty, the strongest or overriding reasons will always be on your side.*

Fifth, I assume that the "strongest" or "overriding" reason is not merely a subjective notion; people can (and sometimes do) make mistakes in weighing up reasons for and against performing an action. For example, a person who judges that moral requirements are often overridden (or outweighed) by personal whims would be making a very serious mistake.

Sixth, it could happen that you were doing your moral duty but other people didn't know that, and hence they might—understandably but mistakenly—judge you to be irrational. For example, let's suppose you've struggled for some time to find gainful employment. You finally land a position in a large insurance company. But, as it turns out, the insurance company operates by routinely paying policyholders less than they are entitled to. Elderly policyholders are particularly targeted, since they are considered "easy marks." Your boss constantly pressures you to cheat the policyholders assigned to you. As a result, you try to "blow the whistle" on your boss, but no one will listen, so you resign. Many of your relatives and friends think you are irrational ("stupid," "crazy") for giving up a job that pays well. But they simply don't realize that you had an overriding moral reason to quit. If they knew that, they would see that you made a tough choice, but one that was, on balance, backed by the strongest reason(s).

I see no way to prove ORT, but I think it is a presupposition shared by nearly all people who take morality seriously. To a person who is serious about morality, the suggestion that we humans have overriding reasons to behave *immorally* is profoundly disturbing, for in that case, doing one's duty would (at least sometimes) be irrational *in the sense that it would involve acting on the weaker reason(s).* And it would hardly be less disturbing to be told that the reasons for acting immorally are *exactly as strong as* the reasons to behave morally; for in that case, from the standpoint of rationality, being immoral is as justifiable as being moral is. In short, if ORT is false, then the *rational* authority of morality is undermined.

Our deep attachment to ORT is revealed in our responses to certain ethical theories. We reject moral theories that blatantly violate our sense that moral requirements override all others. For example, consider the claim that we should always do what is best for *others* ("Love thy neighbor *rather than* thyself").[13] Such a theory entails that I should sacrifice important interests of my own for the sake of relatively minor interests of others—for example, perhaps I should give up my annual vacations for the next decade so that my fellow workers can each add a day to their annual vacations. Since, intuitively, the strongest reasons do not favor giving up my annual vacation, the *alleged* moral requirement doesn't seem to be backed by the strongest reasons; hence, the theory implicitly denies ORT and we reject the theory.

Very well. ORT seems to be true. And indeed it is commonly accepted by theists and nontheists alike. But contrary to what is sometimes suggested, ORT is not a necessary truth. Consider a possible world in which a powerful evil demon rules.[14] The demon sees to it that highly morally virtuous persons are tormented eternally upon death, while the morally lukewarm and wicked are granted eternal bliss. In such a possible world, prudence dictates that one fail to fulfill one's moral duties on occasion. Moreover, when prudential considerations involve avoiding eternal torment, it is extremely plausible to suppose that prudential considerations will provide stronger or weightier reasons than *at least some* moral requirements. If I can avoid eternal torment by performing an immoral act that is not very harmful (e.g., by telling a lie that is wrong but won't cause much harm), and if I will otherwise be damned, then I submit that I have overriding reason to do something immoral.

ORT, then, is widely accepted, but apparently it is not a necessary truth. I now want to show how ORT can be used as a premise in an argument for the existence of God. To do this, I need to argue for the following thesis: *The Conditional Thesis (CT): If there is no God and no life after death, then the Overriding Reasons Thesis is not true.*[15] The case of Ms. Poore is used to support CT:

Ms. Poore has lived many years in grinding poverty. She is not starving, but has only the bare necessities. She has tried very hard to get ahead by hard work, but nothing has come of her efforts. An opportunity to steal a large sum of money arises. If Ms. Poore steals the money and invests it wisely, she can obtain many desirable things her poverty has denied her: a well-balanced diet, decent housing, adequate heat in the winter, health insurance, new career opportunities through education, and so on. Moreover, if she steals the money, her chances of being caught are very low, and she knows this. She is also aware that the person who owns the money is well off and will not be greatly harmed by the theft. Let us add that Ms. Poore rationally believes that if she fails to steal the money, she will likely live in poverty for the remainder of her life. In short, Ms. Poore faces the choice of stealing the money or living in grinding poverty the rest of her life.[16]

Let me make three observations about this case. First, in giving it, I do not assume that stealing is wrong in every case. *Moral rigorism* is the view that simple moral rules such as "Lying is wrong" and "Stealing is wrong" admit of no exceptions whatsoever. I regard moral rigorism as untenable.[17] Second, it seems to me that Ms. Poore has very strong reasons to steal, but not a sufficient *moral* justification. Ms. Poore faces a choice between a life of unceasing poverty and stealing a large sum of money. The level of poverty is highly restrictive but not extreme—she is not starving or homeless, for example. In these circumstances, stealing is surely not *morally* permissible, however prudent it may be. Third, given the features built into the case, it is plausible to suppose that Ms. Poore has overriding reason to steal *assuming that there is no God and no life after death*. On that assumption, she stands to gain a great deal by stealing and to lose comparatively little. For if there is no God (and no life after death), the prudential concerns of this earthly life are weightier than they otherwise would be: Whatever fulfillment one attains must be attained prior to death. Moreover, the following general principle seems quite plausible: *If considerations of prudence and morality conflict, and if the prudential considerations are momentous while the results of behaving immorally are relatively minor, then prudence overrides morality.* And I submit that the Ms. Poore case is one in which prudential considerations are momentous while the results of behaving immorally are relatively minor—if we assume that God does not exist and there is no life after death.

Thus, CT appears to be true. But so does ORT. And together they support the conclusion that *either* God exists *or* there is life after death (or both).

ORT RECONSIDERED

But if the Ms. Poore case works, then doesn't it cast doubt on ORT? At least, from an atheist's point of view, isn't the Ms. Poore case plausibly one in

which the overriding reasons do *not* favor doing what is morally required?
And more generally, wouldn't any example used to support CT provide a reason to reject ORT, at least for an atheist?

If we posit that there is no God and no life after death, then the Ms. Poore
case will give us a reason to reject ORT. But it is hardly fair simply to assume
that atheism is true, when an argument for theism is being offered. And surely
we ought to be reluctant to jettison ORT. It seems deeply intuitive to most
morally serious persons. Furthermore, it is widely accepted by nontheists as
well as theists. Shouldn't we, at this point, at least be open to views that can
allow us to retain both ORT and CT? I think so. If we are proceeding in an
Aristotelian fashion, we certainly won't give up on ORT easily. Moreover, as
we shall see, it is possible for nontheists to accept both ORT and CT without
falling into contradiction.

But isn't it hard to see how ORT could be known? If ORT is known, it is
either known a priori or it is known a posteriori. If ORT is known a priori,
then either it is self-evident or it follows logically from self-evident premises.
A *self-evident* proposition is one that can be known simply by grasping the
concepts involved (such as "All husbands are married"). Surely ORT is not
self-evident. Nor does it appear to be logically derivable from any self-evident premises. On the other hand, if ORT is known a posteriori, then isn't it
an inductive generalization based on specific cases? But ORT isn't known in
this way either, and the Ms. Poore case (along with others like it) indicates
why. And obviously, an argument based on an unknowable premise isn't
worth much. Right?

The epistemological questions regarding ORT are interesting and important, but before we use them as a reason to reject ORT, we had better take a
deeper look. Similar questions can be raised regarding other principles that lie
deep in the structure of our thinking. For lack of a better term, I shall refer to
them as "principles of thought." For example, as Hume pointed out, the following principle underlies our inductive reasoning:

A. *The future will resemble the past.* In a correct inductive inference, it is
probable that if the premises are true, then the conclusion is true. Example:
"In each of the past 25 years, Seattle has had an annual rainfall of over 30
inches. So, next year Seattle will probably have an annual rainfall of over
30 inches." Hume argued that (A) is not known a priori. We cannot see that
it is true simply by grasping the concepts involved. Nor can we derive it
logically from self-evident premises. Can (A) be known a posteriori? Well,
arguments for it would seem to beg the question. "In the past," we may say,
"the future has resembled the past; so this pattern will continue in the future." But clearly, this argument assumes the very point to be proved. Moreover, there are many ways in which the future does not resemble the past

(today isn't exactly like yesterday), but we remain confident that the future resembles the past *in the relevant sense*, and thus that any examples that would appear to undermine inductive reasoning really do not. In the face of an apparent counterexample to (A), we assume that there is an error in the observation-report, or a misperception, or that we have somehow misidentified the correct principles of induction, or that we have misapplied them. And we stick with (A).

Among the principles of thought are principles of credulity. A principle of credulity concerning sense experience might be stated (rather vaguely) as follows:

B. *It is rational for me to accept what my sense experience indicates unless special reasons apply.*[18] Here again the principle is surely not self-evident and not logically derivable from self-evident premises; hence it is not known a priori. Moreover, it is hard to see how (B) can be inferred from experience in a non-question-begging way. Won't any appeal to experience simply presuppose (B)? It would seem so. Also, note that radical skeptics reject (B) outright. But in spite of the puzzles regarding how (B) can be known, most philosophers accept (B) or something similar to it.

Indeed, most philosophers are *firmly* committed to both (A) and (B), or at least to principles along these lines. This commitment continues even when the philosophers find themselves unable to explain how they know the principles. I think we cling to such principles of thought because (a) on reflection they seem to be deeply correct and (b) there would be a kind of intellectual disaster in denying them. But I think something similar can be said about ORT. At least to morally serious persons, ORT is deeply intuitive and there would be a kind of disaster in denying it, since to deny it is precisely to deny the rational authority of morality.

I am not claiming that denying ORT has epistemic ripple effects as far reaching as denying (A) and/or (B). These principles have applications in virtually every area of our thinking, while ORT applies only to what philosophers call our *practical* reasoning. But I think it is quite plausible to suppose that ORT is fundamental to our practical reasoning. And I think we ought to be extremely reluctant to deny ORT: Because ORT is deeply intuitive, we ought to strongly favor philosophical theories that can save it, and to look with suspicion on those that cannot.

One last observation about ORT is pertinent. Many naturalists claim that their metaphysical position grounds or supports morality just as well as theism does. But it seems to me that naturalists who deny ORT cannot plausibly make this claim. They are denying that the strongest reasons always favor doing your moral duty and thus they are denying the rational authority of morality.

THE MORAL ARGUMENT: STAGE II

To this point, I've been defending the Overriding Reasons Thesis and the
Conditional Thesis:

ORT: The overriding (or strongest) reasons always favor doing what is
    morally required.
CT: If there is no God and no life after death, then ORT is not true.

If we accept both ORT and CT, then we must conclude that either God exists
or there is a life after death in which virtue is rewarded (or both). Now, if a
good God exists, moral wrongdoing is sin; and sin alienates one from God.
Moreover, it is never in one's best interests to be alienated from God. Thus,
theism allows us to maintain ORT while accepting CT. However, ORT and CT
leave open the possibility that (i) there is no God but (ii) there is a life after
death in which virtue is rewarded. And this is just the position of many who
accept reincarnation. Of course, naturalists generally reject reincarnation, so
this possibility is apt to be of little interest to them, but since some nontheists
believe in reincarnation, a brief exploration of it may be helpful at this point.[19]

    Given reincarnation, there is life after death. And given a universe governed
by karma, one always receives one's just deserts. For example, if a wicked person lives a prosperous, pleasant life, that person will pay for his or her wickedness in a future life. One never "gets ahead" by doing wrong. In the long run,
wrongdoing leads to misery while virtue leads to happiness. Thus, if there is
no God, but reincarnation occurs under the law of karma, then moral requirements are never trumped by other sorts of considerations and ORT holds.

    However, given that reincarnation and karma hold *in the absence of any
deity*, the universe is governed not only by physical laws (such as the law of
gravity) but by *impersonal* moral laws. These moral laws must be quite complex, for they have to regulate the connection between each soul's moral
record in one life and that soul's total circumstances in its next life, including
which body it has, its environment, and the degree of happiness (or misery) it
experiences. Thus, these impersonal moral laws must somehow take into account every act, every intention, and every choice of every moral agent and
ensure that the agent receives nothing less than his or her just deserts in the
next life. Now, the degree of complexity involved here is obviously very high,
and it serves a *moral end*, namely, justice. But a highly complex structure that
promotes justice can hardly be accepted as a brute fact. Such a moral order
cries out for explanation in terms of an intelligent cause. And if the moral order is on a scale far surpassing what can reasonably be attributed to human
intelligence, an appeal to divine intelligence is justified. Hence, the moral or-

der postulated by nontheistic reincarnation paradoxically provides evidence for the existence of a personal God.[20]

To sum up, ORT and CT, taken together, lead us to conclude that either God exists or there is a life after death in which virtue is rewarded (or both). But a life after death in which virtue is rewarded would itself be an astonishing phenomenon, and one that would call for an explanation in terms of a personal God. Furthermore, the postulate of a perfectly morally good God would render the hypothesis of karma superfluous. For such a God would see to it that no one is penalized for being virtuous in the long run, and that no one gets ahead in the final analysis by doing wicked things.

OBJECTIONS AND REPLIES

There are of course various objections to the moral argument presented above. Let us now turn to them. As with any philosophical argument, there are ways to avoid the conclusion. My strategy will be to show that the ways out all come at a substantial philosophical cost—one is arguably better off accepting the conclusion.

Objection 1. *You have not established the Conditional Thesis. Even if God does not exist, we humans have overriding reason to be moral. Take Ms. Poore, for example. She has overriding reason not to steal, for multiple reasons. She will feel guilty if she steals. And guilt feelings are very unpleasant. Moreover, she will suffer loss of virtue if she steals. But virtue is its own reward; one never gets ahead by destroying one's good moral character.*

The appeal to guilt feelings won't work. First, while guilt feelings play an important role in the motivations of most people, this is not so for everyone. Some people do not have a strong conscience and do not approach life from a dominantly moral perspective. Second, we have to keep in mind that even basically good people occasionally fail in their moral duties. They act selfishly or perhaps fail to act out of laziness or cowardice. And if what they've done isn't too heinous or harmful, they generally forgive themselves and get on with their lives. Ms. Poore might be like that. She might feel some pangs of conscience initially, but "get over it" before long, excusing herself on the grounds that she is in a difficult situation.

True, Ms. Poore will become less virtuous if she steals. And virtue is generally a benefit to those who have it, but is perfect virtue always a greater benefit than any good one might obtain at its expense *if there is no God and no life after death*? Consider the following contrasting cases:

Luke Warme is a morally lukewarm person who happens to be regarded as highly virtuous. He is revered by all, loved by his family and friends, and finds his life enjoyable and satisfying. Verity Sainte on the other hand is a genuinely virtuous person—honest, just, and kind. Unfortunately, because of some clever enemies, Verity is widely regarded as wicked. She is in prison for life on false charges. Her family and friends, convinced that she is guilty, have turned against her. She spends most of her time in solitary confinement.[21]

Who's better off, more fulfilled? To all appearances it is Luke Warme, not Verity Sainte (assuming there is no God and no life after death). And even if virtue is of value for its own sake, it is not the only thing worth having. For example, freedom is valuable, too. Suppose a corrupt warden agrees to release Verity from prison if she will commit just one immoral act—one that is not too harmful. Perhaps Verity can tell a lie that will enable the warden to cover up some unjust favoritism he or she has shown toward one of the prisoners. Or perhaps Verity's accounting skills can be of use to the warden in covering up a misuse of funds. Her choice, like Ms. Poore's, is roughly between a moral stance that ensures enduring misery and a single immoral act that will, to all appearances, provide her with greater fulfillment all things considered.

Objection 2. *But the cases of Ms. Poore and Verity Sainte are rather unusual. You seem to admit that, even if there is no God, moral requirements usually override all other reasons for acting. And that's good enough.*[22]

First, I *am* willing to grant that moral requirements would often or even usually be overriding even if there were no God. For example, in my opinion, murderers generally do not attain greater personal fulfillment by killing (whether or not God exists). Whatever their gains might be, the blow to their character is too great.[23]

Second, however, I do not think it's a small thing to grant that moral requirements are sometimes overridden by self-interest. For in that case it is sometimes irrational to do what one is morally required to do. For reasons I've already given, I think we ought to be extremely reluctant to accept such a result. Bear in mind that the examples I've provided suggest that one has overriding reason to commit some wrong act if one has much to gain (all things considered), one probably won't get caught, and the resulting harm is not great. But it is plausible to suppose that many people face such cases at some point in their lives *assuming there is no God and no life after death*. Thus, it seems to me, rejecting ORT should be "an option of last resort."

Objection 3. *Even eminent theistic ethicists, such as Thomas Aquinas, grant that stealing is not always wrong (e.g., if one is starving, it isn't wrong to steal a slice of bread). Perhaps Ms. Poore is in one of those special circumstances in which stealing is morally permissible. If so, your primary example fails.*[24]

I tried to describe the Ms. Poore case so that she had strong prudential reasons to steal but not a sufficient moral justification. As with any detailed moral example, there is apt to be some disagreement about the impact of adding or deleting various elements. One way to approach this is to distinguish the basic outline of the case from various elaborations thereof. The basic outline is this: Ms. Poore faces a choice between a life of unceasing poverty and stealing a large sum of money. Her level of poverty guarantees a very low standard of living but her poverty is not extreme—that is, she is not starving or homeless. She can steal the money without getting caught. And stealing the money will not produce great harm; it will not impoverish the victim.

I think that most morally serious people would not grant that stealing is permissible for Ms. Poore in the case as outlined here. Just consider what morally virtuous people would say about the case—people who combine (in high measure) such virtues as love, justice, moderation, courage, honesty, and wisdom. Surely such virtuous people, though sympathetic with Ms. Poore's plight, would not judge that stealing is *morally* permissible for her. And I suggest that the judgment of morally virtuous people should be given a lot of weight here.[25]

The case of Ms. Poore, as outlined above, can be elaborated in various ways. For example, we might specify what Ms. Poore will gain if she steals the money. She might gain (a) freedom from financial worry, (b) comfortable housing, (c) medical care for a persistent (but nonfatal) illness, (d) a much-needed vacation, (e) more education leading to fulfilling employment, and so on. But even if we specify these gains, is she permitted to steal, from a moral point of view? Again, if we take the judgments of morally virtuous people as our guide, I think the answer is no.

Let me add that there *are* ways of elaborating the case so that Ms. Poore is permitted to steal. Suppose we rewrite the case so that she has a child who will die without a certain pharmaceutical and stealing is the only way Ms. Poore can obtain the pharmaceutical. In such a case, I grant that stealing is morally permitted. But that is not the type of case I've built my argument on.

Objection 4. *The argument involves the false presupposition that one can be morally virtuous by doing the right thing for merely self-interested reasons.*

This seriously misrepresents my argument. I grant that one is not being morally virtuous if one is doing the right thing for merely self-interested reasons. But the question is rather, what if self-interested reasons are sometimes stronger than moral reasons? What if prudential reasons sometimes override moral requirements? In that case, doing one's moral duty is irrational in the sense that it involves acting on the weaker reason(s). My claim is that, given naturalism, we sometimes have overriding reasons to do what is wrong.

Objection 5. *The argument involves the false presupposition that one is morally required to do X only if doing X is in one's long-term best interests.*

Again, this is misrepresentation. Ms. Poore is *morally* required not to steal. But the problem is that she has overriding reasons (of a nonmoral or prudential nature) to steal. In a nutshell, the problem is that the rational authority of morality is undermined if there is no God and no life after death.

Objection 6. *How does postulating God help? God can't make moral reasons overriding; God can only make it prudent to do what is morally required.*

I partly agree. I've not suggested that God by fiat (or otherwise) lends moral reasons their force. Let's just assume, for the sake of the argument, that moral reasons have whatever force they have independent of God. Nevertheless, what a good God can do is guarantee that moral reasons (requirements) are never trumped by other sorts of reasons. Unfortunately, moral reasons can be trumped assuming naturalism is true. That's the issue I've been trying to draw attention to all along the way. In short, theism enables us to retain both ORT and CT; naturalism does not.

Objection 7. *Suppose there is no God but one nevertheless believes that God exists. Wouldn't one still have overriding reason to do what is morally required? If so, your argument doesn't show that God exists.*[26]

First, even if there is merit in the objection, it hardly lends support to naturalism. Second, merely believing that God exists surely does not make it rational to be moral, for one's belief that God exists might be irrational or unjustified. Indeed, it seems to me that belief in God cannot make it rational to be moral unless one is justified in believing that God exists.[27]

The objection suggests a more complex version of CT, along the following lines (assuming that stage II of my moral argument is successful): "If God does not exist and one does not have a justified belief that God exists, one does not have overriding reason to be moral." The conclusion would then be, "Either God exists or one has a justified belief that God exists." This conclusion is welcome to theists, but can hardly be of comfort to the naturalist.[28]

NOTES

1. This claim is controversial, of course. For example, following in the tradition of St. Anselm, some hold that the ontological argument (by itself) provides adequate reason to believe that God exists. For my questions about the ontological argument, see C. Stephen Layman, *Letters to Doubting Thomas: A Case for the Existence of God* (New York: Oxford University Press, 2007), 236–39.

2. Marilyn McCord Adams, *Horrendous Evils and the Goodness of God* (Ithaca, N.Y.: Cornell University Press, 1999), 180.

3. Science presupposes some other widely held beliefs that cannot be proved and that some people have doubted. For example, as Hume pointed out, in order to employ inductive reasoning, one must assume that *the future will resemble the past*. ("All lemons tasted in the past have been sour. So, the next lemon to be tasted will probably be sour.") And here's yet another type of example: *Laws of nature, such as the law of gravity, hold in regions of the universe that are beyond the range of human observation.*

4. Two clarifications: (A) The phrase "enduring and widely held" invites questions such as "Enduring for how long? And how widely held?" I readily grant that there is vagueness here and I see no way to avoid it. But the longer the beliefs have endured and the more widely they are held, the better. (B) In the midst of philosophical discussion, we often *become aware* that we believe certain things, and we may not have been previously aware of having these beliefs. A belief can be "enduring and widely held," as I am using the phrase, even though many are not *consciously aware* of holding it. For example, most people believe that *if A causes B, then A does not occur after B in time,* but many people hold this belief without consciously entertaining it.

5. I don't mean to suggest that radical skepticism gets a free pass as long as it is held by those employing Descartes' method in a consistent way! Radical skepticism is open to severe objections. For example, suppose you are about to cross the street. You see a truck bearing down on you—or at least it *seems* to you that you see a truck bearing down on you and you have no special reason (beyond Descartes' method of doubt) to doubt that you are seeing a truck. From the standpoint of radical skepticism, *you are no more justified in believing A than B*:

A. A truck is coming down the street.

B. There is no truck coming down the street.

Such a result seems thoroughly unacceptable; and anyone who tried to live consistently with it probably wouldn't last long.

6. In regard to moral knowledge and divine revelation, it is perhaps worth noting that the Bible indicates that some moral truth is available apart from special revelation (e.g., Romans 2:14–15).

7. See Layman, *Letters to Doubting Thomas*, especially chapters 4 ("A Cosmological Argument") and 5 ("A Design Argument").

8. Layman, *Letters to Doubting Thomas*, 215–25.

9. Here I am assuming for the sake of the argument that it is *possible* that God does not exist. If God exists of necessity, as many theologians have held, then God cannot fail to exist. But since I am offering an argument for God's existence, I must of course allow for the possibility that there is no God. For a defense of moral Platonism, see Richard Swinburne's chapter in this volume.

10. For a very carefully argued defense of objective moral truth—a defense that does not rely on theism—see Russ Shafer-Landau, *Moral Realism: A Defence* (Oxford: Clarendon Press, 2003).

11. The main argument presented here is borrowed from two earlier works: C. Stephen Layman, "God and the Moral Order," *Faith and Philosophy* 19, no. 3 (July 2002): 304–16, and "God and the Moral Order: Replies to Objections," *Faith and Philosophy* 23, no. 2 (April 2006): 209–12. I have also borrowed occasional paragraphs from these articles, altering the wording only slightly.

12. Some ethical theories allow for supererogation and some do not. A typical (alleged) example of a supererogatory act would be donating a kidney to a perfect stranger who needs one. Such an act is morally praiseworthy but not morally required, if indeed it is supererogatory.

13. The example is borrowed from Sarah Stroud, "Moral Overridingness and Moral Theory," *Pacific Philosophical Quarterly* 79, no. 2 (1998): 170–89. I take it that "Love thy neighbor *rather than* thyself" is a quite different principle than "Love thy neighbor *as* thyself."

14. According to classical theism, God exists of necessity and is necessarily omnipotent and necessarily perfectly morally good. From this standpoint, there is no possible world ruled by a powerful evil demon. But I am here offering an argument for the existence of God and hence we must for the sake of the argument set aside the assumption that God exists of necessity (i.e., in every possible world).

15. It is perhaps worth noting that CT does not imply that if God exists (or there is life after death), then ORT is true. This conditional will be discussed in the last two sections of the chapter.

16. The case is borrowed from Layman, "God and the Moral Order," 307.

17. I take moral rigorism to be untenable because of examples such as the following: Suppose an innocent person is about to be killed by thugs. I can hide the innocent person and tell the thugs a plausible lie about his or her whereabouts, thus giving the innocent person an opportunity to escape. Most ethicists would agree that lying is morally permissible in such a case.

18. Various kinds of special reasons can rightly cause me to doubt what experience seems to indicate. For example, if my optometrist tells me my eyes are not functioning properly in a certain respect, then I may not trust some of my visual experiences. Similarly, if I have taken a hallucinogenic drug, I may not trust my sense experiences. I might also doubt what my experience seems to indicate on the grounds that the content seems highly improbable based on what I already know—for example, suppose it were to *seem* to me that I see an oak tree *jogging*.

19. As I have defined *naturalism*, it implicitly denies the existence of nonphysical souls. Hence, any version of reincarnation involving nonphysical

souls (e.g., the traditional Hindu view) is inconsistent with naturalism so defined. If I understand correctly, it is characteristic of Buddhists to accept reincarnation while denying (or at least, not affirming) the existence of a nonphysical soul.

20. The main point of this paragraph is borrowed from Robin Collins, "Eastern Religions," in *Reason for the Hope Within*, ed. Michael J. Murray (Grand Rapids, Mich.: Eerdmans, 1999), 206.

21. This thought experiment is borrowed in its essentials from Richard Taylor, "Value and the Origin of Right and Wrong," in *Ethical Theory: Classical and Contemporary Readings*, ed. Louis Pojman (Belmont, Calif.: Wadsworth, 1989), 115–21.

22. This objection has been pressed by Peter Byrne, "God and the Moral Order: A Reply to Layman," *Faith and Philosophy* 23, no. 2 (April 2006): 202.

23. I grant this for the sake of the argument, but the claim can certainly be challenged. Some novels and films seem designed to call it into question. Examples include Patricia Highsmith, *The Talented Mr. Ripley* (1955; repr. London: Vintage, 1999). There is a film version by Anthony Minghella, *The Talented Mr. Ripley* (Miramax Films, 1999). See also the Woody Allen films *Crimes and Misdemeanors* (Orion Pictures, 1989) and *Match Point* (British Broadcasting Company, 2005).

24. This objection has been pressed by Byrne, "God and the Moral Order," 204.

25. See Shafer-Landau, *Moral Realism*, 265–302, for a systematic development of the idea that virtuous persons provide us with a model of reliable moral judgment.

26. I wish to thank Paul Pardi for suggesting this objection to me in e-mail correspondence, September 9, 2006.

27. This is a note for epistemologically informed readers. I am using the word "belief" here a bit loosely, to indicate whatever propositional attitude toward "God exists" is required from the religious standpoint. In ordinary English usage, "belief" may convey greater confidence in the truth of a proposition than is requisite from the religious standpoint, but certainly the requisite propositional attitude is significantly more positive than suspending judgment or remaining neutral.

28. I wish to thank Terence Cuneo, Paul Pardi, and the editors of this volume for helpful advice and comments on various drafts of this chapter.

Chapter Three

Atheism as Perfect Piety

Louise Antony

Dr. Craig's position is that the existence of God is both necessary and sufficient for the existence of objective moral truth—for the reality of right and
wrong. He's wrong on both counts. I'll start by explaining why God is not
necessary for morality, then move on to why God is not enough. Along the
way I'll have some things to say about Dr. Craig's notion of accountability.
Let me introduce all my themes by means of a little autobiography.

I was raised a devout Catholic, but in my first semester of college, as a result of studying philosophy, I came to the conclusion that God does not exist.
I did not take the matter lightly. Indeed, I struggled against the (inevitable)
outcome with all my might, trying without success to defend the classic arguments for the existence of God against the classic objections. In fact, I
think I had ceased to believe a good while before I finally admitted it to myself. What kept me clinging, nominally, to a faith I no longer felt was precisely the worry that William Lane Craig is promoting: the worry that without God, there is no morality.

Since morality had been linked with religion my entire life, I was accus-
tomed to thinking of the two as equivalent. And since I had never considered
giving up religion, I had never even imagined what a world without God
would be like. Now that the course of my reasoning was forcing me to do so,
I was confronting a picture much like the one painted by Dr. Craig: human beings scuttling aimlessly about on an insignificant planet in an unexceptional
region of space-time, living animal lives, devoid of meaning and value. I found
this vision both terrifying and repugnant. I could not countenance nihilism,
particularly at that point in my life, when I was learning so much about the extent of suffering and injustice in the world. I was outraged by the violence my
country was, at that time, perpetrating on the people of Southeast Asia, and

outraged as well by the lies my government told in trying to legitimate it. I was also becoming aware of the huge disparities in wealth and well-being, not only among citizens of the United States, but between well-off people in my country and millions of people outside it. I acquired the concept of "oppression" and saw, as if illuminated by the light of the Gospels themselves, the duty of every decent person to oppose it.

So it seemed clear to me, and clearer than any of the premises in any of the arguments that led to atheism, that there was a right and a wrong. Some actions are morally good, and some are grievously bad. And yet the force of the reasoning against theism was undeniable. The argument that hit me the hardest came from the problem of evil: How could an omnipotent, omniscient, and perfectly good being allow so much suffering in the world?[1] The irony in my thinking at this point—God was necessary for there to be moral evil, yet the fact that evil existed showed that God did not—only added to my confusion. Suffice it to say that I was caught in a psychologically untenable position.

Now I must admit at this point that my turmoil was not entirely about the objectivity of moral value. I was also pretty worried about the fate of my immortal soul. If I stopped believing and my antitheistic reasoning turned out to be wrong, would I be damned? I had read Pascal. He argued that a bet in favor of God's existence was infinitely more rational than a bet against it. If you bet for God, and lose, you lose nothing. If you bet against God, and win, you win nothing. But if you bet against God and lose, you condemn yourself to an eternity of suffering. I was pretty worried about the latter; if someone asked me to place money on it, I might have put it all on theism. But betting is not believing; I can bet on a horse without believing that he'll win.[2]

And so it was that, still in this fearful and unsettled state of mind, I contrived a little argument meant to indemnify my immortal soul against the possibility that God did exist even if I had ceased believing in him. Although I no longer need this argument, I still like it. And despite its perversity, I recommend it to my theistic friends. The conclusion of the argument is that, even if there is a God, it is morally better to *not* believe in him than to believe in him. The reasoning for this conclusion bears directly on the issue of the debate between Craig and Kurtz.

To explain the argument, I must first explain a distinction I was taught as a girl, between *perfect* and *imperfect* contrition. The distinction concerns the possible reasons one might have for being contrite. Someone with perfect contrition is sorry because she or he has offended God by doing wrong; someone with imperfect contrition is only sorry because she or he fears punishment. Imperfect contrition achieves its aim—it is good enough to forestall damnation. But perfect contrition is much preferable, since it bespeaks the best possible motives for repentance—a hatred of sin and a desire to do what is right.

Now I had always felt that my own contrition fell short. It seemed to me that no matter how hard I tried to focus on the inherent evil of my sins, I would find myself thinking instead about what they might cost me. But now, grown up and in the throes of my religious crisis, I was struck by a perverse insight: that the perfect contrition that had eluded me hitherto might finally be achieved *if I became an atheist*. If I didn't *believe* in God, then fear of eternal damnation could hardly be a reason for me to repent anything. If I, as a nonbeliever, felt contrite for having done something wrong, it could *only* be because it *was wrong*.[3] If I ceased to fear God's judgment, then the only possible reason I could ever have for doing good would be *goodness* itself.

Much emboldened, I took my reasoning a step further: Maybe atheism was the *only* way to achieve perfect contrition, the only psychologically possible way for us fallible, selfish human beings to put aside concern for ourselves in confronting our misdeeds. Wouldn't a God who loved what was good be more pleased with creatures who sought that good for its own sake than with those who did so only to curry favor? So much more pleased, in fact, that God would rather his creatures displayed perfect contrition than that they believed in him? (Take that, Pascal!)

The argument, then, in full dress:

1. Perfect contrition (even with unbelief) is more pleasing to God than imperfect contrition (even with belief).
2. The only (psychologically possible) way for human beings to achieve perfect contrition is to cease to believe in God.
3. Human beings ought to do that which is most pleasing to God.

Therefore,

4. Human beings ought to cease believing in God.

Of course, as you might imagine, the doublethink involved here was not long sustainable. "God doesn't exist, but he won't punish me for thinking this"—the contradiction was too transparent to be comforting for long. But making the argument helped me learn something else that did comfort me: *Morality is independent of God*.

How so? In my reflections on perfect and imperfect contrition, I asked myself *why* God preferred the former to the latter. Clearly, to sin is to flout God's commandments, to disobey. And disobedience displeases God. But why? Is it the *mere* fact of disobedience? That seemed hardly possible. Surely God was not like the petty tyrants one sometimes encounters in school—teachers or principals who issue arbitrary commands and prohibitions, just for the exercise, just for the delight of bending another person to their capricious wills. No, I concluded. God's dicta are not arbitrary; God wills only what is *right* and prohibits only what is *wrong*. Disobedience offends him because disobedience entails the commission of a crime. It's the right and wrong he cares about, not that he said do it or don't.[4] It's the goodness, stupid.

I was soon to encounter a text that made all this reasoning explicit and vivid: Plato's dialogue *Euthyphro*. The dialogue begins with Socrates encountering the eponymous young Euthyphro as the latter is on his way to bringing a charge of murder against his own father. His unusual action, Euthyphro explains, is dictated by *piety*. Socrates professes to be puzzled, and, as is his wont, asks Euthyphro to define his terms. Piety, Euthyphro replies, is that which is loved by the gods. But this answer doesn't satisfy Socrates. He presses Euthyphro further: Do the gods love pious acts because they are pious, or are such acts pious because they are loved by the gods? Socrates raises this question because Euthyphro's definition is ambiguous between two readings. On one reading, Euthyphro is saying that being loved by the gods is what *constitutes* piousness. "Pious," on this alternative, is just shorthand for "something the gods love." There is nothing more to understand about the gods' relation to pious acts than this. There is not, or need not be, any characteristic common to all pious acts, other than their being preferred by the gods. In particular, there need be nothing about pious acts that *explains* the gods' preference. The gods may change their preferences on a whim—and frequently did, if Homer and Hesiod knew their stuff. There is thus no sure way of predicting, in advance of expressions of divine favor, whether a given act is pious or not.

The generalization "pious acts are those that are loved by the gods" is thus, on the first reading of Euthyphro's answer, a mere definitional tautology. Now the second reading also entails this generalization, but makes it considerably more interesting. The second reading presumes that there *is* something about pious acts—some substantive property that all pious acts share—that explains why the gods love them. On this view, there is potentially much to understand about pious acts in themselves, and much to understand about the gods in consequence.

Suppose, for example, that it turns out that the pious acts are all and only those that express mortals' devotion, regardless of other features the acts may have. In that case, learning that the gods love pious acts tells us that the gods enjoy being worshipped above all else. A poor woman gives away her meager savings in order to purchase tributes; her children are left to beg in the streets, but no matter—the gods are delighted! Alternatively, imagine that the pious acts turn out to be those that are kind or just. Then we could infer that the gods value kindness and justice, regardless of whether the acts also express devotion. In this case, it would be the woman's foregoing the tributes, and attending to her needy children, that pleases the gods. Once we understand what unifies and characterize pious acts, we can predict with confidence just which acts the gods will, in the future, favor. (Homer's and Hesiod's gods were more like the former, Plato's more like the latter.)

Translated into contemporary terms, the question Socrates is asking is this: Are morally good actions morally good simply in virtue of God's favoring them? Or does God favor them because they are—independently of his favoring them—morally good? It's a question I'd like to put directly to Dr. Craig, because he really seems to be of two minds about the issue. On the one hand, he claims to believe that without God, there would be no morality. On the other hand, he—like all decent religious people—seems to shrink from the logical consequences of saying so.

The moral theory that embodies the first reading of the updated Euthyphro definition is called divine command theory (DCT). It says that what is good is good *only* because God has commanded it; there is nothing *more to* an act's being good than that God commanded it.[5] Theories that endorse the second option—let's call any such theory a divine independence theory (DIT)—contend that the goodness of an action is a feature that is *independent* of, and *antecedent* to God's willing it. God could have commanded either this action or its opposite, but being good himself, commands only the good one. As with the two readings of the Euthyphro definition, both DCT and DIT entail a perfect consonance between the class of actions God commands and the class of actions that are good (or rather, they do so on the assumption that God is perfectly benevolent). The two theories differ, however, on what accounts for this congruence. DCT says that it is God's command that explains why the good acts are good, while DIT says that it is the goodness of the acts that explains why God commanded them. The way to bring out the difference is to consider a case of an act that we'd all antecedently agree is morally wrong—say, torturing an innocent child. If DCT is correct, then the following counterfactual is true: If God had commanded us to torture innocent children, then it would have been morally right to do so.[6] DIT, however, entails the following: If God had commanded us to torture innocent children, then God would not have been perfectly good.[7] Dr. Craig will want to protest that the antecedent of these counterfactuals is impossible, indeed, inconceivable—that God could never condone, much less command, such a thing, that it would be incompatible with his moral nature. But if Craig does so protest, then he reveals himself to be a partisan of DIT after all. Only the theorist who believes that right and wrong are independent of God's commands could have any basis for thinking she or he knows in advance what God would or would not command. If, as DCT says, an act's *being good* just consists in its being chosen by God, then there's nothing about an action in advance of its being chosen or rejected that would enable us to determine what attitude God would take toward it in some other possible world. "Good" for the divine command theorist is *synonymous* with "commanded by God"; we are supposed to lack any conception of what it would be for an act to be good or bad that's independent of our knowledge of what God has commanded. There *is* no good or bad, according to DCT, apart from what God commands. Because that is so, there is nothing that is *inherently* good or bad, and thus nothing that *explains* God's choosing which acts to endorse and which acts to prohibit.

There's another objection to my claim that DCT, if true, would make it impossible to predict what God prefers. The objection is that we could use simple induction: We have lots of examples of the kinds of things God commands; it stands to reason that he would continue to command similar things in the future. This is a perfectly cogent objection. It does point out that if we could find something the commanded acts have in common, then we would have a basis for predicting future commands. The problem with it as an answer to the issue I'm raising, however, is that the one kind of property we *cannot* observe the commanded acts to have in common, if DCT is true, is a *moral* property. According to DCT, remember, to be morally good *just is* to be commanded by God, and so it is not a property that can be observed to be present in advance of God's commands. Even if we discovered that, for example, all of the acts that God commands are acts that ease the suffering of some sentient creature, we would not thereby discover that God commanded those acts because such acts were good. The discovery, for example, would provide no guidance in a case where one could ease one person's suffering by killing her or him, or where the withholding of vital but painful medical treatment would nonetheless keep the patient comfortable.

But let's look at the opposing view. According to DIT, God's choices are both predictable, and—what seems to me more important—explicable. God's choices don't confer goodness upon certain actions; on the contrary, he chooses to command them *because* they are the good ones. This view holds out the possibility that human beings can discover for themselves what is right and what is wrong—that they resemble their Creator in having a capacity for making such judgments. I was certainly taught, growing up as a Catholic, that we have such a capacity—it was called a conscience.

In short, divine command theory is an insult to any God worth worshipping, and to the human beings who worship him as well. DCT makes moral goodness out to be essentially a matter of etiquette. To be correct in etiquette is just to do things in what is the preferred way of doing things, in some cultural group or other. Thus, it's rude to burp loudly after a meal in my culture, but (reportedly) not in some others. There is no objective moral fact of the matter about burping—its rightness or wrongness consists simply in whether it is so regarded by the cultural group in question. DCT is not relativistic in this way, but that's only because it hypothesizes but a single arbiter. God, for DCT, is simply the ultimate Miss Manners.

Another analogy: Think about what it is for something to be "cool."[8] In contemporary American culture, it's probably safe to say that the cool things are the things that popular people like. Why is that so? It might be the case that there is a substantive property shared by all and only cool things, and that popular people are adept at recognizing this property whenever and wherever it is instantiated. More likely, however, the explanation goes the other way: that whatever the popular crowd happens to like *thereby* becomes cool. If that's the case, then there is nothing inherently true about cool things that gives them that status, and nothing about things in themselves that could enable you to predict what will be cool. Anything is potentially cool, and what's cool today may be "so last week" by tomorrow. On analogy, if DCT is correct, then what's "good" is not an inherent property of good things—what gives them their status is simply their having been commanded by God. Just as *Vogue*'s say-so can make brown the new black, a word from God and theft is the new charity.

I doubt that there are many people who really believe DCT. If there were, then there would be fewer interpretative difficulties surrounding those stories in the Bible that depict God commanding actions that we would ordinarily take to be moral atrocities. So what, everyone would say, if God orders genocide (as he does at Samuel 15:1–3)? Or if he commands a father to murder his son (Genesis 22)? God commanded it, so it's good! But of course this is not the attitude most people take toward these stories. Most people struggle to make sense of them in light of the clear moral fact that killing innocent children is wrong. If these acts are wrong, and if God is good, then there must be some mistake; we must be misinterpreting. God must not really have commanded these things, or we must be wrong about what it is that he actually did command. For this sort of exegetical practice to make sense, there has to be an *antecedent* concept of moral rightness driving the interpretation of God's commands.[9]

Even among those who are willing to bite the hermeneutical bullet, and say that, well, yes it *is* genocide and God *did* command it, so it must be right— even then, there is usually some attempt made to reconcile the goodness of genocide *in this particular case* with one's moral qualms about genocide in general. For example, consider God's command that Saul "blot out" the Amalakite nation, slaughtering not only every man, woman, and child, but also every living beast residing with the tribe. *The New Advent Encyclopedia* avers that "if this seem an inhuman command, let us remember the prevailing sentiment that the Amal were 'inhuman and barbarous; a people with such evil customs deserves no mercy.'"[10]

More evidence that most religious people are *not* divine command theorists can be found in common reactions to individuals who claim divine or scriptural justification for the commission of heinous acts. The Bible contains numerous examples of the sort referred to above, cases in which God, apparently, either commands or licenses the performance of immoral acts, so individuals who are inclined for their own reasons to perform such acts often reach for the Bible to justify themselves. Many American proponents of slavery made such appeals. Here, for example, is Jefferson Davis, President of the Confederate States of America:

> [Slavery] was established by decree of Almighty God. . . . It is sanctioned in the Bible, in both Testaments, from Genesis to Revelation. . . . It has existed in all ages, has been found among the people of the highest civilization, and in nations of the highest proficiency in the arts.[11]

Such statements were denounced by Christian abolitionists, who insisted that Christianity entailed the sinfulness of slavery. Jonathan Edwards Jr., writing in 1791, regarded Christian complacency about the slave trade as morally primitive. "Our pious fathers," he wrote, "lived in a time of ignorance which God winked at; but now he commandeth all men everywhere to repent of this wickedness."[12]

More recently, we can consider the cases of religious extremists. Eric Rudolph, a Christian pro-life militant, carried out a series of bombings in which three people were killed and more than a hundred and fifty were injured. He did this, he claims, in obedience to a divine command to save, by whatever means necessary, the lives of innocent children threatened by legalized abortion.[13] His acts were roundly denounced by mainstream Christians, even by those who oppose abortion. The American Life League, for example, in its 1999 "Pro-Life Proclamation against Violence," signed by thirteen religious pro-life organizations, called on "[a]ll perpetrators of violence to recognize that, far from being pro-life crusaders, they are nothing more than common criminals."[14] Ygal Amir, the assassin of Yitzhak Rabin, the Israeli prime minister who signed the Oslo Accords, defended his action by reference to the Talmudic "law of the pursuer" (din rodef), which commands every Jew to kill or to wound severely any Jew who is perceived as intending to kill another Jew.[15] Thoughtful Jews are almost as horrified by the assassin's appeal to the Talmud as by the act Amir sought thereby to legitimize.[16] In all these cases, reflective and morally responsible religious people find reason to reject surface readings of scripture and other authoritative texts when such texts appear to attribute to God edicts that conflict with commonsense morality. But if divine command theory is correct, if there is nothing more to moral goodness than God's preferences, then there can be no rationale for seeking alternative readings of morally troubling texts. There can be nothing "morally troubling" about an endorsement of slavery or a command to vigilante violence, because, according to DCT, there is no moral standard independent of God's will. It is only if—I repeat myself—moral goodness is a property independent of, and explicative of, God's will, that it makes any sense to question apparently immoral commands of God.

I've been arguing that not only is the existence of God not necessary for the existence of morality, but that it is, in a way, an insult to God to think that it is. To think that God is the ground of morality in Dr. Craig's sense is to think that there is no objective moral truth in the sense that we ordinarily take there to be. God's commands cannot, on Craig's view, be explained. The consequence of this picture is one that I know many religious people would find disturbing, and that I would have thought Dr. Craig would find disturbing. The consequence is that there can be no *moral reason* to worship God. The God of DCT is not himself *worthy* of worship, as he would be if he were objectively perfectly benevolent. Since whatever God does is ipso facto benevolent—in just the way that whatever the popular people do is ipso facto cool—the only kind of reason one could have for worshiping him is *prudential*. He's a powerful Guy; there's ample evidence that it's not smart to get on his bad side. He likes worship; we worship—if we know what's good for us.

I would have thought that Dr. Craig would shrink from this consequence, but to my surprise, he seems to embrace it. I'm referring to his extremely puzzling remarks about accountability. He writes, "Even if there were objective moral values and duties under atheism, they seem to be irrelevant because there's no moral accountability" (33). I'm not sure what values and duties are supposed to be "relevant" to, but what Dr. Craig seems to have in mind here is that there is no *point* to doing the right thing, or refraining from doing the wrong thing, unless you are going to be rewarded for it. This bespeaks a sensibility that can understand no other system of motivation than base self-interest. It puts Dr. Craig pretty much in the same camp as the evolutionary psychologists he so disdains. He, like them, finds puzzling the idea that people might actually want to do the right thing *because it is the right thing to do*. Like egoists generally, who think that in every intelligible action we take, we are always, in some way, aiming to benefit ourselves, Craig seems prepared to dismiss the avowed motives often cited by people who do good things: "I just wanted to help," "I wanted her to be happy," or simply, as above, "I did it because it was the right thing to do." Wanting to help, wanting a loved one to flourish, wanting to be just—I don't see what's puzzling or "irrelevant" about such motives—not unless one really thinks that goodness and evil are unintelligible except in the context of a quasi-contract made with a tyrant, where these notions turn out to be synonymous with "what will keep me out of trouble" and "what will get me into trouble." I hope that if I were ever called upon to do so, I would sacrifice my own life for that of one of my children. How could such a sacrifice fail to "have a point?" It would only be pointless if my child's continued existence is itself pointless, and if Dr. Craig were to suggest such a thing to me, he'd see what righteous anger can be summoned by an atheist.

The other thing I find puzzling about Dr. Craig's remarks on accountability is that they seem to put him doctrinally at odds with several of the major Christian denominations. His idea that it is only the carrot of eternal life and the stick of damnation that give moral action a point makes hash of the Catholic distinction between perfect and imperfect contrition, which I explained above. Certainly I was taught, as a girl, that morally right action was right *in itself* and not *because* God would reward it. I was encouraged, generally, to think of the earthly life as a kind of apprentice period, and that part of its point is to get human beings to recognize the good *as* good.

I know that other Christian traditions insist on the same conceptual separation—between doing what is right *because it is right*, and doing it out of fear of punishment. I remember the deeply religious philosopher John Bishop delivering a paper on "triumphalism," in which he argued that a proper religious faith would not depend upon the belief that the good would eventually triumph. I think of that paper often, for I believe it has important lessons for those of us who are engaged, in this world, in such projects as trying to end U.S. imperialism or turning back global warming. These seem very frequently to be lost causes, and it takes enormous courage and commitment to continue the struggle without any rational confidence that one's efforts will be rewarded. But it is a higher, more praiseworthy state of mind to be able to continue to act without promise of success, with only the comfort that one is doing what one can to make things better. Bishop's challenge to "keep faith" even in the face of the dark possibility that all will be lost is, I think, a profound expression of confidence in the moral capacities of human beings.

That said, it is true that Catholicism does promise eternal rewards for good behavior on Earth.[17] But not all Christian denominations do. Lutheranism, Calvinism, and Presbyterianism all hold to the doctrine of *predestination*.[18] According to this doctrine, your eternal destiny is not determined by the quality of your actions while you're on Earth, but rather by a choice God has made for you before you were even born. As Martin Luther explains it, the idea is that human beings are so fundamentally sinful and despicable that absolutely nothing we can do, no number of righteous actions, could ever *warrant* God's granting us eternal life.[19] Grace, faith, and salvation are therefore "free gifts of God," where "free" seems to mean "not necessitated by any reason." Right action does not *earn* one salvation, on this view, in contrast to the (as Luther saw it) corrupt Catholic doctrine of justification by works. I suppose, then, that Dr. Craig must think Lutherans can do no better than atheists in giving moral behavior a point, since it doesn't carry any promise of future reward.

But this last point is really just ad hominem. Dr. Craig can't help it if some Christian denominations have inadequate moral theories—after all, Christian sects say incompatible things about the conditions necessary for salvation, so some of them *must* be wrong. The germane point is this: A demand for accountability is the natural accompaniment to the view that God's commands are the ground of moral obligation. If behaving morally amounts to nothing more than obeying God, then it's perfectly reasonable to ask, "What's in it for me?" Without an independent ground for moral action, a source of value independent of God's command, there simply would be no reason for anyone to obey God other than self-interest. One's reason cannot be that God is good. For on divine command theory, "good" is an empty honorific we apply to the all-powerful Being who issues commands—it cannot be taken to give us any reason in and of itself.

This point leads to the final theme I want to take up in this chapter—Dr. Craig's contention that the existence of God is *sufficient* for morality. We can explore it by looking more closely at the whole concept of obedience in its theological application. Let's look, for example, at the narratives of the Hebrew Bible. Many religious people—Jews, Christians, and Muslims—take these stories at face value, as historically accurate accounts of events that actually transpired. But even nonliteralists believe that these narratives are in some way morally authoritative—that they illuminate the nature of the divine-human relationship. It's worth asking how.

One character in the Bible who seems really to have been an adherent to divine command theory is the patriarch Abraham. God commands him to sacrifice his son, "thine only son, whom thou lovest," and Abraham, without hesitation (he "rose up early in the morning"), grabs Isaac and sets out to slaughter him. There is no record in the text of Abraham's having even considered the possibility that there was some mistake—that it was not God, but rather a perverse demon speaking to him, for example.[20] But then again, why would he? Apparently, for Abraham, there really was no moral standard independent of God's command. In particular, there seems to have been nothing in the *nature* of the command—"Kill your beloved and innocent son, just because I want you to"—that in any way signaled to Abraham that it was not really God speaking to him. God said "Jump"—Abraham said "How high?"

Now do we, as contemporary readers of the ancient story, endorse Abraham's choice? It's clear that *God* is happy with Abraham's choice. After he sends an angel to prevent the death blow to Isaac, God proclaims himself to be well pleased with Abraham. God is glad that Abraham did not act on the basis of any independent conception of right and wrong, glad that he obeyed blindly, that he did not in any way try to second-guess God. Abraham passed a test, and the test, apparently, was to do whatever God wanted, no matter how abhorrent. (If *I* had been writing the Bible, I would have told the story differently—in my version Abraham would have said, "I don't care who you are; that would be wrong and I'm not doing it." And *then* God would have proclaimed himself well pleased. . . .) The examples I cited above, of contemporary public reaction to criminals who claim divine sanction for their crimes—would-be Abrahams—suggests that we do not believe that one should take all apparently divine proclamations at face value, that rather, we think that one should screen any such appearances against one's own independent moral judgments. So what about Abraham? Can anyone other than a proponent of DCT endorse Abraham's choice?

Here's one possibility. Perhaps Abraham is *not* a divine command theorist, appearances to the contrary notwithstanding. Perhaps, instead, he has a *moral* belief that one ought to do what God wants one to do. On this reading, Abraham does possess a moral sense that's independent from God's commands, and this moral sense tells him to defer to God. God's commanding something doesn't *make* it morally right, on this new view; it's just that God is infinitely more likely than Abraham is to know the moral facts of the matter. The analogy here is with the trust that laypersons rationally invest in their doctors: I generally take my doctor's advice (or believe that I ought to) not because I believe that my doctor's ordering something *constitutes it* as medically sound, but rather because I have reason to believe that my doctor is far better placed than I am to recognize what *is* medically sound. I'm prepared for the possibility that my doctor may tell me to do something that doesn't quite make sense to me, and the mere fact that I don't understand why this is medically necessary is not, in itself, any reason to reject my doctor's advice. By analogy, Abraham should be understood as acting on the basis of *trust* in God—he assumes, humbly and faithfully, that God knows what he is doing, and that, somehow or other, it will all turn out for the (morally) best.

This interpretation is, I believe, a very popular one. Its popularity confirms the point I was making above, that many people interpret the Bible in the light of an independent moral standard. But the interpretation raises immediately the question of the *sufficiency* of God's existence for the existence of objective moral fact. The interpretation assumes, I've been arguing, that Abraham has a conscience, a moral sense that allows for the *possibility* of a mismatch between what is right and what God commands. Abraham, in the event in question, does override the initial ruling of his conscience, but his decision is treated by the interpretation as an act of *rational trust*, analogous to my rational trust in following medical advice I don't quite understand. In that case, the plausibility of the interpretation depends on the rationality of Abraham's "moral trust." *Does* he have good reason to think that God knows better what is moral than he does?

We know this much from the Hebrew Bible: People who get on God's bad side are in deep trouble. So Abraham may have had plenty of *prudential* reasons for doing what God wanted him to. But that's not what's at issue here. What we want to justify Abraham's acquiescence is a moral track record for God—an indication that he really is benevolent, and indeed, better placed to know what's right and wrong than we are. Unfortunately, if we take the Hebrew Bible literally, God's record is pretty poor. To begin with, the God of the Hebrews plays favorites (What part of "chosen people" do you not understand?). Even if, as Christians contend, the "New Covenant" with Jesus makes everyone in the world (at least potentially) a member of the "Chosen," God seemed pretty literal-minded about the thing in the days before Christ. The Bible is full of accounts of God's killing, displacing, or otherwise seriously smiting presumably innocent people who had the misfortune of belonging to a tribe whose leaders had threatened to impede his ambitions for the Israelites. Yes, Pharaoh did commit an atrocity by enslaving the Jews (not that slavery per se is unequivocally condemned—the Hebrew kings have slaves, with no evidence of divine disapproval). But what, pray tell, was the crime committed by some innocent Egyptian's first-born son? Collective punishment is a favorite of this God's—we have the Flood, the destruction of Sodom, the slaughter of Alamakites—or how about the condemnation of the entire human race to lives of strife and pain because our remote ancestors broke one single rule? Sometimes, there's not even a pretext that the doomed people are morally at fault: The only "crime" committed by the Canaanites was living in a land that God wanted for his people. (Don't think the lesson is lost on those Jewish and Christian Zionists who believe that Jews have a God-given right to occupy lands inconveniently inhabited by members of a less-favored race.)[21]

One needn't be a literalist about the Bible, as I acknowledged earlier. One can take the view that the stories in the ancient texts were products of their times, and that the moral (or amoral) perspectives they express are not to be taken as a final or definitive guide to moral action. Fair enough. The point is that there is nothing *incoherent* about the picture we get from the literal reading—and that is a picture of an enormously powerful but not particularly righteous God.

It's a well-known but not much emphasized feature of the classic argument from design that it can establish, at most, the natural, as opposed to the moral, powers of God. From the orderliness of nature one can—perhaps—conclude with some warrant that there exists a powerful and intelligent designer of the universe. But there is nothing about nature that testifies to this creator's being, on balance, good. There is certainly nothing in the argument as it's usually stated that rules out the possibility of an indifferent creator, or even a malevolent one. The flip side of this is that the argument from evil, even if completely successful, doesn't establish atheism, but only the absence of *at least one* of the defining features of God as he is usually conceived: It shows that one must give up *either* omnipotence, omniscience, *or* benevolence. Combining the argument from design with the argument from evil yields, it seems to me, exactly the kind of vengeful, despotic God depicted in the pages of the Hebrew Bible.[22]

Obedience to such a God would not be morally virtuous; it would be, at best, prudent. One does not owe allegiance to another being simply because that being is stronger. And it does not matter if the being in question is responsible for your very existence. No one thinks that an abused child is morally obliged to obey an abusive parent, simply because the parent gave the child life. Parents do not own their children, and their right to expect obedience is contingent upon their being benevolent and competent trustees of the child's own welfare.

The question can be asked, then, *Why* ought one to obey God? The fact that this question can be asked, that it's comprehensible, that it makes sense, is sufficient proof that the mere existence of an all-powerful Creator is not enough to generate a realm of moral fact. Perfect benevolence does not follow logically from the other properties of God. Now it might be objected at this point that perfect benevolence *does* follow from the complete concept of God, that is, as "the most perfect being conceivable." That, indeed, is true. If God is so conceived, then the existence of God would be sufficient for the existence of moral value, since there could not be a perfectly good being without there being good to begin with. But this consideration won't help Dr. Craig. In the first place, the existence of *any* morally good being, with *any* degree of virtue is similarly sufficient to establish the existence of objective moral value: There can't be *regular* good people without there being a good to begin with. Secondly, the fact that we can form a concept of a being with a certain set of attributes does not, *pace* St. Anselm, demonstrate the real possibility, much less the actuality, of such a being.[23] Finally, defining "God" so as to entail the truth of the claim "God is good" simply forces a rewording of the original question: Instead of asking "Ought we to obey God?" the question must be rendered this way: "Is the creator of the universe God?"

It is customary in philosophical debates to present not only a positive case for one's own position, but a diagnosis of the errors in one's opponent's arguments. Unfortunately, I cannot do this, for Dr. Craig provides no arguments for his chief contentions. Most glaringly, he offers no argument for the particular claim that there is no morality without God. What he does instead is cite authorities. Sometimes he cites an authority who testifies as to what atheists believe, and sometimes he cites an authority who, speaking as an atheist, proclaims the doctrine Dr. Craig and his experts insist all atheists share. But of course atheists do not all think alike—we have no catechism or creed. Dr. Craig could easily have found many statements by atheists rejecting the claim that atheism entails amoralism (along with arguments supporting that position), but he gives no evidence of having looked for them. Neither does Dr. Craig acknowledge, much less endeavor to answer, the main objection to his own position, the objection found in the *Euthyphro*. I can hardly believe that he has not encountered it before. I have the dark suspicion that Dr. Craig is not really interested in engaging atheists in rational discussion, but rather is speaking exclusively to his theistic contingency, with the aim of reinforcing for them the vile stereotype of atheists so prevalent in contemporary American society. If I've mistaken Dr. Craig's motives, I apologize. But I challenge him to make an honest answer to the arguments that I, and numerous others before me, have made.

In sum: Dr. Craig's view of morality entails a picture of God as some kind of cross between Miss Manners and Tony Soprano—a stern enforcer of arbitrary edicts. I trust that most religious people would find such a picture repugnant, and an insult to the God of their hearts. If belief in Craig's God is the only alternative, I think atheism is far and away the more pious view.

NOTES

1. Actually, as I'll explain below, the argument from evil is not really an argument against the existence of God, but only against his possessing all three of these properties.

2. For an extremely sensitive and moving discussion of this issue, see "Religio Philosophi" by Daniel Garber. It appears in a volume I've edited, *Philosophers without Gods: Meditations on Atheism and the Secular Life* (New York: Oxford University Press, 2007).

3. That's not to say that I couldn't feel rational regret for something without thinking the thing was morally wrong. Obviously, if I chose Door 2, and the grand prize was behind Door 3, I'd feel sorry that I chose Door 2. But I wouldn't feel remorse, or contrition.

4. As I think about it now, I note that my view also makes good sense of a loving God's response to *imperfect* contrition. At first blush, it's not at all obvious why God

would be satisfied with a "remorse" that was really only a form of rational regret, the kind of "sorry" we are when we get stopped for speeding. It is, perhaps, explicable on the view that God is a tyrant. A dictator god, vain about his own power, might find the mortal terror of his subjects sufficiently gratifying that he would grant clemency. But how unappealing a picture! On my alternative view, God is satisfied with imperfect contrition because it shows that the subject has found at least *some* reason to avoid sin (as tickets provide *some* reason to watch one's speed). On this picture, God primarily wants the sinner to cease doing wrong—if it takes *fear* of the Lord to stop him, then so be it.

5. And nothing less, either. That is, it makes no sense to speak of an act's being morally good if God *hasn't* commanded it.

6. Of course, according to scripture, God did command the torture of an innocent child in commanding Abraham to sacrifice Isaac—assuming you will agree with me that it would be a kind of torture for a father to bind his child as for sacrifice and then raise a knife as if to slaughter him, with every appearance of seriousness. I won't press the issue here; more on the significance of this horrific story later. It is irrelevant to the issue here that God prevented the murder from taking place. The point is that he *commanded* murder. I don't see how a divine command theorist can avoid the conclusion that murder was—at least in that instance, and at least for a short period of time, morally good.

7. Just a technical note before the philosophers reading this jump all over me. In standard modal logics, any counterfactual with an impossible antecedent is true. So if it is impossible for God to issue such a command—which it's not, since he did, see previous note, but if it were—then both counterfactuals would be true, vacuously. Results like this are widely regarded as regrettable, insofar as one looks to formal modal logic to reconstruct ordinary reasoning with counterfactuals. I'm going with ordinary intuitions, which do not treat all counterfactuals with impossible antecedents as true, and presuming the viability of some system of relevance or paraconsistent logic for counterfactuals.

8. I'm here adapting an example of Sally Haslanger's. See her "Ontology and Social Construction," *Philosophical Topics* 23, no. 2 (Fall 1995), especially pages 98–103.

9. Of course I must concede that there are *some* people who simply don't have any problem with the idea that God would order the slaughter of thousands of innocent people, but these people prove my point. They are the ones who proudly display the bumper sticker that reads, "God said it, I believe it, and that's the end of it."

10. The author continues, sardonically: "It is plain, however, that we are far from the Sermon on the Mount." See www.newadvent.org/cathen/01377c.htm.

11. See "Speech of Jefferson Davis in Senate Feb. 13 and 14, 1850, on Slavery in the Territories," in *Jefferson Davis, Constitutionalist: His Letters, Papers, and Speeches*, vol. 1, ed. Dunbar Rowland (New York: J. J. Little & Ives, 1923), 286.

12. See Jonathan Edwards Jr., "The Injustice and Impolicy of the Slave Trade," 1791, 29–30, quoted by John Coffey in "The Abolition of the Slave Trade: Christian Conscience and Political Action," an online document from the Jubilee Center. See www.jubilee-centre.org/online_documents/TheabolitionoftheslavetradeChristian conscienceandpoliticalaction.htm#_ftn5.

13. You can read Rudolph's own statement, together with accounts of many other assaults committed by the self-styled "army of God" at www.armyofgod.com/index.html.

14. The Ontario Consultants on Religious Tolerance report that the American Life League issued, in 1999, the "Pro-Life Proclamation against Violence," signed by thirteen pro-life groups. See www.all.org/article.php?id=10357.

15. Israel Shahak and Norton Mezvinsky, *Jewish Fundamentalism in Israel*, 2nd ed. (London: Pluto Press, 2004).

16. Unfortunately, there seems to be considerably less outrage about another exploitation of Halacha—the 1999 killing of twenty-nine Palestinians at prayer by Baruch Goldstein, who claimed justification for the act in Jewish law: The killing by a Jew of a non-Jew under any circumstances is not regarded as murder. It may be prohibited for other reasons, especially when it causes danger for Jews. For more on this see Shahak and Mezvinsky, *Jewish Fundamentalism*.

17. It used to be a little more complicated. When I was growing up, the doctrine of Limbo was in force. Limbo was where unbaptized innocents and righteous people went after they died. They were denied the sight of God, but other than that were perfectly happy. I thought at the time that this was grossly unfair, and have been gratified to learn that the Church has repudiated the doctrine. *I told you so, Sister Daniel Joseph.* . . .

18. And according to Edwin Curley, so ought Episcopalians and Catholics. Predestination is one of the "articles of religion" recorded in the Episcopalian prayer book, and it is a doctrine endorsed by Thomas Aquinas (*Summa Theologiae* I, Question 23). Curley points out that there is ample scriptural support for the doctrine in the writings of the apostle Paul: Romans 8–9. See Curley's "On Becoming a Heretic," in Antony, *Philosophers without Gods*.

19. Martin Luther, "The Freedom of a Christian," in *Martin Luther: Selections from His Writings*, ed. John Dillenberger (New York: Doubleday, 1962).

20. Jewish commentary is explicit about this. The authoritative medieval scholar Rashi says that the phrase "rose up early" means that Abraham "hastened to fulfill the commandment." See www.chabad.org/library/article.asp?AID=8217&showrashi=true.

Thanks to Joseph Levine for bringing this commentary to my attention, and for providing an initial translation from the Hebrew.

21. The history of Jewish appeals to biblical authority on behalf of Zionism dates to the early Zionist period. See John Quigley, *Palestine and Israel: A Challenge to Justice* (Durham, N.C.: Duke University Press, 1990), especially chapter 8, "Kaftans and Yarmulkes." The perspective was emblematized by the slogan, popular in the early days of Zionism, describing the region of Palestine as "a land without people for a people without land" (Quigley, *Palestine and Israel*, 73, citing Amos Elon, *The Israelis: Founders and Sons* [New York: Penguin, 1983], 158–59). As for "Christian Zionism," consider this statement about "evangelical Zionism" from the World Alliance of Reformed Churches: "This is the belief, held by a group of Christians especially in North America, that the modern state of Israel, including its territorial ambitions, has a direct biblical mandate providing a justification for its political and

military actions. A few personalities in North America—such as Jerry Falwell, Pat Robertson and Franklin Graham—have made statements about such beliefs, and also about the nature of Islam, that have attracted wide attention. . . . [Evangelical Zionism constitutes] a grave threat both to the perception of Christian faith by the peoples of this region, and a threat to the understanding of the biblical message by Christians in North America." See www.warc.ch/update/up134/01.html.

22. There are some religious traditions that have responded to this argument by denying the *omnipotence* of God. Advocates of "natural theology," at least as they are represented by Cleanthes in Hume's *Dialogues concerning Natural Religion*, held that God was not all-powerful, only very, very powerful. The editors tell me that this is also the position taken by process theists. I'd be very surprised if this line were at all attractive to Dr. Craig.

23. Once again, for the philosophers: We can allow that if a necessarily existing being is metaphysically possible, then that being is actual (assuming the S5 axiom: if possible, then necessarily possible). But the ontological argument begins with the premise that a necessary being is *conceivable*, and conceivability does not entail—or we needn't concede that it does without further argument—metaphysical possibility. I believe that I learned this argument from Peter van Inwagen, when I was studying the work of Alvin Plantinga with him back in the early seventies, but I am not sure I am remembering correctly. Even if I've rendered the argument correctly, I do not know if he would still endorse it.

Chapter Four

Is Moral Goodness without Belief in God Rationally Stable?

John Hare

In this chapter I am going to comment on the debate between Paul Kurtz and William Lane Craig on the topic, "Is goodness without God good enough?" I will confine my comments about the two debaters to endnotes (see especially notes 1–3, 9, 23, and 25). I will give my own argument in the main text, because I think this will make the argument easier to follow.

There are various ways in which the debaters need to clarify what question they are talking about. I will mention three. First, does "goodness" mean just moral goodness, or all types of goodness?[1] Second, does "without God" mean "without believing in God" or "without the existence of God"?[2] Third, for what is goodness without God supposed to be "good enough"?[3] In this chapter I will assume that the question is about moral goodness (including moral obligation), that the question is about believing in God, and that the question is whether moral goodness without believing in God is good enough for rational coherence. I will defend the position that it is not enough, or, to put this in Kant's terms, that moral goodness without belief in God is rationally unstable.[4] In the first part of the chapter I will be relying on Kantian arguments, although I know that Kant-style moral philosophy is only one of the options. In the second part I will widen the discussion to include moral theories based on virtue and on consequences.

To say that a morally good life without belief in God is rationally unstable is not to say that it is impossible. We can, and do, live with all sorts of rational instability. But such a life is, nonetheless, missing something important. Kant's example is Spinoza, whom he took (perhaps unfairly) not to believe in God but to have led a conspicuously good life, and so to have been in a rationally unstable position.[5] The defect in such a life is that it is unable to provide a defense for commitments that call for defense because they are vulnerable to plausible attack. In the following I will examine two such commitments. Then I will look in the second half of the chapter at three traditional accounts of what is central to moral goodness, and I will try to articulate the role that belief in God plays within each account. The question will then be whether the person who does not believe in God can replace God with something else to achieve the same result within each theory. If not, it will not follow that he or she has to believe in God, but that he or she has to either do so or change his or her moral theory. Given the scope of this chapter, it is bound to be somewhat programmatic and to leave open a number of hard philosophical questions. My goal is to give an overall picture of what seems to me the best way of looking at the relation between morality and belief in God.

1. TWO COMMITMENTS THAT REQUIRE DEFENSE

1a. The Possibility of the Highest Good

The first commitment that requires defense is commitment to the claim that we can be morally good consistently with our own and other people's happiness. "Happiness" is a term full of difficulty, and sometimes philosophers who disagree about the relation between morality and happiness have differing accounts of what happiness consists in. I am not going to try to defend a detailed account of my own. Roughly, what I mean by a happy life is one that achieves enough of its own goals so that it is not characterized by more than a low degree of frustration. Kant ties happiness closely to pleasure, or the overall satisfaction of what we want as creatures of nature (as distinct from moral agents).[6] But we might not count someone as "truly happy" who was on a "pleasure machine," being fed intravenously and receiving nonstop pleasurable sensation during his or her waking hours.[7] I will stick with "achieving enough of its own goals to avoid frustration," recognizing that the term "happiness" can be and has been defined in other ways.

To show the connection between happiness, on this conception, and morality requires some assumptions about morality. I will mention four, without arguing for them. There are many different conceptions of morality; but these four assumptions are common to theories in the Kantian tradition, which is still widely influential. First, morality requires us to share the morally permissible ends of those affected by our actions, in the sense of making those ends our own ends. So, to put this in terms of happiness, morality requires us to try to make other people happy, as long as what they want is not immoral. Second, morality requires us not to rank our own advantage above that of others, just because it is ours; this is because morality requires us to treat all human beings as having the same worth. Third, "ought" implies "can," in the sense that if it is not the case that we can do something, the question whether we ought to do it does not properly arise. Finally, humans have a double motivation, toward our own happiness and toward what is good in itself, regardless of its connection with our happiness; we are not as a matter of fact motivated finally *only* by our own happiness.

The first assumption together with the third imply that morality requires us to believe that it is possible for the people affected by our actions, including ourselves, to be happy in a way that is consistent with each other's happiness. We ought to try to increase each other's happiness, and so we must be able to believe this is possible. The possibility of the general union of happiness and virtue is what Kant calls "the highest good." If we were all morally good, we would be trying to make each other happy, and we would have to be able to believe that we could do so (since otherwise there would be no point in trying). But in this case we would be able to rely on each other's virtue. There would no doubt still be cancer and depression and floods, but at least the victims of these would be surrounded by compassionate caregivers and levees would be built properly, and so on. Our problem, however, is that we do not all seem to be morally good. Since we do not see into each other's hearts, it is hard to be sure about this. But the evidence of how people live suggests strongly that for many people what comes first is their own advantage, and not the happiness of others. Morality, on the conception I am defending (the second assumption), requires us not to rank our own advantage this way. Much of what makes life miserable is the way we treat each other, because we do *not* share each other's morally permissible ends. So the question is how we can continue to believe rationally in the consistent achievability of all this happiness in a world in which we are not all morally good.

Perhaps we cannot. Perhaps the world is morally absurd, in the sense that morality gives us a task that the world inevitably frustrates. We could imagine this situation in terms familiar from Descartes' *Meditations*. He imagines a demon who manipulates the world so that whenever we aim at true belief, we end up with false belief. Suppose instead that a demon manipulated the world so that whenever we aimed at another person's happiness we achieved her or his misery. We would stop trying to do good, just as in Descartes' thought experiment we would end up not trying to achieve true beliefs. This is denied by existentialist philosophers like Jean-Paul Sartre, who hold to a roughly Kantian morality, but who hold also that the world is morally absurd. He holds that if I will for myself, for example, "to marry, to have children, even if this marriage depends solely on my own circumstances or passion or wish, I am involving all humanity in monogamy and not merely myself."[8] Kant would say I am willing it as a universal law. But Sartre thinks that if we are honest with ourselves, we have to recognize that these universal moral projects do not make sense. To live authentically is to realize both that we create these tasks for ourselves, and that they are futile. Sartre does not consider it a serious objection that morality and the world, in his view, do not make sense. The demand to make sense is a symptom, as he sees it, of the very disease he has analyzed. But if we accept the principle that "ought implies can," we have to accept that if we ought to achieve this happiness for all consistent with the virtue of all, then it can be achieved (though not necessarily by our own efforts). The "ought implies can" principle has sometimes been denied, but it lies behind much of our moral practice. We think it is wrong to hold people (for example, children) accountable to standards they are unable to reach, even with the available assistance.

The moral argument I am defending for the existence of God is that some agency that is not merely human is required to produce the possibility of our collective and consistent happiness—that is, of a sufficient number of our collective morally permissible ends being achieved together so that we can be happy together. What is required is the agency of providence, which has powers not merely human. The atheist position is rationally unstable because it cannot provide a good reason for maintaining this hope in the face of the harm we routinely do to each other.[9]

There are two temporal locations for the thought I have just introduced about consistent happiness: present and future. My argument has been that morality requires us to believe in, first, a system *presently* in place by which a sufficiently large number of the morally permissible ends of human beings can be conjointly realized so that they can be happy together. Second, it requires us to believe that there is a possible *future* state in which this realization is achieved. In the biblical tradition, this possible state is expressed as a state in which justice and peace embrace or kiss each other (Psalm 85:10), or alternatively as the kingdom of God.

1b. The Possibility of the Revolution of the Will

The second commitment that calls for defense is the commitment to the claim that it is possible to become morally good people *internally*. I stress "internally" because this argument is different from the previous one, in that the relevant difficulty is not the difficulty of coordinating the achievement of the ends of different people but of achieving a morally good ranking of ends within oneself, within one's own heart. Kant calls this achievement "a revolution" of the will.[10] I mentioned in the previous section that for many people what comes first is their own advantage. According to the fourth assumption I made above, humans are said to have a double motivation: an affection for advantage, which is directed toward one's own happiness and perfection, and an affection for justice, which is directed toward what is good in itself independently of its relation to us.[11] There is nothing wrong with the affection for advantage, on this view, but morality requires that it be ranked *under* the affection for justice. If this ranking is observed, it will have the effect that we do what will be to our advantage only if it is consistent with morality. Morality on the view I am defending requires us to treat all human beings as having the same worth (the second assumption), and so prohibits us from giving any greater initial weight to our own advantage in our decisions about how to live than to the advantage of any other person.[12] This does not mean that a person has to ignore what is good for her or him, or become simply an instrument for the well-being of other people. But our problem is that this kind of impartial benevolence, "counting each person as one and no person as more than one," does not seem natural to us. The term "natural" is tricky here, but I mean to include whatever is given us by natural selection, and so is explained by its contribution to survival and reproduction.[13]

The literature in evolutionary psychology is instructive here.[14] We can find in nonhuman animals precursors, in a sense, of altruism, but we do not find full altruism of the Good Samaritan kind, where the Good Samaritan sacrifices himself for an *enemy* in need.[15] I will call this "Good Samaritan altruism." We find what is called "kin selection," where sterile castes among the social insects forgo reproduction, because there is greater frequency of their genes in the next generation if they stick to their specialized functions. We find so-called reciprocal altruism between nonrelated members of the same species, but this depends upon the probability of mutual advantage and is a kind of tit-for tat. We find various forms of social control, in which rules that are beneficial to the group are enforced by a kind of communal sanction. But all these cases are complicated examples of the affection for advantage, depending upon a special relation between the agent and the recipient. None of them are cases of the affection for justice, which requires the agent's action on behalf of the recipient without regard to the person's special relation to the agent (as friend, family member, or fellow citizen), merely because the recipient is a person in need. If the bottom line in explanation is survival and reproduction, this leaves it mysterious how the affection for justice could get started among human beings.

In the literature there are various responses to this problem, and I will mention four. Some authors deny that morality does in fact require Good Samaritan altruism.[16] Acknowledging that there is no evolutionary basis for such a requirement, and holding that what is good is to satisfy the set of desires that evolution has given us, they hold that Good Samaritan altruism is a utopian import from religious sources, and not suited to human life. A second approach is to acknowledge that we have the impression that we are under objective moral norms, binding on us whether we recognize them or not, but this is an illusion that itself has evolutionary benefits because it enables certain kinds of coordination.[17] A third possibility is to concede the tension between the moral norms and evolutionary advantage, and to hold that there is a level of *cultural* evolution, involving the replication of "memes" or some such unit rather than genes.[18] Finally, there is the possibility that evolution might work at the level of the group rather than the individual organism or the gene.[19] None of these four approaches has yet found consensus support; and while the problem may yet be solved, we can safely make the modest claim that the burden is still on anyone who wants to claim that Good Samaritan altruism has a foundation in natural selection.

If it is true that Good Samaritan altruism is not natural to us in the defined sense, then we require some other answer to the question why we should be moral than that it is natural in that sense. We also need an answer to the question of whether we *can* be moral in a sense that requires Good Samaritan altruism, if our natural capacities predispose us to self-preference. The two questions are linked by the principle that "ought" implies "can," for if it is not the case that we can, the principle tells us that it is not the case that we ought. The problem I am raising here is the problem of what I have elsewhere called "the moral gap."[20] There are actually two gaps involved: the gap between those animals who have only the affection for advantage and humans who have also the affection for justice, and the gap within our own lives between the demand to be moral and our actual performance. A religious answer to the problem of the first gap is that God appears to humans by self-revelation in a way God does not do to other animals, and this revelation can silence the human preoccupation with self in a way that allows love of what is supremely good in itself, namely God. Subsequent to that revelation a preoccupation with self is accountable, or sin. A religious answer to the problem of the second gap is that even though we are born preferring ourselves, God offers assistance to reverse the order of incentives, or the ranking, by regeneration. This means that God is both the source of the moral demand on us and the enabler of our compliance. Augustine says, "God commands some things which we cannot do, in order that we may know what we ought to ask of God."[21]

I will briefly mention three nonreligious strategies to answer the problem. I have discussed them more fully in *The Moral Gap*. The first strategy is to hold our natural capacities where they are on the picture I have just drawn and then to reduce the moral demand in order to fit them. That was the first response I mentioned above, which concludes that Good Samaritan altruism is utopian; but it is not only evolutionary ethicists who have taken this line. Certain kinds of care-theorists have also done so, such as Nel Noddings, who says that we do not have obligations to starving children in Africa because they are not part of our group; we do not even know who they are.[22] A second strategy is to keep the moral demand where it is on the picture I have drawn and then exaggerate or puff up our natural capacity to meet this demand. Both the second and third responses I mentioned above take this strategy, since they claim that we have the natural capacity to be led by the illusion or the self-replicating memes that perpetuate morality. But a more familiar implementation of the strategy is to hold that we have the resources by moral education or social control to make people good. This approach was typical of the optimism about human progress at the end of the nineteenth century. [23] Finally, the third strategy is to hold both the demand and our capacities constant, and then find some naturalistic substitute to do God's work in bridging the resultant gap. One example is the Marxist analysis that our capacities for a good life will be changed if the proletariat takes ownership of the means of production. Another example is internal to evolutionary ethics.[24] We might hold that group selection will produce the genes for universal cooperation, as human groups get larger and eventually include the whole human race. If none of these three strategies work in any of their variants, then either we will have to abandon this traditional picture of morality or we will have to accept theism.

2. THREE TRADITIONAL ACCOUNTS

I want to look in the second half of this chapter at *three* traditional pictures of morality, and the place in each of them for theological premises in their original formulations.[25] Ethical theorists frequently distinguish between theories based on virtue, theories based on duty, and theories based on consequences. Aristotle might be taken as giving us the first kind of theory, Kant the second, and Mill the third. God appears in all three types of theory in their original formulations, but in different ways because of the differences of the theories.

2a. Virtue Theory

A theory based on virtue gives the central role in ethical theory to the idea that the best human life is lived in accordance with the virtues. Plato and Aristotle have theories of this kind, in which God functions as a magnet, drawing us toward the best human life, which is also the life closest to the divine. The image is Plato's,[26] but Aristotle says that God moves everything "by being loved."[27] In Aristotle, the god is the prime mover, who moves other things (by being loved by them) but is without motion in the divine activity itself, which consists in contemplation. Both Plato and Aristotle hold that humans get closest to the divine by contemplation. Thus Plato says of the contemplator, "In so far as human nature is capable of sharing in immortality, he must altogether be immortal, and since he is ever cherishing the divine power, and has the divinity within him in perfect order, he will be singularly happy."[28] Aristotle ends the *Eudemian Ethics* by saying, "To conclude: whatever choice or possession of natural goods—bodily goods, wealth, friends, and the like—will most conduce to the contemplation of God is best: this is the noblest criterion. But any standard of living which either through excess or defect hinders the service and contemplation of God is bad. This is how it is with the soul."[29] But while contemplation is central to the good life, both philosophers also refer to theological premises in regard to ethical (as well as intellectual) virtues. Thus Gregory Vlastos says about Plato that in the *Apology* and the *Euthyphro*, "Piety is doing god's work to benefit human beings."[30] Aristotle says that the good of an individual is a desirable thing, but the good of a city is a greater and more complete thing to obtain and preserve, because "what is good for a people or for cities is nobler and more *godlike*."[31]

The notions of "God" and "divinity" need careful analysis in these texts, and we should not assume that the same notion is in play as in the Abrahamic faiths. But my point is just that theological premises are doing significant work in these ethical systems. These classical virtue theorists held that the best human life is life in accordance with virtue, and that this means being as like God or the gods as we can. To "think mortal because we are mortal" would be, Aristotle warns us, a diminution of our purpose and of the kind of happiness available for us.[32] If we want to construct a virtue theory *without* theological premises, we can do so. But then we will need to look at the role those premises played in the classical forms of the theory, both in ancient Greece and more particularly in medieval versions in all three Abrahamic faiths (where the role is in important respects different from the picture in Greek philosophy, because God is seen as also intervening in human affairs). This will tell us, so to speak, what we will be missing, and where we may need to supply a nontheological counterpart if we want a consistent virtue theory with the same general shape. I suggest that we will be missing two things. The first is the power within our lives of an attraction toward a kind of life that is not merely human. The second is, in a broad sense, metaphysical. The divine life toward which we are attracted on the first picture is a life that is foundational to the way the whole universe is ordered, so that when we live in a way consistent with this attraction we are mirroring in our own lives the order of the cosmos. Without the theism, we will lose this harmony.

2b. Duty Theory

The second picture of morality that I mentioned is found in theories based on duty (sometimes called "deontological theories"), and I have in mind especially Kant's picture. I described some of the features of this picture in the first part of this chapter. In theories of this kind, the central role in ethical theory is given to the moral law, and our duty to live in accordance with it. The role of theological premises in Kant's ethical system has recently been recovering its appropriate level of scholarly attention.[33] He says, throughout his published work, that we have to recognize our duties as God's commands.[34] This does not mean that God's command creates the moral law (which is, Kant thinks, necessary, and so has no creator) but that God is the "author of obligation in accordance with the law."[35] God plays this role because God is sovereign of the kingdom of ends, and has distinct legislative, executive, and judicial roles within this kingdom. One of God's roles is to secure the real possibility of the highest good, the union of human virtue and happiness, which Kant thinks the moral law requires us to pursue. We are, he thinks, not merely rational beings but bodily creatures with complex bodily needs (the satisfaction of which is happiness), and ethical systems that merely tell us to be virtuous and to be indifferent to everything else fail to acknowledge our full humanity. But Kant says that we cannot see how the union of virtue and happiness can be accomplished by merely human agency. It requires that the physical world be under the governance of a being who also wills in accordance with the moral law. In other words, it requires God. Kant has the view that if we ought to do something, it must be the case that we can do it. So if we ought to pursue the highest good, it must be achievable.[36] But if it is not achievable by merely human agency, we must believe in a nonhuman agent who can achieve it.

A second role for theological premises in Kant's system is that God gives us "a higher assistance inscrutable to us," which enables us to overcome the radical evil with which we are born.[37] This radical evil is our propensity to prefer happiness to duty, and Kant thinks this propensity is innate. His view is that we are born with both the predisposition to good (including respect for the moral law) and the propensity to evil, which prevents the predisposition to good from issuing, as it otherwise would, into a good life. These two opposite tendencies are, he thinks, ranked in our original condition so that the propensity to evil prevails. In order to overcome the propensity to evil, we require what Kant calls "a revolution of the will," which reverses the ranking of happiness and duty, so that we put duty first. But because we are born preferring our happiness, we do not have the power in ourselves to accomplish this revolution, and it requires divine assistance. If we construct a duty-based theory without these theological premises, what will we be missing? I suggest two things. The first is a belief in providence, a belief that the world is under the final control of goodness rather than evil or indifference, so that it is (despite abundant evidence to the contrary) hospitable to the moral life. The second is a belief that we can overcome the evil within ourselves, even though we do not seem to have the power within ourselves to do so.

2c. Consequentialism

The third picture of morality I mentioned is found in theories that give the central role in ethical theory to the assessment of consequences. The most famous version of this kind of theory is utilitarianism, and the most famous utilitarian is John Stuart Mill, who said that our aim in the moral life should be to assess what will produce the greatest happiness of the greatest number, and then to produce this.[38] He defines happiness in terms of pleasure (including higher pleasures as well as lower), but utilitarians have usually not followed him in this and have talked instead of the maximization of, for example, preference-satisfaction. The first person to state the utilitarian principle was Francis Hutcheson, who said, "That action is best, which procures the greatest Happiness for the greatest Numbers," and proposed God as the model of benevolence thus construed.[39] He defined "natural" goods as giving us personal or selfish pleasure, and "moral" goods as advantageous to all the parties affected. Since this leaves a possible gap between the two kinds of good, we need some assurance that morality and happiness are coincident. Hutcheson thought that God has given us a moral sense for this purpose, which gives us pleasure when we aim at and achieve moral goods, so that we end up making ourselves happy as well. Mill faced the same difficulty of the gap between morality and happiness (pleasure), since he thought we are motivated only by pleasure. In his *Three Essays on Religion* (published posthumously) he proposes the following answer, "The indulgence of hope with regard to the government of the universe and the destiny of man after death, while we recognize as a clear truth that we have no ground for more than hope, is legitimate and philosophically defensible." Without such hope, we are kept down by "the disastrous feeling of 'not worth while.'"[40] Henry Sidgwick saw the same problem as Mill about the gap between morality and happiness. He rejected Hutcheson's introduction of the moral sense and held that the only workable solution was to bring in a god who desires the greatest total good of all living things and will reward and punish in accordance with this desire. Sidgwick was not sure whether this entitled us to believe in God, just to get this solution to a problem within ethical theory. This depends on whether, in general, it is reasonable to accept certain principles (such as the uniformity of nature) that are not self-evident and that cannot be proved, but where "we have a strong disposition to accept them, and . . . they are indispensable to the systematic coherence of our beliefs."[41]

The last utilitarian I will mention is R. M. Hare, who brings theological premises into his theory in two ways. The first is that he constructs the model of a person who can do moral thinking properly, with access to all the relevant information about what actions will have what consequences for the satisfaction of the preferences of all the people affected, and with complete impartiality between all these people. We humans are defective in both these ways. We do not have all the relevant information and we are biased toward ourselves and those close to us. R. M. Hare humorously calls his model moral thinker "the archangel," but he recognizes that archangels (by the relevant religious doctrines) sometimes fail morally, and he elsewhere talks about God for this role.[42] The second way he brings in theological premises is by pointing to the assumption within the moral life that the world is the kind of place in which it is worthwhile trying to be morally good. He calls this "a faith in the divine providence."[43] At the close of *Moral Thinking*, he says, "If morality is to be a viable enterprise, [we have to] believe that if we adopt moral purposes and principles we stand a reasonable chance of carrying them out and not perishing uselessly in the process. And I myself would bring up any children that I had charge of accordingly. This is the secular equivalent (or not perhaps so secular) of seeing that they are, as the Marriage Service puts it, 'christianly and virtuously brought up.'"[44]

If we construct a consequentialist moral system without theological premises, what will we be missing? I suggest two things. The first is that we will need a model of good moral thinking, which mere human beings do not provide. The theory needs the idea of a perfect moral thinker, by approximation to whose thinking we can measure our own success.[45] This is a conceptual point. The picture of moral thinking within utilitarianism originated with Hutcheson's construal of God's benevolent love for God's creation, and the theory still requires such a picture of the ideal even where the *existence* of such a God is denied. The second point is like the first point about duty-based theories. We will need a way to bridge the gap between happiness and morality that Hutcheson, Mill, Sidgwick, and R. M. Hare all observed. Some nontheistic doctrine of providence will be required, and it is not at all clear what that could be.

In all three pictures of morality I have tried to point to two features that theism contributed to the original versions, one feature being, in a broad sense, metaphysical and one being internal to ethical motivation. The two features are different in each of the three cases, because the pictures are different. But theism in each case ties the ethical and the metaphysical together. In each case, the way we ought to live harmonizes in some way (different in the different theories) with the way the universe is, beyond ourselves and our choices. Perhaps this is one function of most religion, sufficiently vaguely formulated so as to cover the varieties in metaphysical and ethical positions within the world's various faiths. At least that is a hypothesis worth checking. Whether there are versions of the three pictures of morality I have described that can survive the deletion of the original theological premises can only be settled by looking at proposed candidates, one by one. This is not a project appropriate for this chapter.[46] If the chapter has succeeded, it has shown, in the first half, that one traditional kind of morality involves commitments that require theological premises in their defense, if they are to be rationally stable. In the second half I have tried to show the place that theological premises held in the original versions of the main types of ethical theory we are familiar with. This has the potential advantage of showing where nontheist versions of these theories will have to find substitutes for God's work if they want to delete these premises.

NOTES

1. Both debaters assume that the question is confined to moral goodness. But there are many other types of goodness (e.g., beauty and pleasure) and a theistic value theory needs to examine the different relations of God to all these different types of value. Moreover, a full theory would need to distinguish between God's relation to moral goodness and to moral obligation.

2. This is a major issue between Kurtz and Craig. Craig agrees that it is possible to be morally good without believing in God, but he holds that this leaves the main question of the debate untouched. Kurtz thinks that Craig has conceded here the central point of the humanist agenda. This difference between the two of them is intelligible if we assume that for Kurtz, since there is no God, the key difference in reality is between those who do and those who do not believe in God. He therefore spends most of his time arguing that those who, like him, do not believe in God, can be morally good people, can get through messy situations without being bound by simple absolute principles, can contribute to political discussion without making disputes more intractable, and so forth. For Craig, on the other hand, God's existence is not merely real but necessary. His project is to trace the objective relation between this existence and moral goodness of various kinds, independently of our subjective beliefs about the relation. The result of this difference between the two debaters is that to a surprising extent they are talking past each other. This is itself a significant indication of how hard it is to do this kind of debate well.

3. Neither debater discusses this explicitly, but they seem to have different opinions about it, deriving from the differences discussed in the previous footnote. Kurtz seems to mean, "good enough for a good life for individuals and societies." Craig seems to mean something like, "good enough to provide the necessary conditions for a sufficient foundation."

4. The term "unstable" is from N. T. Volckmann's notes to Kant's *Natural Theology*, 28:1151 in the Berlin Academy Edition. I am indebted to Patrick Kain for the ref-

erence, and for subsequent discussion. See Kain, "Interpreting Kant's Theory of Divine Commands," *Kantian Review* 9, no. 1 (May 2005): 128–49, n. 32.

5. The discussion of Spinoza comes at various places, but most importantly in the third *Critique*, at 5:452.

6. Immanuel Kant, *Critique of Practical Reason* 5:22. In *Practical Philosophy*, trans. and ed. Mary Gregor (Cambridge: Cambridge University Press, 1996).

7. See R. M. Hare, *Freedom and Reason* (Oxford: Clarendon Press, 1963), 125–29.

8. Jean-Paul Sartre, *Existentialism and Human Emotions* (Secaucus, N.J.: Citadel Press, 1957), 18.

9. The argument I have given is essentially Kant's argument for the need to believe in God if we are to believe in the real possibility of the highest good. The argument can be put in Craig's terms as an argument that without theism (or at least a belief in providence) we get moral nihilism, once we are realistic about our human tendency to prefer our own advantage to the good of others.

10. Immanuel Kant, *Religion within the Bounds of Mere Reason* 6:47. In *Religion and Rational Theology*, trans. and ed. Allen Wood and George di Giovanni (Cambridge: Cambridge University Press, 1996).

11. I have detailed the account by Duns Scotus of this double motivation in *God and Morality: A Philosophical History* (Oxford: Blackwell, 2006), 87–110.

12. I say "initial weight" because the same worth produces the same weight in decisions about how to live given the same access to knowledge about what the advantage of each person consists in, and the same ability to procure that advantage. Since these are not in fact the same, decisions about how to live can give somewhat greater weight to the agent's own advantage, but not nearly as much greater weight as the affection for advantage unrestrained by the affection for justice would endorse.

13. The "contribution" can be indirect, if the phenomenon is a by-product of something else that has a direct impact on survival or reproduction. See John Cartwright, *Evolution and Human Behavior* (Cambridge, Mass.: MIT Press, 2000), 39f.

14. I have given an account of some of this literature in "Is There an Evolutionary Foundation for Human Morality?" in *Evolution and Ethics: Human Morality in Biological and Religious Perspective*, ed. Philip Clayton and Jeffrey Schloss (Grand Rapids, Mich.: Eerdmans, 2004), 187–203.

15. The reference of the phrase "the Good Samaritan" is to a story told at Luke 10.

16. I have in mind Larry Arnhart's *Darwinian Natural Right: The Biological Ethics of Human Nature* (Albany, N.Y.: SUNY Press, 1998). See also his revised view in "The Darwinian Moral Sense and Biblical Religion," in Clayton and Schloss, *Evolution and Ethics*, 204–20.

17. See Michael Ruse, "Evolutionary Ethics in the Twentieth Century," in *Biology and the Foundations of Ethics*, ed. Jane Maienschein and Michael Ruse (Cambridge: Cambridge University Press, 1999); also see Ruse, *Taking Darwin Seriously* (Oxford: Blackwell, 1986), and Ruse, *Can a Darwinian Be a Christian?* (Cambridge: Cambridge University Press, 2001). I have discussed his view in "Evolutionary Naturalism and Reducing the Demand of Justice," in *Religion in the Liberal Polity*, ed. Terence Cuneo (Notre Dame, Ind.: University of Notre Dame Press, 2005), 83–94.

18. Richard Dawkins is the originator of meme theory, and Daniel Dennett enthusiastically endorses it in *Breaking the Spell: Religion as a Natural Phenomenon* (New York: Viking, 2006). Meme theory has not, however, found widespread acceptance, and there are serious problems in finding identity conditions for the units required by the theory. There is an interesting predecessor theory, with a recognition of some of the difficulties, in Donald Campbell, "Comments on the Sociobiology of Ethics and Moralizing," *Behavioral Science* 24 (1979): 37–45.

19. The classic text is Elliott Sober and David Sloan Wilson, *Unto Others: The Evolution and Psychology of Unselfish Behavior* (Cambridge, Mass.: Harvard University Press, 1998). But the theory of group selection has not yet found widespread acceptance among biologists. See again Dennett, *Breaking the Spell*, 184f.

20. John Hare, *The Moral Gap* (Oxford: Clarendon Press, 1996).

21. *Grace and Free Will*, 759, in *Basic Writings of Saint Augustine*, ed. Whitney J. Oates, vol. 1, *A Select Library of the Nicene and Post-Nicene Fathers of the Christian Church*, ed. Philip Schaff (New York: Random House, 1948).

22. Nel Noddings, *Caring: A Feminist Approach to Ethics and Moral Education* (Berkeley: University of California Press, 1984). A care theory locates care as the central component of the moral life.

23. This is the suggestion made by Kurtz, whose language is surprisingly close to that of J. S. Mill. Kurtz holds that "each person has the ability to determine his or her own meaning fully," and whether we choose to live morally depends on whether we receive proper moral education. Thus the humanist manifesto of 1933 says, "Man is at last becoming aware that he alone is responsible for the realization of the world of his dreams, that he has within himself the power for its achievement." But it is doubtful whether we know how to make people good through moral education, and the optimism of the late nineteenth century did not survive the twentieth, in particular the Second World War, in which the people who carried out the massacres and Holocaust were the most educated people in the world's history to that point. Moreover, meaning is probably not the sort of thing that an individual can create, for reasons Wittgenstein describes. See Ludwig Wittgenstein, *Philosophical Investigations*, trans. G. E. M. Anscombe (Oxford: Blackwell, 1963), 243–68.

24. See note 19 for a difficulty with this proposal. Even if we accept the idea of group selection, it is not clear that it can operate in the absence of conflict between groups.

25. One reason for doing this is that Kurtz makes a number of historical claims that need to be challenged. He says, for example, that modern secular humanism has precursors in Socrates and Kant. Unfortunately these historical claims cannot be properly evaluated without extensive reference to the texts of Plato and Kant, in order to describe their views of the relation between ethics and theology. There is not space for that here. I have given a much fuller treatment in *God and Morality: A Philosophical History*.

26. *Ion* 536a. In *The Collected Dialogues of Plato*, ed. Edith Hamilton and Huntington Cairns (Princeton, N.J.: Princeton University Press, 1961).

27. *Metaphysics* XII, 7, 1072b3. In *The Complete Works of Aristotle,* vol. 2, ed. Jonathan Barnes (Princeton, N.J.: Princeton University Press, 1984).

28. *Timaeus* 90c, in *Collected Dialogues of Plato*, ed. Hamilton and Cairns.

29. See *Complete Works of Aristotle*, ed. Barnes, vol. 2.

30. Gregory Vlastos, *Socrates: Ironist and Moral Philosopher* (Cambridge: Cambridge University Press, 1991), 176 (from, e.g., *Euthyphro* 13e10–11 and *Apology* 30a).

31. *Nicomachean Ethics* I, 2, 1094b10, emphasis added. In Barnes, *Complete Works of Aristotle*, vol. 2.

32. *Nicomachean Ethics* X, 7, 1177b31f. In Barnes, *Complete Works of Aristotle*, vol. 2.

33. See a number of papers in *Kant and the New Philosophy of Religion*, ed. Chris Firestone and Stephen Palmquist (Bloomington: Indiana University Press, 2006).

34. See, for example, *Critique of Practical Reason* 5:129, in *Practical Philosophy*, trans. and ed. Gregor.

35. In *Practical Philosophy*, trans and ed. Gregor. See also Patrick Kain, "Self-legislation in Kant's Moral Philosophy," *Archiv für Geschichte der Philosophie* 86, no. 3 (2004): 257–306.

36. The duty to work toward the highest good is internal to the present life (by the first assumption I detailed in the first part of the paper), even if the realization should not be expected until the next life.

37. *Religion within the Bounds of Mere Reason* 6:45. In Kant, *Religion and Rational Theology*, trans. and ed. Wood and di Giovanni.

38. Utilitarianism faces the difficulty of how to adjudicate between strategies that give a greater total happiness and a greater average happiness, but for the purposes of the present chapter I do not need to comment further on this.

39. *Inquiry* II, III, VIII, 177–78. In *British Moralists 1650–1800*, vol. 1, ed. D. D. Raphael (Oxford: Clarendon Press, 1969).

40. J. S. Mill, *Three Essays on Religion* (London: Henry Holt, 1874), 249–50.

41. Henry Sidgwick, *The Methods of Ethics* (Indianapolis, Ind.: Hackett, 1981), 509.

42. R. M. Hare, *Moral Thinking* (Oxford: Clarendon Press, 1981), 34, 45–46.

43. R. M. Hare, "The Simple Believer," in *Essays on Religion and Education* (Oxford: Clarendon Press, 1992), 23. He says that this faith "is matched by a feeling of thankfulness that all is well," referring to Julian of Norwich: "All shall be well and all manner of things shall be well."

44. R. M. Hare, *Moral Thinking*, 205.

45. See Thomas Carson, *Value and the Good Life* (Notre Dame, Ind.: Notre Dame Press, 2000). He makes the point in detail that the model of full information and impartiality internal to many forms of utilitarianism requires thinking of the position God would be in, if there were a God.

46. I have done some work on this project in *God and Morality*, and less formally in *Why Bother Being Good?* (Downers Grove, Ill.: InterVarsity Press, 2002).

Chapter Five

Why Traditional Theism Cannot Provide an Adequate Foundation for Morality

Walter Sinnott-Armstrong

In his debate with Paul Kurtz, William Lane Craig spends most of his time on his second contention, which is the conditional claim that if theism is false, then we do not have a sound foundation for morality. Others in this volume have replied to that contention, and I have replied elsewhere.[1] In my view, what makes it morally wrong to murder, rape, steal, lie, or break promises, for example, is simply that these acts harm other people without any adequate justification. I can't help but believe that it would be morally wrong for some- one to cause such unjustified harm to me. There is no reason why I would have any more rights than any other person. Hence, it must also be morally wrong for me to cause such unjustified harm to them. This harm-based moral- ity has no need of God, so it provides a sound (though modest) foundation for morality even if theism is false. I do not see how Craig meets such obvious objections to his second contention in this volume or anywhere else, so I will not bother to discuss it further here. I will, instead, focus on Craig's first con- tention. When I refer to his contention from now on, his first contention is the one I will have in mind. My strategy will be to analyze what Craig himself says about his first contention in order to determine whether he provides any reason to believe it. He does not.

CRAIG'S CONTENTION

Craig's first contention looks straightforward: "If theism is true, we have a sound foundation for morality" (30). Don't be fooled by this simple language. This contention is anything but simple.

What kind of theism is Craig's contention about? Is he saying that just any old theism provides a sound foundation for morality? What about belief in Zeus? Of course not. Craig is claiming that monotheism, not polytheism, provides a sound foundation for morality. Is his contention about every monotheism? Probably not. If there is one god, but that god is evil or only partly good, then monotheism is true, but it is hard to see how such a defective god could provide a sound foundation for morality. Maybe Craig's contention is that we have a sound foundation for morality if traditional theism is true—that is, if there is an all-good, all-powerful, all-knowing god. However, the bare claim that there is some all-good, all-powerful, all-knowing god does not tell us which things are good or bad. If you think that homosexual love is morally good, then you will think that an all-good god allows it. If you think that homosexual love is morally bad, then you will think that an all-good god forbids it. Either way, the mere claim that God exists and is all-good, all-powerful, and all-knowing cannot provide a sound foundation for any view about whether homosexual love is morally good or bad. In order for theism to provide a sound foundation for morality, we need to add specific claims about what God likes or is like.

This point raises another question: Who are "we" in Craig's contention? Relative to each other, different traditional theists add incompatible claims about God's nature and commands, but false doctrines cannot provide a sound foundation for anything. Imagine that we and they agree that God is all-good, all-powerful, and all-knowing, but we think God dislikes homosexual love, and they think God likes homosexual love. On the basis of these beliefs about God's nature, we believe that God forbids homosexual love, and they believe that God allows homosexual love. Then, if our version of theism is true, we might have a sound foundation for our moral beliefs, but they do not have a sound foundation for their moral beliefs. And if their version of theism is true, they might have a sound foundation for their moral beliefs, but we do not have a sound foundation for our moral beliefs. Either way, some traditional theists do not have a sound foundation for morality. To have a sound foundation for morality, one must believe the right version of traditional theism. Craig's contention is, then, incorrect if it means, "If *any* theism is true, we have a sound foundation for morality." To be defensible, Craig's contention must mean, "If *our* theism is true, we have a sound foundation for morality."

Craig might reply that he is talking about a different kind of foundation. Philosophers often speak of foundations and foundationalism in epistemology. An epistemic foundation for a belief is what makes someone justified in believing it. In contrast, an ontological foundation for moral wrongness is what constitutes moral wrongness or what makes acts morally wrong. Craig sometimes suggests that he is concerned with epistemic foundations for moral beliefs, such as when he says "we have" a foundation instead of "there is" a foundation. His contention then means that if theism is true, something makes us justified in believing that certain specifiable acts are morally wrong. That can't be accurate, however, since even if theism is true, we might not be justified in believing it is true. A bare truth cannot make us justified in believing anything if we are not justified in believing that truth. Thus, Craig's contention can't be correct if it refers to epistemic foundations. Hence, I will assume from now on that Craig's contention is about ontological foundations. His contention is then about the existence of moral values, duties, and accountability, not about anyone's justified belief in them.

Finally, what kind of morality is Craig's contention about? It can't be about moral claims that Craig's opponents deny. If theists argue that there is no sound foundation for moral restrictions on homosexuality or abortion if theism is false, then nontheists can accept that conditional contention as long as they think there are no legitimate moral restrictions on homosexuality or abortion. Presumably, then, Craig's contentions are both about common morality that is shared by theists and nontheists, including moral restrictions on murder, rape, theft, cheating, lying, and promise breaking.

Craig also specifies that his topic is objective morality, but what does that mean? Craig tells us twice: "To say that there are *objective* moral values is to say that something is good or evil independently of whether *anybody* believes it to be" (30, my emphasis) or "regardless of whether *we* think so or not" (30, my emphasis). The difference between these definitions will become important later. For now what matters is that Craig's contention means that, if his Christian theism is true, there is a sound ontological foundation for common moral values, duties, and accountability that exists independently of what we think or anyone thinks.

OBJECTIVE MORAL VALUES

What is the sound foundation for moral values, according to Craig? He writes,

> On the theistic view, objective moral values are rooted in God. He is the locus and source of moral value. God's own holy and loving nature supplies the absolute standard against which all actions are measured. He is by nature loving, generous, just, faithful, kind, and so forth. Thus if God exists, objective moral values exist. (30)

That's all Craig says about objective moral values before he goes on to the separate topic of moral duties. If he gives any reason here to believe that theism provides a sound foundation for moral values, it must be found within this passage. So let's look at this passage carefully.

What is this passage supposed to accomplish? It might be only a profession of faith. However, a mere profession of his faith does not show that Craig or anyone else has any reason at all to believe his contention about moral values. To show that, Craig needs an argument. So I will assume that he is trying to give an argument in this passage.

What is Craig's argument? It seems to run like this: (1) If theism is true, then God is loving, generous, just, faithful, kind, and so forth. (2) These qualities are objective moral values. Therefore, (3) if theism is true, then God has objective moral value. (4) If God exists and has objective moral value, then objective moral values exist. Therefore, (5) if theism is true, then objective moral values exist.

One problem with this argument is that, if theism is simply the belief that some god or other exists, then premise (1) is questionable. Even if theism is true because some god exists, that god still might not be loving, generous, just, faithful, or kind. Indeed, all of the evil in the world suggests that God might not be loving, generous, just, faithful, or kind. Job might well wonder how faithful God is to those who are faithful to Him.

Premise (1) might, however, be only about traditional theism. Then it might seem obvious that, if traditional theism is true, God is all-good, and it is good to be loving, generous, just, faithful, and kind, so God must be loving, generous, just, faithful, and kind. This line of reasoning assumes that it is good to be loving, generous, just, faithful, and kind, so this argument begs the question if it is supposed to show that objective values exist. Craig might respond that he is talking about a God who is defined to be loving, generous, just, faithful, kind, and so forth. However, Craig also defines God as all-good, so his combined definition would be inconsistent if it were bad to be loving, generous, just, faithful, or kind. One way or another, if premise (1) is about traditional theism, then it already assumes certain values and begs the question.

The next premise is that God's qualities of being loving, generous, just, faithful, kind, and so forth are objective moral values. Craig did not state this premise openly, but this suppressed premise is necessary to make his argument valid. Without this assumption, Craig could not argue from his premise that God has these qualities to the conclusion that God has objective moral value. But this suppressed premise again begs the question. Craig's argument is supposed to show that, if theism is true, then we have a sound foundation for objective moral values. Instead, Craig's premise just assumes that there are objective moral values—specifically, that it is morally good to be loving, generous, just, faithful, kind, and so forth. Since this argument assumes what it is supposed to prove, it cannot provide a sound foundation for anything.

Of course, you and I might agree that these qualities have objective moral value. However, our agreement does not show that objective moral values really exist, much less that objective morality has a sound foundation, even if God exists. If Craig is supposed to be arguing for a conclusion, he cannot legitimately assume his conclusion, even if everyone agrees to it.

Another problem with this argument is that, even if God does exist and does have qualities with objective moral value, this conclusion about God has nothing directly to do with us humans here on earth. Even if God is morally good, that does not show that any humans or human actions are morally good (or morally bad, for that matter). Craig suggests that his argument is supposed to show something about human life when he refers in the same paragraph to the objective moral evil of the Holocaust. However, nothing about the Holocaust follows from Craig's claim that God exists and has objective moral value.

Craig's reply lies in this sentence: "God's own holy and loving nature supplies the absolute standard against which all actions are measured" (30). But, first, why believe this additional claim? Some theists might in fact believe it, but that does not give anybody any reason to believe it. Second, it is not clear how we are supposed to know God's infinite and incomprehensible nature well enough to use it in real life as a standard for measuring the value of all things. God is supposed to be a mystery, and a mystery cannot be a useful standard. Third, God is so different from us that what is good for him might not be good for us. Even if it is good for God to be faithful or punitive, for example, it does not follow that it is good for us humans to be faithful or punitive. We are so different from God in so many ways that God's standards of goodness might be very different from our own standards of goodness, as theists themselves often suggest when trying to explain how a "good" God could allow so much apparently unjustified suffering in the world. For all of these reasons, Craig's argument in this passage cannot show that there is any sound foundation for any moral values that are relevant to humans, even if God does exist.

OBJECTIVE MORAL DUTIES

Craig goes on to talk about duties. All he says here on that topic is this:

Second, *if theism is true, we have a sound basis for objective moral duties*. To say that we have *objective* moral duties is to say that we have certain moral obligations regardless of whether we *think* that we do. On the theistic view, God's moral nature is expressed toward us in the form of divine commands that constitute our moral duties. Far from being arbitrary, these commands flow necessarily from his moral nature. On this foundation we can affirm the objective goodness and rightness of love, generosity, self-sacrifice, and equality, and condemn

as objectively evil and wrong selfishness, hatred, abuse, discrimination, and oppression. (30)

In this passage, Craig endorses a traditional version of a divine command theory of morality: "divine commands . . . constitute our moral duties." This
claim is not about only *some* of our moral duties. Craig's claim is about *all* of
our moral duties. Each and every moral duty is supposed to be constituted by
a divine command. If Craig's claim were not universal in this way, then he
could not defend his other contention, that there would be no objective morality if theism were false. If even part of morality is not based on divine commands, then that part of morality has a sound foundation even if theism is
false. Thus, Craig has to apply his view to all moral duties.

What does Craig mean by "constitute"? As philosophers normally use this
term, it signals a very strong relation. If a divine command constitutes our
moral duty not to rape, for example, then what makes it morally wrong to rape
is just that God commanded us not to rape. Moreover, whenever God commands us to do (or not to do) any act, we have a moral duty to do (or not to
do) that act.

I find this view incredible. If God commanded us to rape, that command
would not create a moral requirement to rape. Of course, Craig says that God
never would or could command us to rape. However, it is not clear how Craig
knows this or how an all-powerful God could be limited in this way. After all,
God is supposed to have commanded Abraham to murder his son, or, at least,
try to murder him. Moreover, even if God in fact never would or could command us to rape, the divine command theory still implies the counterfactual
that, if God did command us to rape, then we would have a moral obligation
to rape. That is absurd.

There is a much more plausible foundation for morality. It seems obvious
to me, and to everyone who does not start with peculiarly religious assumptions, that what makes rape morally wrong is the extreme harm that rape
causes to rape victims. This secular foundation makes morality objective. If
what makes rape morally wrong is harm to rape victims, then whether rape is
wrong does not depend on whether I or rapists believe that rape is wrong. It
also does not depend on whether anyone wants to rape. Regardless of anyone's desires and moral beliefs, rape causes harm to the victim, and that harm
makes rape wrong. This secular foundation, thus, makes morality every bit as
objective as the divine command theory.[2]

Indeed, the harm-based foundation makes morality even more objective than
does Craig's divine command theory. Recall that Craig defined moral values as
objective only if they exist "independently of whether *anybody* believes it to be
so" (30; my emphasis). Later he defined moral duties as objective if and only if

they hold "regardless of whether *we* think so or not" (30; my emphasis). Perhaps Craig intended "anybody" to mean only "any one of us," but my point is just that these definitions, taken literally, capture distinct levels of objectivity. Craig's divine command theory makes moral obligations fit the second definition. On his view, moral obligations are independent of "whether we think so." However, Craig's divine command theory does not make moral obligations objective in the first way. After all, God is someone. Thus, if morality depends on what God thinks, then it is not independent of whether anyone thinks so, and then morality is not objective according to Craig's first definition. But morality does depend on what God thinks, according to Craig's divine command theory. If God did not think rape was morally wrong, then it would not be morally wrong, since God knows all moral truths. Moreover, if God did not think that rape was morally wrong, then God would not command us not to rape, and then rape would not be morally wrong, according to his theory. Craig claims that God's divine commands express God's moral nature, but that does not solve the problem here. Even if it is part of God's nature to think what he thinks about rape, morality is still not independent of what God thinks, on Craig's view. In contrast, the secular harm-based view makes morality independent even of what God thinks. If God somehow thought that rape was not morally wrong, and if God forgot to command us not to rape, or even if God commanded us to rape, none of that would make any difference. Rape would still be morally wrong, because it would still harm rape victims. In this way, the secular foundation makes morality objective in a way that Craig's divine command theory does not.

Craig might respond that morality does not have to be objective in this strong way. However, I am just applying his own original definition. At the very least, he should stop saying that morality cannot be objective on a secular view. The opposite is true: Morality is even more objective on a secular view than on a divine command theory.

The secular view is also preferable on grounds of simplicity. Like the secular view, the divine command theory must recognize harm and its relevance to morality. Then the divine command view adds a new supernatural level to its theory of morality. That added complication brings no benefits for the objectivity of morality, as I just argued. We should prefer simpler views when we have no reason to complicate matters. Hence, we should prefer the secular view.[3]

Besides, Craig gives no argument at all for his divine command theory. You can't show a sound foundation for morality simply by announcing a theory without any reason to accept that theory. Craig's theory assumes that we have a moral duty to do whatever God commands us to do. But, even if there is a God who issues commands, why are we morally required to obey God's commands? One common answer is that we owe God gratitude for creating us.

But children should also be grateful to their parents for creating them, and yet children do not have a moral obligation to do everything that their parents tell them to do. Another common answer is that God will punish us if we disobey him. That would give us a strong prudential reason to obey, but that reason would still not be a moral duty. I might have a reason to obey the commands of a tyrant who will punish me if I disobey, but I still do not have any moral duty to do whatever that tyrant commands. A final common answer is that God the father knows best, so, if God tells us that an act is morally wrong, it is. But how do we know that God is always correct? How do we even know what God commands? Unless we have some independent reason to believe that certain acts are morally wrong, we have no reason to believe that God is correct when he indicates to us through his commands that those acts are morally wrong. This answer cannot, then, tell us why we morally must obey God's commands. Without any reason to accept that assumption, we have no reason to accept Craig's divine command theory.

What's worse, Craig's divine command theory is vulnerable to a cavalcade of devastating objections. First, as Plato showed long ago in his dialogue *Euthyphro*, divine command theories fall into a dilemma. Let's assume that God commanded us not to rape. Did God have any reason to command this? If not, his command was arbitrary, and then it can't make anything morally wrong. On the other hand, if God did have a reason to command us not to rape, then that reason is what makes rape morally wrong. The command itself is superfluous. Either way, morality cannot depend on God's commands.

Craig tries to fend off this standard objection when he says, "Far from being arbitrary, these commands flow necessarily from his moral nature" (30). However, that dogma does not solve the problem. It might be part of the nature of a god in some religion to command everyone to drink wine on Sunday, but that command is still arbitrary. The fact that a command flows necessarily from the nature of the commander does not make that command any less arbitrary if it is arbitrary that the commander has that nature rather than another nature. Craig might respond that God has his nature essentially and necessarily, so it is not contingent that God commands us not to rape. However, commands can be arbitrary even if they are not contingent. It could be an essential part of the nature of Bacchus, the Greek god of wine, to like wine. Nonetheless, if Bacchus commands us to drink wine, that command would still be arbitrary in the sense that there would be no reason for that command. It might even be part of the essential nature of Satan to command us to rape, but that command is still arbitrary, because it is not supported by any reason. Craig might complain that I am missing his point, which is that God's nature is essentially moral, that is, morally good. That is why God's essential nature necessarily leads him to command us not to rape. However, this response assumes that rape is bad on independent grounds. If rape were not bad, then the claim that God is all-good would not imply that God commands us not to rape. Of course, I agree that rape is bad, but this supports my position, not Craig's. Even if it is God's essential nature necessarily to command us not to rape, that command remains arbitrary unless there is some reason for that command, such as that rape is bad on independent grounds. But, if there is such an independent reason, then, as I said, that reason is what makes rape morally wrong, and the command itself is superfluous. So morality cannot be constituted by God's commands.

A second objection is that the divine command theory makes morality childish. Compare a small boy who thinks that what makes it morally wrong for him to hit his little sister is only that his parents told him not to hit her and will punish him if he hits her. As a result, this little boy thinks that, if his parents leave home or die, then there is nothing wrong with hitting his little sister. Maybe some little boys think this way, but surely we adults do not think that morality is anything like this.

Indeed, to call Craig's theory childish is insulting to children. Children know better. Larry Nucci found that almost all Amish teenagers said that if God had not commanded them not to work on Sunday, then it would not be wrong to work on Sunday. However, over 80 percent of these Amish teenagers said that, even if God had made no rule against hitting other people, it would still be morally wrong to hit other people.[4] This shows that even teenagers who were brought up in a strict religious way recognize that morality has a sound foundation outside of God's commands.

Of course, they might be mistaken. Still, when so many people (adults and teenagers, secular and religious) agree that morality does not depend on commands either by parents or God, then the burden of proof must lie on those who claim otherwise. Craig has not even tried to carry this burden.

A third objection is that the divine command theory makes morality unknowable. To see why, consider whether it is immoral to eat pork. If the divine command theory is correct, we cannot answer this question simply by pointing out that eating pork causes harm to pigs or to us, unless we already know that God commanded us not to cause such harm. We also cannot know whether it is immoral to eat pork on the basis of others' testimony or our own moral intuitions if we have no reason to think that their testimony or our intuitions map onto divine commands, and we cannot have any such reason without knowing what God commanded. Thus, on Craig's theory, we cannot know what is morally wrong if we cannot know what God commanded. Unfortunately, however, we have no sound way to determine what God commanded. Of course, Craig thinks he has a way. He thinks he can prove by reason alone not only that God exists but also that God has many of the features that traditional Christianity attributes to God. However, his arguments for God's existence are faulty, as I have shown elsewhere.[5] In any case, even if Craig could show that God exists, that still would not help at all in determining what God commands. Theists often tell us what God commands, as if they knew, and the commands that they ascribe to God are often (though not always) plausible. However, what makes us and them accept that God commands those actions rather than others is that we already and independently had a reason to believe that certain acts are immoral. Assuming God is good, of course God would command us not to rape. But the only way we know God would issue that command is that we already know rape is wrong. There is no way to know what God does or would command without already knowing what is morally right and wrong.

The most common response by Christians is that we know divine commands through the holy scriptures. Unfortunately, the Bible contains some horrible moral messages about slavery and killing nonbelievers:

As for your male and female slaves whom you may have: you may buy male and female slaves from among the nations that are round about you. (Leviticus 25:44, English Standard Version; see also Exodus 21:7–11)

Slaves, obey your earthly masters with fear and trembling, with a sincere heart, as you would Christ. (Ephesians 6:5, English Standard Version; see also 1 Timothy 6:1)

If your brother, the son of your mother, or your son or your daughter or the wife you embrace or your friend who is as your own soul entices you secretly, saying, "Let us go and serve other gods," . . . you shall not yield to him or listen to him, nor shall your eye pity him, nor shall you spare him, nor shall you conceal him. But you shall kill him. (Deuteronomy 13:6–9, English Standard Version; see also 2 Chronicles 15:13 and Luke 19:27)

So Joshua struck the whole land. . . . He left none remaining, but devoted to destruction all that breathed, just as the Lord God of Israel commanded. (Joshua 10:40)

In addition, there is the great flood, where many innocent children were supposed to have been killed by God. Of course, there are also some very nice passages and messages in the Bible. Like most books written by humans, the Bible is a mixture of good and bad. As such, it cannot serve as a reliable guide to morality. If we follow all of the Bible, we will be led astray into immorality. On the other hand, if we pick and choose which Bible passages to follow, then we need to use our prior moral views to guide our choice. Either way, the Bible cannot provide a sound foundation for morality or for knowledge of morality.

Last but not least, the divine command theory makes morality *hard-hearted*. Divine commands by their nature allow no exceptions for the sake of human welfare. If God commands us to kill nonbelievers, then, according to the divine command theory, that command becomes our moral duty no matter how much suffering it will cause to innocent people. God is supposed to have taken account of that suffering before he issued the command, so, if there were justified exceptions, God would have said so.

This defect of divine command theories comes out in contemporary religious opposition to research using embryonic stem cells. Almost nobody opposes embryonic stem-cell research except on the basis of religious views. Those who do oppose embryonic stem-cell research claim that it is morally wrong no matter how much good it would do. Even if embryonic stem-cell research is needed to cure juvenile diabetes, to enable paraplegics and quadriplegics to walk again, and so on, as many doctors claim, it would still be morally wrong if what makes it wrong is simply that God commanded us not to do it. This view of morality has separated morality from human suffering by basing morality on commands coming from another world. Such a view is callous. Nobody would accept it if they did not already hold strong religious beliefs.

Many good Christians would reply that God commands us not to harm others and to help others in need. Those commands are not hard-hearted. Maybe not, but suppose that parents command their son to be nice to his little sister. Their son is then nice to his sister, but only because his parents ordered him to be nice to her. If they had not commanded him to be nice to his sister, then he would not be nice to her. This boy might not seem hard-hearted, but his motivations are far from ideal. Analogously, anyone who helps and refrains from harming others just because God commanded them to do so might not be hard-hearted, but their motivations are far from ideal. It would be better for them to help and refrain from harming other people out of concern for those other people. Many Christians do, of course, help others because they care about those others. But that only shows that they are not really following the divine command theory. They are, instead, following a harm-based morality. That is wonderful, but it cannot save the divine command theory from the charge of being hard-hearted.

MORAL ACCOUNTABILITY

Craig ends with moral accountability:

> Third, *if theism is true, we have a sound basis for moral accountability*. On the theistic view, God holds all persons morally accountable for their actions.

Evil and wrong will be punished; righteousness will be vindicated. Despite the inequities of this life, in the end the scales of God's justice will be balanced. (31)

What does Craig mean by "accountability"? In a factual sense, people are accountable for their actions when they will *in fact* be punished for misbehavior. In a normative sense, people are accountable when they *deserve* to be punished for misbehavior.

Craig seems to have the first sense in mind. Otherwise he could not legitimately infer from "evil and wrong *will* be punished" (my emphasis) to any conclusion about accountability.

In the factual sense of "accountable," a sound foundation for accountability would be a sound reason to believe that wrongdoers really will be punished. Craig believes this, which is no surprise. However, he gives no reason to believe that this prediction is true. On some theistic views, such as in Judaism, there is no hell in which wrongdoers are punished. Many Christians also do not believe in hell. Thus, Craig's claim is not held by all theists or even all Christians. It is a central part of Craig's theism, but he cannot show that his brand of theism provides a sound foundation for such accountability just by saying that he believes it. Mere assertion cannot show that any foundation is sound.

Maybe the Bible is supposed to show that wrongdoers will be punished. But why believe the Bible's prediction? Traditional Christianity tells us that Christ died for our sins, and that we will be forgiven if we confess and turn to Christ. If so, many wrongdoers will not be punished after all. Moreover, as we saw (Deuteronomy 13:6–9), the Bible tells believers to kill nonbelievers. By commanding such killing, the Bible suggests that if you kill such a nonbeliever, you will not be punished. You might even be rewarded. But actually it is morally wrong, not right, to kill another person just because that other person tries to convert you to another religion. Hence, the Bible does not say that all people who do what really is immoral will be punished. Finally, the Bible is filled with stories, such as the great flood and the destruction of Sodom and Gomorrah, in which whole groups of people are punished, even though some of those people were too young to have been morally guilty of anything bad enough to warrant a death penalty. Because of stories like that, the Bible cannot support the prediction that only wrongdoers will be punished or, as Craig says, "righteousness will be vindicated." If innocent people get punished along with guilty ones, then this kind of accountability gives no incentive to avoid wrongdoing. As a result, the Bible cannot provide a sound foundation for moral accountability in the first sense.

Craig's claim still might seem defensible with the other sense of "accountability." In that normative sense, people are accountable when they *deserve* to be punished for their misbehavior. What is necessary for such desert? Common sense suggests that people deserve to be punished for wrongful acts only if they are able to know that those acts are wrong. When people do acts that are wrong, but they have no way to tell whether those acts are wrong, then those people do not deserve to be punished. It is not their fault. This simple point creates serious trouble for divine command theorists. They claim that acts are morally wrong only because those acts violate divine commands. But then people who do not and cannot know what God commands them to do also do not and cannot know which acts are morally wrong. Hence, they cannot deserve to be punished.

To see the point, consider a possible divine command not to work on Sunday (or Saturday, for that matter). People who had never heard that command could not know that it is morally wrong to work on Sunday, so they should not be held morally responsible if they do work on Sunday. God might build into them a natural aversion to working on Sunday, but they still would not know that it is morally wrong, because they would have no idea what makes it morally wrong to work on Sunday, and they would have no reason to believe that their aversion reflects moral wrongness if moral wrongness is constituted by divine commands.

Now compare horrible murderers who lived before Jesus and never had access to a Bible or to Christian beliefs. If the divine command theory were correct, then these murderers could not know that it is morally wrong to murder. But then they would not deserve to be punished. That's absurd. Of course, these murderers deserve to be punished, even if they had no access to any divine command. The reason is that these murderers could know that it is wrong to murder on the basis of the harm to their victims. If harm is the basis of wrongness, these murderers can know what is wrong and can justly be held responsible. But if the basis for moral wrongness really were divine commands, then these murderers could not know that murder is morally wrong and, hence, they could not be justly held responsible or punished.

Divine command theorists usually reply at this point that God implanted in everyone a natural ability to see what is right or wrong. That is supposed to explain how our ancient murderers could know that their acts were wrong. However, this response just admits the point. We know which acts are wrong by seeing the harm they cause, not by thinking about divine commands. The best explanation of moral accountability in the second sense turns out to be completely secular, contrary to Craig's claim.

Craig concludes this section with a different argument:

> We can even undertake acts of extreme self-sacrifice that run contrary to our self-interest, knowing that such acts are not empty and ultimately meaningless

gestures. Thus, the moral choices we make in this life are infused with an eternal significance. (31)

This passage suggests that acts of self-sacrifice are empty and ultimately meaningless unless they have some kind of eternal significance. Such a view robs us of any incentive to improve this finite world. We would have more reason to destroy this finite world in the search for an eternal heaven. If this is the best that theism can do, then it cannot provide a sound foundation for anything that deserves to be called morality.

Instead, the meaning of an act of self-sacrifice lies in its benefits to others. Self-sacrifice that does not help anyone is meaningless, but self-sacrifice that aids others gets meaning from the fact that it does aid others. Sure, the people who are aided will eventually die, but that does not imply that nothing was accomplished. Their lives went better because of the sacrifice. That matters to any caring person.

Moreover, it is not clear why self-sacrifice is meaningful on Craig's own traditional theistic view. Suppose that I sacrifice myself to help someone else, and I go to heaven. Still, if I had not sacrificed myself, I would have confessed my sins, and God would have forgiven me, so I would have gone to heaven anyway. Then my act of helping the other person was not "infused with eternal significance" after all, because it had no effect on my eternal life or on God's glory. The only way to avoid this result is to deny that God forgives those who turn to him after sinning. That would be a harsh doctrine contrary to traditional Christianity. Hence, it turns out that self-sacrifice does not have eternal significance on Craig's own view.

CONCLUSION

I have argued that Craig fails to provide a sound foundation for any of the aspects of morality that he mentions: moral values, moral duties, and moral accountability. Of course, other theists might try to give better arguments for a religious view of morality. I don't see how they could avoid all of the problems in Craig's account without leaving traditional Christianity far behind. In any case, even if morality could be shown to rest on theism in some other way, Craig has failed badly in his attempt to provide a theistic foundation for morality.[6]

NOTES

1. William Lane Craig and Walter Sinnott-Armstrong, *God? A Debate between a Christian and an Atheist* (New York: Oxford University Press, 2004), especially pages 32–36.

2. As I said in my opening paragraph, this harm-based view refutes Craig's other contention that, if theism is false, we do not have a sound foundation for objective morality. My point here is, instead, that the divine command theory is undermined by the availability of a better foundation for objective morality.

3. Thanks to Robert Garcia and Nate King for this point.

4. Larry Nucci, "Children's Conceptions of Morality, Social Conventions, and Religious Prescriptions," in *Moral Dilemmas: Philosophical and Psychological Reconsiderations of the Development of Moral Reasoning*, ed. C. Harding (Chicago: Precedent Press, 1986).

5. Craig and Sinnott-Armstrong, *God?* chap. 2.

6. For helpful comments, I am grateful to Larry Crocker, Robert Garcia, Nate King, Doug Linder, and Thalia Wheatley.

Chapter Six

Theism, Atheism, and the Explanation of Moral Value

Mark C. Murphy

I will first comment briefly on the ambiguity of the debate topic, and indicate what precisely is objectionable about Paul Kurtz's epistemological interpretation of it. I will then turn to the issue upon which William Lane Craig focuses—that concerning the "grounding," "foundation," or "explanation" of moral value. Here I will question the adequacy of Craig's argument for the superiority of theistic to atheistic explanations of moral value by sketching a nontheistic explanation that fares no worse than Craig's as an account of moral value. I conclude by making a concession to Craig's view on the issue of moral obligation, though I will argue that this is a concession that a defender of Kurtz's view need not be unhappy to make.

1.

The question debated by Paul Kurtz and William Lane Craig is "Is goodness without God good enough?" and while this formulation enjoys the benefits of pithiness and suggestiveness, it bears far too many possible meanings to ensure that the debaters come into argumentative contact with one another. In asking whether goodness without God is good enough, one thing that one might be asking about is the character trait of being morally good, that is, what it takes to be a morally good person; by contrast, one might be asking about goodness as such, about the existence or exemplification of the property *good*. Again, in asking whether goodness without God is good enough, one thing that one might be asking about is whether God's existence is a necessary condition for the presence of goodness (in whatever sense the questioner has in mind); by contrast, one might be asking about whether *belief* that

God exists is a necessary condition for the presence of goodness (in whatever sense the questioner has in mind). So, in asking whether goodness without God is good enough, we might be asking (1) whether one can be morally good without believing that God exists; or (2) whether one can be morally good if God does not exist (for example, whether one can be morally good unless God providentially orders the universe, or assists us in acting well through sanctification)[1]; or (3) whether there can even be such a thing as goodness—that is, can there be any such property as being good, or can the property of goodness be exemplified—without God's existing.

Kurtz fixes on (1)—almost, but not quite, to the exclusion of (2) and (3). There is nothing wrong with disambiguating an ambiguous question and then offering a persuasive answer to the particular disambiguation chosen. The difficulty is that the question with which Kurtz almost exclusively concerns himself is not a particularly interesting, live question. If we ask whether atheists can be morally good people, then on any view that is currently defended by more than a few cranks, the answer is: *of course* atheists can live lives that are, *in large measure*, morally upright, even extraordinarily admirable or heroic. (I return to the italicized qualification in a moment.) What makes Kurtz's interpretation of the debate question a poor one is not that the plain sense of the debate topic rules it out, but that if there is going to be a debate, one would expect it to be on a live question about which there is disagreement between the debaters.

There is a way that Kurtz could have formulated (1) so that it would have been a live and interesting question. (1) asks whether one can be morally good without believing that God exists, and above I noted that on (1) Craig and Kurtz are perfectly in agreement that atheists can, in large measure, live admirable lives. Kurtz might reformulate (1), though, as (1*): Can atheists live *fully* admirable lives? Here Kurtz and Craig might very well part ways. Most theists would deny that an atheist can live a *fully* admirable moral life. The reason that most theists would deny this is that most theists think that we have duties to perform actions that take God as their intentional object. (An intentional object is just what an intentional state—believing, desiring, hoping, liking, admiring, hating, etc.—is about.) For example, most theists think that we ought to thank God for God's great goodness to us; and that we ought to obey God by performing the acts that God has told us to perform and refraining from those acts that God has forbidden us to perform; and that we ought to worship God on account of God's greatness. But these are actions that are not available to the atheist. The atheist cannot thank God for God's great goodness to us, if the atheist denies that there is any such being as God that has shown us great goodness; the atheist cannot obey God, if the atheist denies that there is any such being who can give commands; the atheist cannot worship a being for that being's greatness, if the atheist does not even believe that this being exists. So (1*), unlike (1), really is a live question, for it is a live question whether the atheist could be completely morally good, whether his or her atheism can, as such, prevent him or her from living a completely admirable moral life.

Now, Kurtz might well think that atheism cannot prevent one from living such a life, but he offers no evidence for this claim. To offer such evidence one would have to show either that there is no such being as God[2] or that even if there is such a being, there are no moral duties that require having God as an intentional object. While there is a way, then, to make Kurtz's epistemological reading of the question interesting, he does not in fact address that version of the question.

Another way to put the point is that the debate question is not ambiguous only about the sort of goodness in question, or about whether it is God's existence or belief in God's existence that is under consideration. It is also made ambiguous by the "good enough" locution. If something is said to be good enough, it is good enough for some purpose. If I say my car is good enough, it makes a difference whether I mean "to get to the store" or "to win the Indianapolis 500." If Kurtz wants to say that the moral goodness that is available to humans even without belief in God is good enough for leading generally morally decent lives, lives that morally sensible human beings would look upon with some admiration, then we should acknowledge the truth of what Kurtz says and move on. (This is what Craig rightly recommends, several times, though seemingly without effect.) If Kurtz wants to say that lack of belief in God does not rule out perfect moral goodness, then what he is saying is highly debatable, but nothing that he has said in his contribution goes toward proving this very interesting and controversial claim. Kurtz is either repeating what we already know or flatly asserting, without supporting argument, what is unsettled and worth discussing.

2.

Craig claims that the theist can, while the atheist cannot, account for three phenomena: the morally good, the morally obligatory, and the morally culpable. Without God, there can be no value of the distinctively moral sort; there can be no obligations of the distinctively moral sort; and the conditions under which one can genuinely be morally culpable for violations of moral duty cannot obtain. I will not focus on Craig's arguments concerning moral culpability. What I want to talk about is Craig's thesis that a grounding for moral value and moral obligation is needed, and that this grounding can be provided only by theism.

There is much in Craig's argument that is underdeveloped,[3] and I will begin by trying to fill in some of the background in a way that I hope is faithful to Craig's intentions and views. The two central notions that Craig employs without explanation are, on one hand, that of a "grounding" or a "foundation," and on the other, that of morality itself. Let me say something about how I think Craig understands the notion of the moral, and then turn to that of a grounding or a foundation.

When Craig sets himself to answer the question of goodness without God, he does not set himself to the task of showing that every sort of value that is familiar to us human beings requires a theistic grounding. No: It is specifically *moral* value—moral goodness, moral obligation, and moral responsibility—that requires such a grounding. As far as Craig's argument goes, there may be true statements of goodness, obligation, and responsibility that can be adequately grounded without appeals to theism[4]—perhaps the truth of *My vacuum cleaner is really good*, *Americans in the 1850s were legally obligated not to aid fugitive slaves*, and *I am responsible for the club's dues payments* are examples. But the reason why they are examples of goodness without God, on Craig's view, would be that the goodness ascribed to my vacuum cleaner is not moral goodness, the obligation not to assist runaway slaves was not a moral obligation, and my responsibility to the other club members is not moral responsibility.

What are the distinctive marks of the moral, on Craig's view? I take it from his contribution to the debate that there are at least four such marks: universality, objectivity, normativity, and other-directedness. The domain of the moral is characterized in *universal* terms: All rational beings, or at least all human beings, are governed by the morally valuable. The domain of the moral is characterized *objectively*: Whether a state of affairs is morally valuable, or an act is morally obligatory, or a person is morally culpable does not depend on what any individual human or any group of humans thinks about the matter. The domain of the moral is characterized *normatively*: When a state of affairs is morally valuable, then an agent has reason to care about it, or pursue it; when an act is morally obligatory, then an agent has reason (perhaps decisive reason) to perform it; when a person is morally responsible for something, then he or she has reason to protect or promote it. The domain of the moral is *other-directed*: At least some of the states of affairs that are morally valuable or actions that are morally obligatory bear directly on other people and their well-being, and we are morally responsible for not caring adequately for or not fully complying with our obligations toward these others. When we say, then, that the relief of suffering is morally valuable, we are saying that for all human beings, the relief of suffering is something that there is reason to care about and to work toward. When we say that it is morally obligatory to refrain from killing the innocent, we are saying that all human beings have strong, even decisive, reason to refrain from killing the innocent.

The second idea to which Craig appeals is the idea of a grounding or foundation. Craig understands the question of goodness without God to be an ontological question—a question about what exists, and about how the various things that exist are related to one another. When we ask what grounds the existence of some thing x, we are asking whether there is some thing y that is more ontologically basic than x and explains x's existence. If we ask, for example, about whether language has a foundation or grounding, we are likely to appeal to persons and their interaction as more ontologically basic and as explaining the phenomenon of language. No doubt there are a number of questions that one could ask and puzzles that one could raise about what counts as explanation, about when explanation is called for, and so forth. But I will leave that to the side for the moment.

Craig's claim is that theism has the resources to appeal to something more ontologically basic than moral value—that distinctive form of value that is objective, universal, normative, and other-directed—that can explain its existence, whereas atheism lacks such resources. So, goodness—that is, moral goodness—without God cannot be good enough, for without God there is no explanation for moral goodness at all.

How does Craig's argument work? The idea is that theism can appeal to God's nature and God's commands to explain moral goodness and moral obligation.

> [I]f theism is true, we have a sound basis for *objective moral values*. . . . On the theistic view, objective moral values are rooted in God. He is the locus and source of moral value. God's own holy and loving nature supplies the absolute standard against which all actions are measured. He is by nature loving, generous, just, faithful, kind, and so forth. Thus if God exists, objective moral values exist. (30)

Moral obligation also appeals to God as its source, but instead of thinking of the standard as God's intrinsic nature, it is God's commands that serve as the grounding for moral obligations.

The atheist, however, lacks such a foundation for moral value: for the atheist, the only plausible grounding for morality is human beings; but without God, there is no "reason . . . to regard human flourishing as in any way significant" (31). We humans are not special; we are, rather, just "accidental by-products of nature" (31) with nothing that sets us apart or makes us particularly worthy of concern. Our moral values are, on this perspective, simply "by-products of sociobiological evolution" (31), and so we have no justification for thinking of our moral beliefs about value and obligation as tracking any objective facts or for thinking that we have reason to curtail pursuit of our interests for the sake of the interests of others. Morality is just an illusion conjured by natural selection.

So, on Craig's view, theism has a plausible way to account for the presence of objective, universal, normative, other-directed value; atheism does not. In evaluating the success of Craig's argument, one might call into question the conception of moral value that Craig is working with: One might deny that moral value genuinely requires universality, or objectivity, or normativity, or other-directedness. This will not be my approach. I will take this conception of the moral for granted, and ask whether Craig has succeeded in showing that moral value is explainable within a theistic world but not within an atheistic one. I will roughly sketch a nontheistic account of moral value—nontheistic because it is available to atheists and to theists who think that moral value can be given an informative nontheistic grounding—and I will argue that Craig's theistic account succeeds in explaining moral value no further than this account does.

It is rather strange that Craig takes his account of atheistic metaphysics of morals from sociobiological accounts of morality. If one were introduced to moral philosophy by Craig's debate contribution, one would think that most contemporary moral philosophers affirm the sociobiological account of moral value with which Craig tries to saddle the atheist. But while most contemporary moral philosophers are not theists, almost none of them accepts the sociobiological account of morality. And it is obvious why most moral philosophers do not accept this wrongheaded view. If we start only with the facts of evolution, we will never extract from it any normativity—we will never be able to cross the gap simply from a story about how our species in fact evolved to any claims about what we genuinely have reason to favor or promote. The atheistic account of moral value that Craig offers is no account of moral value at all, but an account of the *appearance* of moral value. Perhaps it would serve for a more enlightening comparison to sketch a nontheistic alternative that attempts to preserve moral value rather than just the appearance thereof.[5]

Here is a suggestion. The atheist can appeal—this is an appeal toward which Kurtz himself gestures—to the notion of *prudential* value as the more ontologically basic category, which can serve as a grounding for moral value, both of goodness and rightness. To flesh out this suggestion, I'll now make the relevant distinctions between prudential and moral value, indicate why Craig himself seems committed to the view that prudential value without God is good enough, and then indicate why prudential value is sufficient to play any grounding role that Craig is in a position to require of the atheistic account.

To be prudentially valuable is to be *good for* a subject. To be prudentially valuable is to be what makes a subject well-off, what makes his or her life go well, what constitutes his or her well-being, what contributes to his or her flourishing. Prudential value can be as *objective* as can be: Whether one is well-off is not determined by the subject's own judgments of well-being—I can be very well-off and not realize it, and I can be very badly off and not realize it. (Indeed, one sign of the objectivity of prudential value is the fact that we argue about what really makes for well-being.) Prudential value is *universal*: It is plausible that we can give a general account of what makes all humans well-off, whether it is done in terms of desire-satisfaction, or pleasure, or some list of goods such as health, knowledge, friendship, aesthetic experience, and so forth. Prudential value is *normative*: Surely we have reason to care about our own well-being (and Craig's argument about accountability[6] presupposes that we have such reasons).

Prudential value is similar to moral value in its objectivity, universality, and normativity, but it is to be contrasted with moral value in its directedness. Prudential value is "self-directed"—it is, as I said, what is good *for a subject*. Moral value, by contrast, is what is good *simpliciter*—good not for someone, but (as Sidgwick was to put it) "from the point of view of the universe."[7] If my well-being is first and foremost a reason for *me* to pursue it, what is morally good is a reason for *anybody* to pursue it. There may well be interesting connections between the prudentially valuable and the morally valuable—indeed, I will discuss them in a moment—but it does seem clear that we distinguish conceptually between what is good for a person and what is just morally good.

Suppose that I put forward the bold propositions: There is such a thing as my being better- or worse-off; and there is such a thing as your being better- or worse-off. Indeed, I'll give cases. It is, other things equal, worse for me to be in excruciating pain than not to be in excruciating pain. Ditto for you. If you want to try to doubt this, have someone close your hand in a vise, or press it against a hot stove, and ask yourself again whether you would be better-off with your hand released from the vise or off the burner.

Now suppose that our debate topic were "Is prudential goodness without God good enough?" and we were to ask whether we can make any sense out of the idea of prudential value without appealing to God. We would not be able to appeal to any of the arguments that Craig made in this debate: Nothing that he says calls into question the idea of a form of value that is universal, objective, and normative that can be explained without appeal to God.[8] When Kurtz suggests that the ethics of humanism is ultimately about flourishing—that is, it bottoms out in prudential value—Craig does not challenge him to make sense out of the notion of human flourishing without appeal to theistic explanation; he challenges the claim that this could serve as an adequate grounding for ethics, because Kurtz does not give a justification for the other-directedness of moral value.

Craig's silence on whether there can be prudential goodness without God might be, I allow, merely a by-product of the debate format: It is more straightforward to challenge the move from prudential to moral value than to challenge prudential-goodness-without-God, and the limitations of debate formats direct one to pursue lines of argument that are more straightforward. But I think that Craig is probably well-advised not to fight about prudential-goodness-without-God. Look, for example, at the way that God's nature is supposed to serve as our standard of moral value on Craig's view. It is God's kindness, God's love, God's generosity, and so forth, that are to serve as our standard. Now, how God's goodness can serve as a standard for our own is a very, very tricky matter, but that is not my worry here. My point is that if God's stance toward us is to serve as our standard for moral value, then there must be some prior notion of prudential value. For God to love us is for God to value us and want *our good*. For God to be kind to us is for God to act in ways that serve *our well-being*. For God to be generous toward us is for God to be abundantly gracious in bestowing upon us goods that make us *better-off*. The very virtues of God to which Craig wants to appeal to provide a grounding for moral value presuppose an independent and prior conception of prudential value.

The first step of an appropriate nontheistic explanation of moral value is to appeal to prudential value. The second step is to connect prudential with moral value. If a grounding for moral value is needed, the nontheist might say, then the grounding is to be found in prudential value. What makes a state of affairs morally valuable (or disvaluable) is grounded in what makes people better- (or worse-) off. (For example, what makes the state of affairs *suffering's being relieved* morally good is that people are made better-off when their suffering is lessened; what makes the state of affairs *poverty's being on the increase* morally bad is that poverty tends to make people worse-off.) What makes a trait of character virtuous (or vicious) is grounded in what makes people better- (or worse-) off. (For example, what makes the trait *courage* a virtue is its making people better able to act to sustain the well-being of people in community.) What obligations people have is grounded in what makes people better- (or worse-) off. (For example, if we have an obligation to aid the poor, it is because by acting to aid the poor people will be better-off; if we have an obligation not to lie, it is because lying is the sort of act that tends to the undermining of people's well-being.) There is plenty of room, even within this particular nontheistic account, for argument about how the relationship between prudential and moral value is to be described — whether, for example, what is required is to maximize well-being, or to refrain from intentionally destroying it, or simply to respond to it in an intelligent way. But, of course, there will be variations like this within Craig's proposed theistic view as well; both Craig's theistic view and my proposed nontheistic view are on a par on this point.

If I understand Craig's view correctly, his objection would be in the second step—the move from prudential to moral value. How do we explain in atheistic terms, Craig asks, why one should care about someone else's flourishing, someone else's well-being? Kurtz's remarks here strike me as unhelpful, for by implication they give up on the universal normativity of moral value. He answers Craig's challenge by mentioning the brute fact that humans tend to care about each other (35). But this is a disastrous response—as it stands, it is completely incapable of explaining the universal normativity of the moral. If I happen to care about my fellow humans, then I will act for the sake of their well-being. But I might very well just not. I might be a sociopath. Or I might just be tired or lazy or selfish. It is not just that Kurtz lacks the means to motivate such people. It is that he has no basis for saying anything normatively charged about their laziness or selfishness—that they are doing something bad, that they ought not to do so, that what they are doing is unreasonable.

How do we move from someone's well-being being a reason for him or her, to its being a reason for anyone? Craig suggests that the atheist cannot say anything helpful here, for the atheist simply denies that the human is special in any way that would help to explain why the human should care about other humans' well-being and even be under duties with respect to them. But here, again, it is hard to see why any atheist would swallow this pill. Even if, on the atheistic view, the processes that brought into existence the kind *human* are no different from the processes that brought into existence the kind *lion* or the kind *slime mold*, the kind *human* is obviously a distinct sort of organism, and distinct in ways that are obviously ethically significant. To take one example: human beings possess *reflective* and *objectivizing* intelligence, which enables them to call their inclinations into question and to see themselves as one person among others. It is no surprise that nontheistic accounts of moral value—whether Kantian, utilitarian, virtue theoretic, or natural law—have focused on this feature of human beings in explaining the basis of the distinct normativity of ethical judgment.[9]

Now, Craig might well object that the appeal to prudential goodness, and the distinctive features of reflective, objectivizing intelligence, are not sufficient to offer an adequately informative explanation of moral value. This explanation of moral value, Craig might say, is just not good enough. One might, on Craig's behalf, put the worry as follows. *There is such a thing as prudential value* and *humans have the capacities of reflective and objectivizing intelligence* do not together logically entail *there is such a thing as moral value*. In other words, one can, without contradiction, affirm both *there is such a thing as prudential value* and *humans have the capacities of reflective and objectivizing intelligence* while denying *there is such a thing as moral value*. But if the standard for explanation here is logical entailment—*p* explains *q* only if *p* logically entails *q*—then Craig's theistic account fails as well. For *God exists* plainly does not logically entail *moral value exists* (where, recall, to say that moral value exists is to assert the existence of a form of value exhibiting objectivity, universality, normativity, and other-directedness).

Perhaps what Craig has in mind is some sense of explanation that does not require straightforward logical entailment. How exactly is the existence of a just, loving, and kind—not to mention omnipotent, omniscient, and provident—Creator supposed to explain the presence of moral value? How can we get an informative explanation of the presence of universal, objective, normative, other-directed standards of evaluation and action by appeal to God's existence?

Craig does not say. Or, if he does say, it is unclear what it is about his answers that is supposed to be helpfully explanatory with respect to moral value. Of moral value, we are told that "God's own holy and loving nature supplies the absolute standard" (30); of moral obligation, we are told that "divine commands . . . constitute our moral duties" (30). We might take these remarks as statements that *it is morally good to conform to God's nature* and *it is morally obligatory to adhere to God's commands*. I think that both of these claims are, reasonably interpreted, true. But by no stretch of the imagination would these count as *explanations* of moral value and moral obligation; they are *assertions* that particular moral values and moral obligations exist.[10]

Alternative theistic explanations may also be rejected. We may put to the side as obviously mistaken any views that appeal to God's rewards and punishments. If the story here is just about God's rewards and punishments—that is, that we will be rewarded for acting for the sake of others' well-being, and punished for acting contrary to their well-being—then we have not moved from having reasons to look after our well-being to having reasons to look after others; we are still governed ultimately only by reasons of our own well-being rather than also by reasons of others' welfare.

We can also put to the side as obviously mistaken any views that appeal simply to God's infallibility in moral matters. We might be tempted to say: Well, if there is a God, and God loves human beings, then we know that human beings are lovable, and that gives us reason to love them. This argument trades on a confusion between the ontology and the epistemology of morals. That God loves human beings—and of course God's loving is appropriate—does not obviously *give* us reason to love them, or at all *explain* why we have reason to love them. All it shows us is that we have *reason to believe* that we ought to love them. This, again, is epistemology, not metaphysics. For all we know, the ground of morality could be anything. Finding out that God loves us is like finding out that God believes that Fermat's Last Theorem is true—it tells us that Fermat's Last Theorem is true, but it does not tell us anything about the metaphysics of mathematical truth. If we know that God loves us, that can give us reason to believe that we are in some way lovable; it does not bear on the issue that Craig is interested in—that is, why we are lovable.

Craig's theistic view fails if the appeals to God as explanatorily powerful are merely assertions of moral value and moral obligation, for that is no explanation at all. Craig's theistic view fails if the appeals to God are just invocations of self-interest, for that does not explain moral value at all. Craig's theistic view fails if the appeals to God are just invocations of God's superior reliability in moral matters, for that appeal would explain only a source of our knowledge about moral value rather than explain the very existence of moral value. Perhaps what Craig means to say—his brief discussion of moral obligation suggests this—is that moral value and moral obligation are just to be *identified* with theistic states of affairs: *being morally valuable* just is *being favored by God*; *being morally obligatory* just is *being commanded by God*. The sense of explanation at stake is that of informative identification, as we explain the nature of water by identifying it with H_2O or explain the nature of heat by identifying it with molecular motion. While I am sympathetic with this project of informative identification,[11] and I agree that it can count as genuinely explanatory, this argument is a failure when wielded against the nontheist. For the nontheist can reasonably enough suggest that moral value can be informatively identified with states of affairs involving prudential value: (e.g.) *to be morally valuable* is *to be or serve someone's well-being*; (e.g.) *to be morally obligatory* is *to promote as fully as possible overall well-being*.[12]

My main point, then, is that Craig's argument bites back. If he raises the demands on what counts as an adequate ground for moral value so that the atheist cannot meet it, the theist cannot meet it, either. If he lowers the demand on what counts as an adequate ground of moral value so that the theist can meet it, then the atheist can meet it as well. Or, to put the point more modestly, Craig has not offered us any reason for thinking anything to the contrary.

3.

I want to conclude by making a concession to Craig's views on the theistic grounding of morality. I have argued so far that nothing in Craig's account gives us any reason to think that a theistic grounding for ethics is any more plausible than a nontheistic grounding, where to ground something is to offer an explanation for some phenomenon in more ontologically basic terms and the ethical phenomena in question are demarcated by their exhibiting universality, objectivity, normativity, and other-directedness. But this leaves open the possibility that there are some moral states of affairs that do include elements beyond these four demarcating features, and that require theistic explanation.

Craig may well be right that the notion of moral obligation requires a theistic grounding. Here I am not taking back any argument that I have made so far. If moral obligation is just about universal, objective, other-directed rules of conduct with which we have exceptionally strong reasons to comply, then we have not seen any reason to suppose that a theistic grounding is called for. But if moral obligation is not adequately set apart in terms of these features, then there is space for Craig to reassert his position.

The argument that moral obligation goes beyond these four features has been made impressively in recent work by Robert Adams. On Adams's view, all obligation—whether moral or not—involves an irreducible social element,[13] involving actually made demands by one party in the social relationship on another.[14] It is the fact that a demand is actually made that gives sense to the notion that one *has to* perform an action, rather than merely that it would be good, even the best, or (importantly) most reasonable to do it.[15]

Adams's clearest argument for the ineliminably social character of obligation appeals to conceptual connections between moral obligation and guilt and between guilt and demands made in social relationships. For an action to be morally obligatory is, on Adams's view, to be an action that one properly incurs guilt for failing to perform.[16] But guilt is social: to be in a state of guilt is, at least in part, to have strained or ruptured one's relationships with some others.[17] Thus Adams takes it to be the case that for an action to be morally obligatory it must be an action to which the failure to perform sets one at odds with another party. And Adams takes it that the particular way in which one sets himself or herself at odds with another in cases of violated obligations is by the knowing failure to conform to the other party's demands or requirements.[18]

Craig's appeal to accountability fits well with Adams's account of obligation. While holding one responsible in terms of punishment is one way to hold someone responsible for their actions, as Adams allows and Craig emphasizes, there may well be others; indeed, one can be held responsible just by there being someone who has the right to rebuke and censure or even think ill of another for performing or failing to perform some action. Now, suppose that Adams is right about the social character of obligation. It does not seem to follow from an act's being the best, or even the most reasonable, thing to do that one who fails to perform that action is thereby subject to censure. It does, however, seem to follow from an act's being obligatory that one who fails to perform that action is thereby subject to censure. It is therefore not sufficient to account for obligation wholly in terms of what is most reasonable to do. To account for the social element, we need to know who it is that has the power to hold humans (universally!) subject to censure for failing to perform their moral obligations. It is very plausible that the only being who is a good candidate to hold persons responsible across space and time is God.

So there may well be a theistic explanation available for some moral phenomena—in particular, that of moral obligation—where there is not a good nontheistic explanation available. Should someone who defends a view like Kurtz's be inclined to resist this argument? He or she might very well try to resist the argument by rejecting the allegedly social character of obligation, arguing instead that obligation can be captured in some formal account of reason, for example. But even putting that possibility to the side, I do not think that the defender of a wholly nontheistic ethical view should be greatly bothered by this sort of argument. Suppose that we simply jettison the notion of moral obligation—what's wrong with that? The nontheistic ethicist, I have argued, can still talk about morally good and morally bad states of affairs; he or she can still talk about what it takes to be a morally good or a morally bad person; he or she can still talk about what is reasonable or unreasonable to do from a moral point of view; and he or she can still talk about obligations in other contexts—legal, cultural, social roles, and so forth. If the nontheistic moral philosopher is denied the concept of the morally obligatory, he or she may well claim that it is a piece of conceptual baggage that ethics is better off without.[19]

NOTES

Acknowledgments. I am grateful to the students in my God and Morality course at Georgetown University in Fall 2006 for their comments on an earlier draft of this chapter, and for helpful discussion throughout our time together. I owe thanks also to Nathan King and Robert Garcia for their extensive and useful criticisms and suggestions.

1. A nontechnical but challenging treatment of (2) from a theistic perspective can be found in John E. Hare, *Why Bother Being Good?* (Downers Grove, Ill.: InterVarsity Press, 2002), 34–94; for a treatment from an atheistic perspective, see Erik J. Wielenberg, *Value and Virtue in a Godless Universe* (New York: Cambridge University Press, 2005), 68–97, 127–42.

2. Kurtz makes some remarks about the problem of evil (35). But these remarks seem to understate massively the theistic resources available to deal with the problem.

See, for example, Alvin Plantinga, *God, Freedom, and Evil* (Grand Rapids, Mich.: Eerdmans, 1978) and Peter van Inwagen, *The Problem of Evil* (New York: Oxford University Press, 2006).

3. I don't mean this as a criticism; the parameters of a debate preclude the sort of development that is adequate for philosophical assessment.

4. This is actually a bit trickier than it might first appear, for many theists will want to deny that *any* true statements that are about things distinct from God can be fully explained without appeal to God. But Craig clearly seems to think that there is something special about the way that morality requires a theistic foundation, something that goes beyond the way that other states of affairs require theistic explanation.

5. Here I respond on behalf of the atheist to Craig's challenge by offering an alternative nontheistic explanation of moral facts. One might, however, simply reject Craig's challenge by holding that the domain of the moral is *autonomous*, lacking a grounding in anything more fundamental than it. For gestures at such a view, see Wielenberg, *Value and Virtue*, 51–53.

6. Craig, 33. That there is such a thing as prudential value and that each of us has reason to care about his or her own well-being is presupposed both in the claim that self-sacrifice is stupid within the atheistic worldview and in the claim that self-sacrifice can be worthwhile within the theistic worldview.

7. Henry Sidgwick, *The Methods of Ethics*, 7th ed. (Indianapolis: Hackett, 1981), 382.

8. At one point Craig does seem to suggest that the mere fact that the various interests a species has is due to natural selection calls into question the objectivity of any form of value that is based upon it (31–32). But this is absurd. Why would the fact that the pain mechanism has a particular contingent evolutionary history call into question the objectivity of the judgment that it is bad for a creature to be in excruciating pain?

9. For example: Christine Korsgaard's Kantian account of moral obligation characterizes moral obligation in terms of those constraints on conduct that reflective beings like us must acknowledge if we are to act at all (*The Sources of Normativity* [New York: Cambridge University Press, 1996], 90–166), and Thomas Nagel's Kantian view on which moral reasons are made possible by our capacity to view ourselves as simply persons among other persons (*The Possibility of Altruism* [Princeton., N.J.: Princeton University Press, 1970], 80–124); Henry Sidgwick's utilitarianism is grounded in our capacity to see the good not just from one's own perspective but "from the point of view of the universe" (*The Methods of Ethics*, 379–88); Alasdair MacIntyre's account of the virtues takes the distinctive human virtues to be those of "independent practical reasoning," the perfection of our capacities of reflective thought as oriented to action, which makes possible the important thought, with respect to the plight of the less fortunate, "this could have been us" (*Dependent Rational Animals* [Peru, Ill.: Open Court, 1999], 55–128, 100); and John Finnis's natural law theory moves from prudential to moral value in part through practical reason's capacity to grasp the forms of good not just as worth seeking for oneself, but as fulfilling any persons (*Natural Law and Natural Rights* [New York: Oxford University Press, 1980], 106–9).

10. Remember, to explain moral value is to account for it in terms of something more ontologically basic than it; so one cannot explain moral value by an appeal to moral value, for moral value cannot be more basic than itself.

11. For a very powerful attempt by a theist to provide an account of the nature of the good and obligatory in theistic terms via informative identification, see Robert M. Adams, *Finite and Infinite Goods* (New York: Oxford University Press, 1999), 13–82, 231–76.

12. I do not mean to endorse these particular identifications. The point is not that these particular identifications of moral value and moral obligation are correct, but that the nontheist can embrace as fully as the theist the task of offering an informative identification of the moral, though in terms of prudential value rather than in terms of facts about the divine nature or divine will.

13. Adams, *Finite and Infinite Goods*, 233.

14. Adams, *Finite and Infinite Goods*, 245–46.

15. Adams, *Finite and Infinite Goods*, 232.

16. Adams, *Finite and Infinite Goods*, 238.

17. Adams, *Finite and Infinite Goods*, 239.

18. Adams, *Finite and Infinite Goods*, 246.

19. This is G. E. M. Anscombe's claim in "Modern Moral Philosophy"; there she argues that the idea of moral obligation has sense only within theistic contexts of ethical discourse and that those who work outside such contexts should jettison that idea as a mere survival. See "Modern Moral Philosophy," *Philosophy* 33 (1958): 1–19.

Chapter Seven

Empty and Ultimately Meaningless Gestures?

Donald C. Hubin

Many have sought in God a supernatural vindicator of the virtuous—an otherworldly being to right the evident wrongs of this world. In the debate that spawns this collection, William Lane Craig joins those with such a conception of God's role, asserting:

> On the theistic view, God holds all persons morally accountable for their actions. Evil and wrong will be punished; righteousness will be vindicated. Despite the inequalities of this life, in the end the scales of God's justice will be balanced. We can even undertake acts of extreme self-sacrifice that run contrary to our self-interest, knowing that such acts are not empty and ultimately meaningless gestures. (31)

Craig goes on to claim that if theism were false, then even if there were objective moral values and duties:

> [T]hey seem to be irrelevant because there's no moral accountability. . . . Given the finality of death [on the humanist view], it really does not matter how you live. Acts of self-sacrifice become particularly inept on an atheistic worldview. Such altruistic behavior is merely the result of evolutionary conditioning that helps to perpetuate the species. A firefighter rushing into a burning building to rescue people in danger or a policeman who sacrifices his life to save those of his comrades does nothing more praiseworthy, morally speaking, than an ant that sacrifices itself for the sake of the ant heap. On an atheistic view this is just stupid. . . . The absence of moral accountability from the philosophy of atheism thus makes an ethic of compassion and self-sacrifice a hollow abstraction. (33)

The desire to see justice prevail in the world is a common one and the belief that it *must*, in the end, do so, is much easier to maintain if one accepts

the existence of a cosmic enforcer of morality. Craig goes far beyond expressing a wish for ultimate justice or grounding his belief in a divine retributor on this wish. He implies (without argument, I think) that without such divine retribution (both punishment of evil and reward for virtue), genuinely
altruistic actions—actions that involve "extreme self-sacrifice" and "run contrary to our self-interest"—would be "empty and ultimately meaningless gestures."

Au contraire! Far from conferring meaning and significance on altruistic
acts of genuine self-sacrifice, the thesis of theism (as understood by Craig)
undermines the very possibility of such actions; as a result, belief in such a
theism renders problematic any ethic grounded on self-sacrifice. In what follows, I will develop and defend three theses:

- First, if Craig is right in asserting that theism implies that "evil and wrong
  will be punished" and "righteousness will be vindicated," then acts of
  morally laudable, altruistic, *genuine* self-sacrifice are not consistent with
  the thesis of theism. Such acts are possible only if righteous self-sacrifices
  sometimes go unrewarded. The very possibility of these actions depends on
  the absence of universal perfect moral accountability.
- Second, again on Craig's understanding of "theism," an ethic that imposes
  a requirement of altruistic genuine self-sacrifice is especially problematic.
  Such ethics can be advocated by theists like Craig only in a rather bizarre,
  and perhaps insincere, manner.
- Finally, I will examine the presuppositions of Craig's claim that on an atheistic worldview, acts of extreme self-sacrifice are "particularly inept" or
  even "stupid" and challenge the truth of that assertion.

In developing and defending these theses I will accept without challenge
some of Craig's claims—even some I believe to be false. For example, I will
accept the assumption that theism entails the existence of a divine rectifier—
one who, in the end, "rights all wrongs," compensating for all unjustified
harms and wrongfully acquired benefits. I would use "theism" more broadly,
but I have no desire to enter into the debate concerning the definition of
"God" and whether or not such a compensatory function is entailed by that
definition. If it is not, then my arguments will apply only to those theists who
accept this particular view of God's role. My arguments do not apply to those
theists who believe that God does not "right the scales" morally speaking,
even if they believe that God is the source of moral values and the ground of
moral duties.[1] Perhaps more surprisingly, if my arguments are correct they
will apply with equal force to a conceivable atheistic view (though it is one
that, to my knowledge, no one has endorsed). Since the arguments turn not on

whether God exists or not but on whether, for each person, perfect moral compensation obtains, the arguments will apply with equal force to an atheistic view that holds that, by some conceivable mechanism, such perfect moral compensation obtains. It is hard to imagine a plausible story about how this would occur within a thoroughly naturalistic worldview, which is precisely what makes the thesis of theism attractive to those yearning for assurance of such justice. But the important point is that the problems I will raise for Craig's view arise from his commitment to this kind of perfect moral compensation. God enters the picture only in the alleged role of guarantor of this measure of compensation.

The defense of my thesis will also require me to distinguish between the virtue of altruism and the existence of morally laudable acts of altruistic self-sacrifice. I do not deny that the virtue of altruism is compatible with the existence of a god who ensures perfect moral compensation. The virtue of altruism concerns the agent's motivations for actions. Altruistic motivation, even purely altruistic motivation, is independent of the possibility (and even the believed possibility) of morally laudable acts of genuine self-sacrifice. So, even if it were true that there are no morally laudable actions that result in a long-run net loss to the agent and even if the agent believes this, she or he could still be motivated by—and indeed motivated *only* by—altruistic considerations. Thus, regardless of whether God exists and functions as a divine retributor, a person may be motivated altruistically and may, in virtue of this, be worthy of the praise typically offered for altruism. What the existence of such a god renders impossible is not the virtue of altruism but the existence of morally laudable acts of altruistic self-sacrifice.[2]

ESCHATOLOGICAL MORAL COMPENSATION

I understand moral compensation to obtain when the costs wrongfully borne (or the benefits wrongfully enjoyed) by a person are offset by the imposition of corresponding benefits (or costs) in such a way as to leave that person at least as well off as she would have been had the wrongful costs (or benefits) not existed.[3] Eschatology is the branch of theology that studies "final things"; individual eschatology concerns the final things for the individual: an afterlife, divine judgment, and so forth. I understand the thesis of eschatological moral compensation (EMC) to be the thesis that, for each individual, divine intervention in an afterlife will ensure that there is perfect moral compensation: "Evil and wrong will be punished; righteousness will be vindicated. Despite the inequalities of this life, in the end the scales of God's justice will be balanced" (31).[4]

The thesis of eschatological moral compensation provides motivation and consolation to many. For some who might otherwise be tempted toward immorality, the belief in perfect moral compensation may well provide a motive for complying with the outward requirements of morality. One seldom goes wrong in assuming that self-interest is a strong motivator, even if it is not the only one. And, many who are troubled by the suffering of loved ones find consolation in the thought that there is, in the end, compensation for such suffering. Finally, it is easier for some people to endure the unjust burdens in their own lives if they believe that, ultimately, justice will prevail.

But the thesis of eschatological moral compensation comes with costs. And one is extremely surprising. It is this: If the thesis is correct, then—contrary to what practically all of us believe—there *are no* actions that are both morally laudable and genuinely self-sacrificial. Let me begin to clarify this claim by distinguishing it from three other claims that I do not assert:

- *Impossibility of self-sacrifice.* EMC entails that there are no actions by which a person diminishes his well-being for the sake of some other end.
- *Impossibility of altruistic acts.* EMC entails that there are no altruistic actions.
- *Impossibility of altruistic acts of self-sacrifice.* EMC entails that there are no altruistic acts that involve genuine self-sacrifice.

While the truth of any of these claims would cause serious problems for Craig's theism, I do not defend any of them. Here's why.

Impossibility of self-sacrifice. I do not assert that the thesis of eschatological compensation entails that there are no actions by which a person diminishes his well-being for some other end. It does not. If "self-sacrifice" means only diminishing your well-being for some other end,[5] then there is no incompatibility between EMC and the existence of self-sacrifice. Indeed, on a traditional Christian eschatology of punishment for unrepented sins, sinning is a paradigmatic act of self-sacrifice, in the sense of being an action through which one diminishes one's overall, long-term well-being for some other purpose—perhaps immediate gratification or gaining power. But it is not a *morally laudable* act of self-sacrifice; it is not morally justified or morally praiseworthy. My interest is not in the relationship between EMC and acts that sacrifice well-being generally; it is in the relationship between EMC and *morally laudable* acts of self-sacrifice.

Impossibility of altruistic acts. I do not assert that EMC is incompatible with the existence of altruistic actions. As I have already suggested and will discuss more fully later, the concept of *altruistic* action concerns the agent's motivation for acting. Altruistic motivation is motivation grounded in the direct (as opposed to instrumental) concern for the well-being of others. The truth of EMC does not render altruistic acts impossible. Even if there is divine reward for right actions and punishment for evil ones (and, indeed, even if one knew this fact), one might well act partly or wholly out of a direct motivation for the well-being of others.

Impossibility of altruistic acts of self-sacrifice. Finally, I do not assert that EMC precludes the existence of altruistically motivated acts of genuine self-sacrifice. Since altruistic acts are actions motivated by direct concern for the well-being of others and self-sacrificial acts are those that result in long-term net disbenefit to the agent, altruistic acts of self-sacrifice will be possible if, and only if, it is possible for agents to perform acts that result in such long-term disbenefit out of direct concern for the well-being of others. The consistency of EMC with the existence of such actions is a complicated matter. However, if it is possible for an agent to act from altruistic motivation in a way that incurs some local cost to him and does not call for divine moral compensation, then altruistic acts of self-sacrifice are consistent with EMC. Some might think that this is possible, perhaps in cases in which the altruistically motivated action is not, despite its motivation, a morally laudable one. Since altruistic motivation is consistent with extremely selective concern for the well-being of others, there could clearly be such cases. So suppose that, in order to save a loved one who has committed a terrible crime from going to prison, I falsely confess to the crime and, as a result, am convicted and punished for the crime. I neither expect, nor do I receive, any worldly benefit from my action; I am motivated only by considerations of the well-being of my loved one. To underscore the wrongness of this action, we can imagine that I correctly anticipate that, not being punished, my loved one will repeat the crime, thus harming another innocent person. In this case, I have intentionally incurred some personal harm in order to benefit my loved one based on an altruistic motivation for *this person's* well-being. However, the act chosen to effect this end imposes morally impermissible costs on other innocent individuals and, arguably, violates moral constraints on actions. If we believe, as seems plausible, that the action is morally forbidden despite its altruistic motivation, then the costs it incurs for the agent may not be compensable under the terms of EMC. The result will be that my altruistic action will result in a long-term net loss in my well-being. In a case like this, then, EMC allows for the existence of altruistically motivated acts of genuine self-sacrifice.

The matter is complicated by the possibility that the altruistic motivations of the agent are sufficient to provoke divine reward, even if the action chosen is, and was known by the agent to be, morally impermissible. If the altruistic motivation itself is sufficient to trigger divine reward for the costs incurred by the agent, even where the altruistically motivated action was morally impermissible, my arguments will, if successful, show that EMC is incompatible with the existence of altruistically motivated acts of genuine self-sacrifice in general. However, I do not pursue this issue here. My concern is with the consistency of EMC with *morally laudable* acts of genuine self-sacrifice. I am not concerned with the consistency of EMC with the existence of acts of self-sacrifice generally, with the existence of altruistic acts generally, or with the existence of altruistically motivated acts of self-sacrifice.

The term "self-sacrifice" involves the self in two respects. Acts of genuine self-sacrifice are acts of sacrifice *of* the self and *by* the self. Variations on the hackneyed example of falling on a hand grenade illustrate the point: Intentionally falling on a hand grenade to save the rest of one's platoon is a standard example of an act of self-sacrifice; pushing a platoon-mate onto a hand grenade to save oneself and the rest of the platoon is not an act of self-sacrifice either for the pusher or the one pushed.

More importantly to my argument, genuine acts of self-sacrifice involve genuine costs to the agent. Where there is no cost, there is no sacrifice, regardless of the motives, beliefs, or intentions of the agent. These other factors bear heavily on questions of the praiseworthiness of the agent and, perhaps, our moral evaluation of the course of conduct the agent undertakes. But without cost, there is no sacrifice and, so, no self-sacrifice.

To clarify this point with an example, consider a participant in Stanley Milgram's famous experiments concerning obedience to authority. In these experiments, volunteers believed that they were assisting researchers investigating how aversive responses affect memory. These volunteers (called "teachers") quizzed people they believed to be other volunteers ("learners") and pressed buttons that the teachers believed gave electric shocks to the learners for incorrect answers. In fact, the learners were confederates of the researchers and they were only pretending to receive shocks. The teachers were the true subjects of the experiments, which were designed to explore the willingness of people to engage in behavior that is believed to be harmful to others—behavior they would ordinarily avoid—when that behavior is sanctioned by authority figures. Now, imagine that one of the actual subjects, a "teacher," rebels against the urging of the experimenters to increase the level of the shock applied and attempts to "rescue" the learner with whom he is working. He pulls the electrodes from this person's body as the electrical charge is apparently being applied, and he does this in the firm belief that he will experience the shock himself as he removes the electrodes. In fact, though, as he removes the electrodes, he feels nothing. This man's act may well be altruistic. He exhibits a disposition to endure a harm himself in order to spare another from further harm and this may well be, as altruism requires, from an immediate and direct concern for the well-being of the other person.

If so, he is morally praiseworthy. We want to say many of the same things about him as we would about a person who actually experienced the painful shock in order to save another. But, there is one thing that we can say about a person who actually experienced the shock to save another that we cannot say about our imagined rebellious subject: our rebellious subject *did not* engage in an act of self-sacrifice. He was disposed to; he was willing to; indeed, he tried to engage in an action that he believed to be one of self-sacrifice. But he did not sacrifice for another.

A personal cost is necessary for self-sacrifice. And, it has to be a *net* cost to the individual. Local costs that are compensated are not sacrifices. We often speak of someone sacrificing to get through law school, medical school, or even a graduate program in philosophy. But if these sacrifices are amply rewarded by a welcomed financial success or, more plausibly in the last case, by some sort of psychic satisfaction, they don't constitute a genuine sacrifice of the self. They are, instead, investments in the future and ones that reap an ample return. They may involve self-control, but they do not involve self-sacrifice.[6] There is an important difference between someone who works sixty hours a week in order to accumulate enough money to go to college and qualify for a career that he will find richly rewarding and a person who does the same in order to put his children through college with no expectation of any personal reward.

In the sorts of cases just alluded to, the agent typically anticipates the benefit that compensates for the period of sacrifice; indeed, this anticipated benefit plays a role in motivating the sacrifice. Let's consider a case that is otherwise similar but does not involve such anticipation of future benefit.

Helpful Worker 1: Herb works at an amusement park emptying trash cans. He is a contract worker, paid solely based on the number of bags of trash he hauls out of the park. One day he sees a child, crying because she is separated from her parents. Herb parks his pickup, buys the child an ice cream cone, and spends an hour walking around with the child until she finds her parents. As he does so, he thinks from time to time about the loss of income he is causing, but it's hard for Herb to steel his heart against a child's tears. What Herb doesn't know is that the manager of the amusement park, in an attempt to help encourage employees to be more helpful to customers, has just instituted a (so far unannounced) program of bonuses for employees who show extraordinary customer care. Herb's altruistic action has been caught on the park's security cameras and the manager decides that a great way to announce the new program would be by giving Herb a $10,000 surprise bonus and publicizing this award to all employees. Let's assume that the only cost Herb incurs from his action is the direct loss in performance pay and that this is far more than adequately compensated for by his cash reward.

Herb is motivated altruistically, we will assume, and he anticipates a net loss to himself from his altruism. But he is wrong. He does suffer a local loss. His next paycheck is less than it would otherwise have been. Herb does not, though, suffer a net, long-term loss. His act of helping the child is not one of self-sacrifice. This is true even though his act is one that shows his *willingness*—indeed, his *intention*—to engage in self-sacrificial behavior for others. Herb is praiseworthy. What he has done is right and laudable. But he has not sacrificed for another.

Now the problem for EMC is pretty clear. If, after all, there is a deity that effects full moral compensation in each life, then it is impossible for anyone to engage in morally laudable self-sacrifice. Even if EMC is true, there can, of course, be acts that involve sacrificing one's well-being. Imposing a cost on yourself through action that is not morally laudable would involve such a sacrifice. The truth of EMC, furthermore, poses no problem for the existence of altruistic actions. And, finally, even if EMC is true, it appears possible for there to be altruistic acts of genuine self-sacrifice.[7] But the truth of EMC means that any morally laudable act that involves a local—in this case, worldly—sacrifice will be adequately rewarded and, so, involve no net, long-term sacrifice to the agent. It is the very nature and function of God's role (as assigned by Craig) as a cosmic retributor to ensure that worldly losses incurred from right action are not net, long-term losses for the agent.

Craig worries that atheism "makes an ethic of compassion and self-sacrifice a hollow abstraction." (33) But if theism implies EMC, as Craig appears to believe, then theism grounds any ethic of self-sacrifice on an impossibility.[8]

THEISTIC SELF-SACRIFICERS AND ALTRUISTIC THEISTS

So far, I have been discussing some implications of the truth of EMC. I turn now to the question of the implications of *belief* in EMC. First, some clarificatory comments on my use of terms like "theistic self-sacrificers" and "altruistic theists."

For argument's sake, I have granted Craig's assumption that theism implies EMC. But, even granting this, it is still an open question whether it is possible for a theist to deny EMC. We ordinarily assume that acceptance of a theory does not require belief in all of the logical implications of the theory. We are not, after all, logical saints and some of the logical implications of a theory may be hidden to even the most penetrating minds. On the other hand, if a theory is defined by a specific thesis or that thesis is an obvious implication of those that define the theory, it is hard to understand what it would mean to say that someone accepts the theory but not the thesis in question. I have no idea whether Craig takes the thesis of EMC to be definitional of "theism" or, if not, to be such an obvious implication of the theory that anyone who could be said to understand the theory would see the implication. If so, then my use of the terms "theistic self-sacrificers" and "altruistic theists" can be taken at face value given this (I think) idiosyncratic account of "theism." He may believe, on the other hand, that EMC is a subtle, nonobvious implication of theism. If so, my terminology may be misleading unless we understand the entire discussion to be about those theists who are close enough to logical sainthood to understand that EMC is an implication of theism. Let us restrict our attention to those theists I shall call "clear-headed theists." What I'm interested in is the implications of belief in EMC, and I'm using "clear-headed theist" or "theist" as shorthand for a theist who accepts EMC.

The theist (in the clear-headed sense) believes that all morally laudable acts that involve local sacrifices of the agent's well-being will be, at least after death, fully compensated for in such a way that the agent will not suffer—at least as a result of performing the act in question—a net, long-term decrease in well-being. Does this mean that a theist cannot engage in morally laudable acts of genuine self-sacrifice? Of course not. For the theist may be wrong about the existence of God (understood now as one who secures perfect moral accountability). In that case, the local, worldly sacrifice of well-being may well be a net, long-term sacrifice. So, a clear-headed theist can certainly engage in morally laudable acts of genuine self-sacrifice provided his theism is false. But a clear-headed theist cannot *intend* to engage in such actions. Believing, as he does, that any morally laudable act that involves a local sacrifice will receive complete compensation, he cannot consistently believe that he will suffer a net, long-term decrease in well-being as a result of performing a morally laudable act that causes a local decrease in his well-being. Thus, he cannot consistently believe that he is able to engage in an act of morally laudable genuine self-sacrifice because he is committed to the belief that there are no such actions. Indeed, if he understands the implications of his brand of theism, he will believe that nothing he can do will be an instance of morally laudable altruistic self-sacrifice.[9] And, if he believes that he cannot perform such an action, he cannot intend to perform such an action.[10]

It is worth reminding ourselves that this argument applies only to clear-headed theists—those who see that their theory implies EMC and that EMC implies that no morally laudable altruistic act will result in a genuine self-sacrifice for the agent. Those theists who fail to appreciate that a consequence of their views is that they are unable to engage in acts of morally laudable altruistic genuine self-sacrifice can still intend to engage in such actions. They can do so in the same sense that I can accept the axioms of Euclidean geometry and, nevertheless, intend to prove that the interior angles of a triangle in Euclidean space do not sum to 180 degrees. Which is to say, they can do so only as a result of confusion.[11]

The confusion in question would have to be relatively obvious, too. We are understanding a theist, as Craig apparently does, to be someone who accepts the thesis of EMC. In order for such a person to intentionally engage in a morally laudable act of genuine self-sacrifice, she or he would have to believe both that all morally laudable acts of (short-term) self-sacrifice are at least adequately compensated by divine reward in an afterlife *and* that her or his intended act of (short-term) self-sacrifice would not be so compensated. Clear-headed theists accept the thesis of EMC and understand that it implies that there are no acts of morally laudable genuine (long-term) self-sacrifice.

This makes a theistic ethic of self-sacrifice extremely problematic. Such an ethic would require actions that clear-headed theists cannot intentionally perform. This point should be troubling for someone like Craig, but we must be careful not to misstate the problem. It is important to see that even clear-headed theists can be altruistic; theistic belief does not rule out altruistic actions. Remember that altruism concerns the agent's motivation and it is manifestly possible for someone to be motivated altruistically even if she or he believes that her or his altruistically motivated action will not result in a long-term net disbenefit to herself or himself.

We can illustrate these points by considering a variation on the story about Herb, the helpful worker.

> *Helpful Worker 2:* Henrietta works at the same amusement park as Herb. Like Herb, she sees a lost child and stops her work to help the child find his parents. This is a morally laudable thing to do and results in lowered productivity for Henrietta and, as a result, a decrease in her paycheck. Unlike Herb, Henrietta has heard of the manager's reward program and she fully expects to be richly rewarded under it.

Suppose that, unknown to Henrietta, the manager has ended the employee reward program. Then her laudable act of helping the child find his parents involves, let us assume, not just a local reduction in well-being as a result of her diminished paycheck, but a net, long-term reduction in her well-being.[12] On this variant of the story, Henrietta is analogous to a theist who engages in a laudable, genuine (net, long-term) self-sacrifice unknowingly because, contrary to her belief, EMC is false. It is important to note that she may well be motivated altruistically. Henrietta may be adequately motivated by direct concern for the well-being of the child. The generous financial reward she expects under the manager's program may not play any role in her decision to stop work to help the child. Or, it may play a role but not a necessary one.

That is, Henrietta may well feel *additional* motivation to help the child given the prospect of reward, but be sufficiently motivated to help even in the absence of this prospect. In either case, her action is altruistic. But, so long as she believes that she will be adequately compensated for her assistance, she cannot *view* her action—at least in prospect—as one of altruistic self-*sacrifice*. Just like a clear-headed theist, Henrietta is fully convinced that her action will not be one of morally laudable self-sacrifice. She cannot, therefore, intend such an action. And, this is true even if, as it turns out, it is an act of self-sacrifice.

If it is known that, in helping the child, Henrietta cannot intend to perform an act of morally laudable self-sacrifice, then any demand that she help the child as an act of morally laudable self-sacrifice is a strange demand—what I will call a "deviant demand." The standard point of issuing a demand is to secure compliance through intentional action. The typical point of demanding that my children clean up their rooms is to get them to clean their rooms as a result of forming an intention to clean their rooms. Demands can, though, be issued with nonstandard purposes. So, as a Marine drill instructor breaking in new recruits, I might well pick out the weakest of them and demand, threatening punishment for failure, that he do fifty push-ups, knowing full well that he cannot comply and, moreover, that he knows that he cannot. All of the following seem true of this case:

- The recruit cannot intend to satisfy my demand. If he drops to the floor and begins doing push-ups, it cannot be with the intention of doing fifty push-ups. He might have the intention to do as many push-ups as he can, perhaps to show me his resolve in the hopes of ameliorating his punishment. But he cannot intend to do what he firmly believes he cannot do.
- I cannot intend that my demand be satisfied. That is to say, whatever my intention in issuing the demand, it is not the intention that the demand be met. This results from my knowledge that the recruit cannot do the task I've demanded of him.
- I cannot intend for the recruit to intend to do fifty push-ups. If I know that the recruit cannot complete fifty push-ups but do not know that he is aware that he cannot, I could intend my demand to create in him the intention to do fifty push-ups. However, since I know that the recruit knows that he cannot satisfy the demand I've made, I cannot even intend that my demand cause him to intend to do so.[13]

What might my intention be in issuing the demand? Perhaps I intend to send a message to the entire group that any failure is unacceptable and will be met with punishment. Perhaps I intend to brand the unlucky recruit as a weakling for the group to despise and define themselves in contrast to. However we fill in the story, my demand has a nonstandard or deviant purpose for two independent and individually sufficient reasons: I believe that what I demand is not within the capability of the recipient of the demand, and I believe that my demand cannot cause in the recipient an intention to satisfy the demand.

This is what I mean by a deviant demand. A demand of Henrietta that she engage in a morally laudable act of self-sacrifice would be a deviant demand, if it came from someone aware of her inability to perform such an action and, as well, to intend to perform such an action.

Similar things can be said of the case of an ethic that requires or encourages acts of self-sacrifice. In a world where EMC is true, the demands of such an ethic are deviant; their point cannot be to secure compliance; compliance is impossible. And the demands of such an ethic, when addressed to an audience of known, clear-headed theists, could not have the point of typical moral demands. These demands could not be intentionally followed by clear-headed theists. If the point of advocating such a morality were to cause the audience to intend to follow it, the advocacy would make sense only if the expectation was that the audience would give up its theism or, at least, the clear-headed version of it.

This means that a theist of Craig's sort, one who accepts EMC, is in a rather awkward position to promote an ethic of self-sacrifice. Such a theist will be advocating actions that she or he knows to be impossible. She or he knows that the moral demands she or he asserts cannot be met, and that the like-minded theists to whom she or he addresses these demands can intend to meet them only if they are confused about the implications of their theism.

BEYOND EMPTY AND
ULTIMATELY MEANINGLESS GESTURES

What is, perhaps, most disquieting about Craig's view of the relation between morality and the existence of God is his thought that what he calls "moral accountability" is necessary for morality to be anything but an empty and meaningless gesture or a hollow abstraction. Craig's claim that objective moral values can exist if, and only if, God exists is philosophically problematic. It seems to rest on a simplistic, though unanalyzed, conception of what it would mean for something to be objective. The same is true of his assertion that God's existence, and only God's existence, can provide a sound basis for objective moral duties. But Craig's idea that "moral accountability"—by which he means perfect eschatological moral compensation—is necessary for

morality to be meaningful and important is not only philosophically problematic; it is morally troubling.[14]

To many nontheists—as well as, I imagine, to many who would consider
themselves theists of a different stripe than Craig—it seems bizarre to assert
that unless there is perfect eschatological moral compensation, "it really does
not matter how you live." If my children suffer as a result of my neglect, then
my children suffer. That is enough for it to matter to me how I act with respect to my children. Indeed, for many it is precisely because there is no guarantee of perfect moral compensation that it matters so much how we live our
lives. If I really believed that every unjustified harm would garner compensation in the end, the unjustified harms I cause would seem *less* troubling for
their effect on the victim. If, in the end, victims of unjustified harm receive
perfect compensation, it seems less urgent that I help those who are victim-
ized by others. At least the urgency of my assisting them doesn't seem to be
grounded in considerations of their long-term net well-being. Perhaps it is
grounded in considerations of my own; perhaps I can secure eschatological
reward for such assistance. But *their* well-being seems of less intrinsic concern. It is precisely the absence of perfect moral compensation that makes the
unjustified harms to others so morally urgent and the sacrifices that we make
to help others so laudable.

But Craig thinks otherwise. On his view, if there is no eschatological moral
compensation, self-sacrifice "is just stupid." In nonphilosophical settings, the
charge of stupidity covers a broad range of disparate errors. Craig says little
to help us understand what, precisely, he means by the charge or why he
thinks it justified. But the context suggests that lying behind Craig's yearning
for perfect moral accountability is more than the fear that psychological egoism, or something close to it, is true. Lying behind Craig's yearning is an acceptance of some form of *normative* egoism.

To establish this point, let me explicitly define some terminology I've already used. I have argued that EMC is incompatible with the existence of
morally laudable altruistic acts of genuine self-sacrifice. Given this, it is difficult to evaluate Craig's suggestion that (presumably morally laudable) altruistic acts of self-sacrifice make sense and are not stupid on his theistic
view. There can be no such acts to praise, if EMC is true. But there are certainly acts that appear to those of us who do not accept EMC to be genuine
acts of self-sacrifice, and some of these are morally laudable and altruistically
motivated. These are the morally laudable altruistically motivated acts that receive no worldly compensation. For those who reject otherworldly compensation, these acts involve genuine self-sacrifice. Let us call the acts that *appear* on the atheistic worldview to be acts of genuine self-sacrifice "worldly
self-sacrificial"—they involve costs not compensated for in *this* world. Using

this terminology allows us to leave open the question of whether these acts are *genuinely* self-sacrificial. If they are morally laudable and altruistically motivated, the believer in EMC says "no"; the EMC denier says "yes."

Now, why does it appear that Craig is committed to some form of normative egoism? First, let's distinguish normative egoism from descriptive egoism (which includes psychological egoism). Normative egoism offers us a theory of how people *ought* to act; descriptive egoism purports to describe human behavior or, more commonly, human motivation. The most common descriptive egoist theory, psychological egoism, holds that human motivation is exclusively egoistic—that the only considerations that move humans to act are considerations of benefit to the self. It's easy to see why one would find it desirable for there to be widespread belief in perfect eschatological moral compensation if this is your theory of human motivation. Such moral compensation achieves by external brute force what many philosophers have sought by philosophical argumentation: the perfect reconciliation between self-interest and morality. Even if one rejects, as surely we should, the thesis of psychological egoism, it would be Pollyannaish to deny that there is more than a little selfish motivation in humans or that this motivation can often lead people to act in morally reprehensible ways. Even on a much weaker, and correspondingly more plausible, theory of human motivation such as what Gregory Kavka calls "*predominant* egoism,"[15] one can see the attractions of widespread belief in a divine retributor.

But no descriptive theory of human behavior or psychology will result in the conclusion that, in the absence of perfect moral compensation, altruistic acts of worldly self-sacrifice are "stupid." That is clearly intended as a normative judgment; purely descriptive theories of human behavior and motivation will not provide adequate warrant for such judgments. To justify a charge that altruistic acts of worldly self-sacrifice are stupid on a worldview that denies EMC, one needs a normative claim. It must be the case that when such acts are thought by the agent to be (morally laudable, altruistically motivated) acts of *genuine* self-sacrifice, they necessarily fall short of what is required by some *norm* of action—a norm the failure to satisfy warrants a charge of stupidity. And, since Craig clearly doesn't believe that such acts are stupid on the assumption of the theistic worldview he embraces, he must believe that this norm of action is met when EMC is true.

But what norm would condemn an act of morally laudable altruistic worldly self-sacrifice on the atheistic worldview that rejects EMC and not condemn such an act on the assumption of EMC? It seems that the only sort of norm that would allow us to condemn these acts on the atheistic view but not on Craigian theism would be some sort of normative egoism.

The best-known variant of normative egoism, *ethical* egoism, isn't quite right for this purpose. Ethical egoism is the view that the morally right thing for an agent to do is what will promote his long-term well-being. Ethical ego-ism would condemn as *immoral* all acts of (unnecessary) genuine self-sacrifice. But the charge Craig is making here is not a moral one. He does not seem to believe that the atheistic worldview entails that altruistic acts of worldly self-sacrifice are immoral, much less that *morally laudable* acts of altruistic worldly self-sacrifice are immoral (whatever one could mean by that asser-tion). He claims not that, on the atheist's worldview, such acts are immoral, but that they are stupid.

Now, with some trepidation at taking this speculative step, I suggest that Craig means by this charge that, on the atheistic worldview, acts of (morally laudable altruistic) worldly self-sacrifice do not "make sense," that they are not "the thing to do." He is endorsing a norm of evaluation, I'm suggesting, in what Allan Gibbard calls a flat, flavorless way.[16] When he implies, by call-ing them stupid, that on an atheistic view, morally laudable acts of altruistic worldly self-sacrifice ought not to be done, he is expressing his endorsement of norms of action that condemn the doing of such acts.

And what is it about such acts that he condemns? Since he does not simi-larly condemn such actions given the assumption of EMC and the only dif-ference between these two background assumptions is whether worldly self-sacrificial acts are *genuinely* self-sacrificial, it appears that the norm that Craig is embracing here is a norm condemning genuine self-sacrifice. His idea appears to be that *worldly* self-sacrificial behavior makes sense (is not stupid) only if it is not *genuinely* self-sacrificial. It is this thought that I allege is morally troubling. It is a challenge to any demand made on our actions that is grounded ultimately in the well-being of others. If acting for the well-be-ing of others without a guarantee that this will result in a personal benefit—or worse, with the full expectation that it will not—is really stupid, what are we to say of the virtue of altruism?

An act of worldly self-sacrifice, undertaken by someone who rejects EMC (and, indeed, even one who denies any otherworldly rewards and punish-ments at all) will seem stupid, only if we think that consistency with self-in-terest is a requirement of "nonstupidity." But why should we accept this? A father may value his children's well-being above his own. Unless this very value is stupid,[17] there is manifestly no stupidity in such a man sacrificing his worldly well-being for that of his children, even in the full expectation that this will result in a long-run, net harm to himself.

It is important to see that Craig's thought that atheism renders acts of worldly self-sacrifice stupid is not implied by the rest of what he says about moral ac-countability, or even what he says about the relation between morality and God in general. One can believe that God is the source of all moral value, that it is only with the existence of God that there can be moral duty, that only God's ex-istence can ensure moral accountability, and even that such moral accountability is essential for moral motivation—one can believe all of these things and still deny that acts of *genuine* (long-run, net) self-sacrifice for the benefit of another would be stupid if EMC were false. One can hold that such an act of altruistic *genuine* self-sacrifice would be a fine and noble thing, which "like a jewel, . . . would still shine by its own light, as a thing which has its whole value in itself."[18]

CONCLUSION

The assurance of "moral accountability"—which seems plausible only on a theistic worldview— is, Craig claims, required for an adequate morality, that is, for a morality that doesn't render "acts of extreme self-sacrifice . . . empty and ultimately meaningless gestures" (31). What we have seen, though, is that the sort of moral accountability Craig apparently accepts, perfect eschatological moral compensation (EMC), has damaging implications for the ethics of self-sacrifice. EMC renders morally laudable acts of genuine self-sacrifice impossible. Furthermore, when addressed to a known believer in EMC, the demands of such a morality are necessarily "deviant" in the sense that they cannot be issued with the intention that they be followed. And, finally, the absence of the assurance of moral accountability does not render altruistic acts of worldly self-sacrifice "stupid" unless one accepts a troubling form of normative egoism. When, with full conviction that there are no other-worldly rewards or benefits, an agent engages in an act that he or she believes will involve worldly self-sacrifice for the benefit of another, he or she need not be acting stupidly or engaging in an empty, meaningless gesture. On the contrary, if the agent values the well-being of the others more than he or she values his own well-being, he or she is acting sensibly and rationally. And to have such values is not to be stupid; it is to love others as oneself.

NOTES

Acknowledgments. For help in thinking through these issues and helpful comments on drafts, I'm grateful to Daniel Hubin, David Merli, and Julie Carpenter-Hubin and to the editors of this volume, Robert Garcia and Nathan King.

1. I believe that the debate between Paul Kurtz and William Craig gets framed unhelpfully when Craig follows what he alleges to be Kurtz's use of "theism" as holding necessarily that "moral values are grounded in God." I use "theism" more broadly, in such a way that theism is consistent with secular moralism, the view that moral values are independent of God's existence.

2. Because my argument does not raise a problem for the *virtue* of altruism, a theist who believes that God ensures perfect justice may see the problems I raise as providing reasons for rejecting act-oriented ethical systems in favor of a virtue-oriented ethical system. What morality requires, one might insist, is that we act virtuously, not that we sometimes engage in acts of self-sacrifice. I'm grateful to Robert Garcia and Nathan King for pointing this out to me.

3. This roughly follows the notion of compensation that Robert Nozick embraces in *Anarchy, State, and Utopia* (Totowa, N.J.: Rowman & Littlefield, 1981), 57. It is subject to all of the problems that he "shamelessly" ignores there. Our purpose is not to hone the notion of moral compensation to be a fine-tuned philosophical instrument. Rather, we are trying to get a rough handle on a concept that plays a role in Craig's argument.

4. Some theists believe that rewards and punishments in the afterlife are infinite. This opens up the possibility of both reward and punishment that would be, on most accounts of retributive justice, out of line with the acts that provoked them. I leave aside many thorny theological matters here and note only that Craig seems committed to the view that wrongdoers receive *at least* enough divine punishment to offset any gain from their wrongdoing and those who engage in morally laudable self-sacrifice receive *at least* enough reward to offset their costs in this world.

5. The word "sacrifice" has its origins in religious rituals involving the presentation of gifts to deities. I'm assuming, though, that in this context we are using it in a secular sense that involves intentionally giving up something of value for oneself for some purpose other than one's own good.

6. To be sure, matters are a bit more complex if we adopt a Parfitian view of a person's survival through time. On Derek Parfit's view, the relation in which we stand to future stages of our lives is more like that in which we stand to other persons than we ordinarily suppose. (See Derek Parfit's *Reasons and Persons* [Oxford: Clarendon Press, 1984] especially Part IV.) I set these difficulties aside with only the reflection that Parfit's view of personhood through time would provide little solace for Craig in this context. EMC depends on a very strong theory of individual identity not only throughout, but beyond, one's natural life.

7. This is subject to the worries previously expressed: If the altruistic motivation calls for moral compensation by God—compensation sufficient to outweigh the personal cost of the action—then EMC will pose problems for altruistically motivated acts of genuine self-sacrifice.

8. Because Craig doesn't offer an explicit definition of "an ethic of compassion and self-sacrifice," this charge may be challenged. The charge makes the (reasonable, I think) assumption that such an ethic would require the existence of morally laudable, altruistic acts of self-sacrifice.

9. It is not as if such a theist is incapable of, say, throwing himself on a hand grenade to save his platoon mates. But his belief in EMC and his clear-headedness about its implications imply that he cannot see this as an act of morally laudable, altruistic genuine self-sacrifice. Some of the properties of actions are determined by the history or the future course of the universe. Furthermore, my beliefs about the nature of my actions are constrained (if I'm thinking clearly) by my beliefs about the past and future of the universe. If I am an executioner assigned to impose the death penalty

on a person I am firmly convinced is innocent, I can carry out the execution, of course, but I cannot view my action as one that extracts retribution. If I am a doctor who is giving immunizing inoculations for a disease that I am convinced is extinct, I can inject the serum, but I cannot view my actions as being ones that prevent contraction of the disease.

10. Matters are complicated if we allow degrees of belief. If one only "mostly believes" that one is unable to bring about a result, it may still be possible for him to intend to bring it about. His intention is, then, predicated on a belief that he mostly rejects (if he is consistent in his beliefs).

11. I'm indebted to Daniel Hubin for pushing me to see how a defender of EMC could still intend to perform actions of morally laudable genuine self-sacrifice.

12. This need not be so, of course. Most people derive psychological rewards from helping others, and so reductions in income that result from helping others may not be reductions in overall well-being. We are, in these examples, using decrease in income as a proxy for decrease in well-being.

13. The matter is a bit more complex than this, but not in a way that affects the argument I'm making. The complexity is this: I could know that someone believes that he cannot perform an action but believe that my demanding that he do so would change this belief. Perhaps he trusts me not to demand anything of him that he cannot do. Then, I could intend that my demand cause in him an intention to perform the action by also causing in him the loss of the belief that he cannot perform it. (If I believe that my demand could actually create in the recipient the ability to perform an action he was otherwise incapable of performing, then a similar point could be made with respect to the last point.) However, this will offer little consolation to a defender of EMC who advocates an ethic of self-sacrifice. The demands of that ethic would avoid being deviant only if they could succeed in causing the recipients to give up their belief in EMC. For theists, that would mean causing them to not be clear-headed theists.

14. It's worth a reminder that Craig sees the issue of moral accountability as separate from the issues of whether there can be objective moral values and duties. And, he believes that moral accountability raises an *additional* problem for the atheist. He says, "If theism is false, what is the basis of moral accountability? *Even if there were objective moral values and duties under atheism*, they seem to be irrelevant because there's no moral accountability" (33, emphasis added).

15. Gregory Kavka, *Hobbesian Moral and Political Theory* (Princeton, N.J.: Princeton University Press, 1986), 64–80.

16. Allan Gibbard, *Wise Choices, Apt Feelings* (Cambridge, Mass.: Harvard University Press, 1990), 6–9.

17. Craig may think that holding this value is stupid if one rejects EMC. But this simply pushes back one level his troubling normative egoism. So, instead of (or in addition to) using long-run self-interest as a test for the nonstupidity of actions, he would be employing it as a test of the nonstupidity of an agent's values.

18. Immanuel Kant, *Fundamental Principles of the Metaphysic of Morals*, trans. Thomas Kingsmill, chap. 1. Available online at etext.library.adelaide.edu.au/k/kant/immanuel/k16prm/prm2.html.

Chapter Eight

What Difference Does God Make to Morality?

Richard Swinburne

I'm not going to discuss whether or not there is a God (that's something I've argued for a lot over the years), but simply whether if there is a God, that makes any difference to morality. Against William Craig, I shall argue that the existence and actions of God make no difference to the fact that there are moral truths; but, against Paul Kurtz, I shall argue that the existence and actions of God make a great difference[1] to the content of morality, the seriousness of morality, and our knowledge of morality. I assume a standard Western account of the nature of God as essentially eternal, omnipotent, omniscient, perfectly good, creator and sustainer of the universe and all that it contains (from moment to moment), the kind of God affirmed by Christianity, Judaism, and Islam as well as some other religions.

1. NECESSARY MORAL TRUTHS

Actions may be morally good, bad, or indifferent. Among good actions are those that are obligatory, and ones that go beyond obligation and that we call "supererogatory." I am obliged to pay my debts, but not to give my life to save that of a comrade—though it is supremely supererogatorily good that I should do so. The obligatory are those that we are blameworthy for not doing, the supererogatory are those that we are praiseworthy for doing. Likewise among bad actions, there are those that it is obligatory not to do—these are wrong actions; and there are bad actions that are not wrong, which I call infravetatory. It is wrong to rape or steal, yet it is bad but not wrong to watch many low-grade thrillers on TV rather than read one or two great works of literature.

Quite clearly some moral judgments (that is, judgments that some particular action or kind of action is morally obligatory or wrong or whatever) are true and others are false. As a result of experience and reflection, it is evident to almost all of us at the beginning of the twenty-first century that genocide is morally wrong, and so is suttee and so is slavery; and it is morally obligatory to keep your promises—at any rate when it causes you little trouble, barring quite extraordinary counterconsiderations. And so on, and so on. And if those of some other culture think otherwise, they are obviously mistaken— just as obviously mistaken as are solipsists and flat-Earthers. In morals, as in everything else, we must believe that things are as, overwhelmingly, they appear to be. We start our construction of a worldview from what seems most evident, including the immediate deliverances of sense (e.g., "I am now giving a lecture") and of memory (e.g., "Two days ago I was in England"), universally held beliefs (e.g., that the earth is millions of years old), and obvious truths of reason (e.g., $2 + 2 = 4$). Although allowing the theoretical possibility of error, it is on the foundations of these basic beliefs that we must construct a worldview; for no foundations are surer than the most evident ones, and these include some of the most obvious moral beliefs. If some philosopher's theory of meaning or knowledge has the consequence that there cannot be moral truths or that we cannot know what they are, then we must reject that theory since it will be more obvious that genocide is wrong than that his or her theory is true.

Now the moral properties (moral goodness, badness, etc.) of particular actions (picked out in terms of who did them where and when) are supervenient on their nonmoral properties. What Hitler did on such and such occasions in 1942 and 1943 was morally wrong because it was an act of genocide. What you did yesterday was good because it was an act of feeding the starving. No action can be just morally good or bad; it is good or bad because it has certain other nonmoral properties—those of the kinds that I illustrated earlier. And any other action that had just those nonmoral properties would have the same moral properties. The conjunction of nonmoral properties that gives rise to the moral property may be a long one or a short one. It may be that all acts of telling lies are bad, or it may be that all acts of telling lies in such and such circumstances (the description of which is a long one) are bad. But it must be that if there is a world W in which a certain action *a* having various nonmoral properties (for example, being an act of killing someone to whom the killer had a certain kind of relation) was bad, there could not be another world W* that was exactly the same as W in all nonmoral respects, but in which *a* was not bad. A difference in moral properties has to arise from a difference in nonmoral properties. If a certain sort of killing is not bad in one world, but bad in another world, there must be some difference between the two worlds (in social organization or the prevalence of crime, for instance) that makes for the moral difference. Moral properties, to use the jargon, are supervenient on nonmoral properties. And the supervenience must be logical supervenience. Our concept of the moral is such that it makes no *sense* to suppose both that there is a world W in which *a* is wrong and a world W* exactly the same as W except that in W* *a* is good. It follows that there are logically necessary truths of the form "If an action has nonmoral properties A, B, and C, it is morally good," "If an action has nonmoral properties C and D, it is morally wrong," and so on. If there are moral truths, there are necessary moral truths—general principles of morality. I reemphasize that, for all I have said so far, these may often be very complicated principles—such as "All actions of promise breaking in circumstances C, D, E, F, and G are wrong," rather than just "All actions of promise breaking are wrong." All moral truths are either necessary (of the above kind) or contingent. Contingent moral truths (e.g., that what you did yesterday was good) derive their truth from some contingent nonmoral truth (e.g., that what you did yesterday was to feed the starving) and some necessary moral truth (e.g., that all acts of feeding the starving are good).

So what makes it the case that promise keeping and truth telling (possibly subject to some qualifications about circumstances) are obligatory, and killing someone (except perhaps an enemy combatant in a just war or a criminal justly sentenced to death) is morally wrong? My answer is simple—the very nature of the act itself. An act of killing being an act of killing (not in specified circumstances) entails that it is morally wrong. Just as a surface could not be blue without having something in common with a surface that is green, which something is being colored, so promise keeping and truth telling could not be what they are without having in common that they are (possibly subject to qualifications) both morally obligatory.

We acquire a sense of morality (i) by being told that such and such actions are obligatory or good-beyond-obligation, and by our parents praising us for doing the latter and blaming us when we fail to do the former; and (ii) by being told that certain other actions are wrong or bad, and by our parents blaming us for doing the former, and praising us for failing to do the latter. As with all fundamental concepts, be it "cause" or "believe" or "deduce," we need to be shown or have described to us many instances of their correct application as well as their logical relations to other concepts (such as the concepts of praise or blame) before we can grasp the concepts. The paradigm instances of the "morally obligatory" (or whatever) will fall into describable kinds—keeping promises, not telling a lie, feeding our own children, and so forth. Once we have in this way via particular instances or kinds of instances, grasped the concept of the "morally obligatory," we can come to recognize that some of the instances by which we have been introduced to it are rather different from the others, and if blame is an appropriate response to the failure to perform the former it is not an appropriate response to failure to perform the latter. We might be told that fighting a duel to defend one's honor is morally obligatory. But through reflection on many other possible situations we may come to derive a general principle that someone's life is a very valuable thing, so valuable that it should only be taken from them to save a life or perhaps in reparation for a life that they have taken away; that is, that no one should ever try to kill anyone except to prevent them killing someone or perhaps as a punishment for killing someone. So we conclude that even if it is appropriate to blame someone who does not kill in a war to save the lives of his or her fellow soldiers, it is not appropriate to blame someone for failure to fight a duel to defend his or her honor. This kind of reflection can lead each of us and (over the centuries) the whole human race to improve our grasp of what are the necessary truths of morality. But if someone started with paradigm cases of actions that he or she calls "morally obligatory" that had nothing in common with what most of us regard as morally obligatory, I see no reason to suppose that he or she has a concept of moral obligation. Suppose that a person were introduced to the concept of "moral obligation" only by being told that it is "morally obligatory" in all circumstances to walk on alternate paving stones, to touch your head three times before getting out of bed in the morning, and to do actions of other kinds that we would think (barring special contingent circumstances) to be morally indifferent; suppose further that this person was blamed for not doing such actions. Surely we would regard this person as not having been introduced to the concept of moral obligation. The difference between this person and the rest of us would be not that we and he or she have different views about which actions are morally obligatory, but that he or she would not have the concept of moral obligation. There has to be a measure of agreement about what are paradigm cases of actions that are morally obligatory, good, and so on, for disputants to have a common concept about the further application of which they are in disagreement. What I have described as the method by which we can reach agreement about what are the necessary truths of morality is of course the method of "reflective equilibrium" as described by John Rawls.[2]

Disagreement about the necessary truths of morality is disagreement about which actions are similar in the right ways to paradigm instances of the morally obligatory, good, and so forth, such that those actions are themselves morally obligatory, good, and so forth. We may acquire a full grasp of the necessary truths without realizing their consequences for us through ignorance of the contingent truths that determine their application. I may believe that it is good to give money to feed the starving but not believe the TV news when it tells us that people are starving in Africa, and so may not realize that it is good to give money for food for Africans. Moral disagreement about the contingent truths of morality is easier to resolve when it does not depend on disagreement about necessary truths. But there is no reason to suppose that disagreement about necessary truths is not resolvable when there is enough agreement about paradigm cases such as to allow for serious reflection on and experience of actions whose moral status is disputed. Such reflection and experience can enable us to see whether the disputed actions have enough of the right features in common with paradigmatically (say) morally obligatory cases of actions such that the disputed actions are themselves morally obligatory.

Theists and most atheists alike are introduced to this common concept of morality by being shown many of the same paradigm cases—both are shown, for example, that keeping promises, talking to the lonely, and so on, are morally good actions; and they recognize these are morally good actions in virtue of what is involved in making a promise or being lonely. If theists and atheists did not have this common understanding of what makes many actions morally good or bad, we would not agree so much about which actions are good, or be able to dispute—as so often we can—about the morality of particular actions. Hence theists and atheists may agree—as clearly they do—both about the moral status (good or bad, as the case may be) of many particular actions, and also about the reasons why those actions have the moral status that they do. The existence of God makes no difference to the fact that there are necessary moral truths.

2. GOD'S EXISTENCE AND CONTINGENT MORAL TRUTHS

But the existence and actions of God do make a great difference to what these truths are. Among the necessary moral truths, which atheists as well as theists may come to recognize, is that it is very good to reverence the good and the wise who are truly great, and obligatory to thank and please benefactors. If there is a God, he is all-good, all-wise, and truly great, and for that reason alone it is very good to worship him. But God is also our supreme benefactor. He is so much more the source of our being than are our parents. God keeps us in existence from moment to moment, gives us knowledge and power and friends—and all the help that other benefactors give us arises from God sustaining in them the power to do so. Hence it becomes a duty to thank God abundantly. But to properly thank others involves showing that you know who they are and what is their relation to you. You must take them seriously. So thanking God will involve rendering the kind of thanks appropriate to the all-good, all-wise source of everything; that means that grateful worship is a dominant obligation. That there is a God is a contingent truth (logically contingent, that is, neither it nor its negation entails a contradiction. It is no doubt necessary in other ways). So it becomes a contingent moral truth that we have a dominant obligation to give God grateful worship.

All the Western theistic religions claim that God has issued specific commands to humans, among them the Ten Commandments. The first and obvious way to please benefactors is to obey their commands. It is in virtue of the necessary truth that beneficiaries have a duty to please benefactors that parents who are not just biological parents but are nurturing and educating parents have certain rights over their children while they are still young to command them to do certain things — to do the family shopping, for example — and the command creates an obligation that would not otherwise exist. Such parents are our greatest earthly benefactors. It follows that if children have limited duties to obey parents, humans have obligations far less limited in extent to obey God. His command will make it contingently the case that some action that otherwise would be only supererogatorily good or morally indifferent is now obligatory; and his forbidding it will make an action contingently wrong when previously it was only infravetatorily bad or morally indifferent. But there are, I suggest, other necessary truths (and so other contingent truths) of morality that relate the obligatory or the supererogatorily good to features of human situations not connected with divine command or commendation.

There are, however, limits to the rights of parents over children — parents do not have the right to command children to serve them day and night — and so, beyond a certain point, parental commands would impose no obligation. Likewise (though the main argument of this chapter in no way depends on this view), my own view is that God's rights over us are also limited, even more narrowly than by the fact that God cannot command us to do what we are obliged (in virtue of some other necessary moral truth) not to do — such as to torture children just for fun. God has the right to demand a lot from us by way of service to others and worship — but if he chooses to create free rational beings, I suggest, thereby he limits his right to control their lives. If there are such limits, it will then follow that in virtue of his perfect goodness, God will not command us to do actions beyond those limits — for to command what you have no right to command is wrong.

What God does not command, he may commend. And since (perhaps up to a limit) it is supererogatorily good to please benefactors more than you are obliged to, God's commendation can make an action supererogatorily good, even when it does not make it obligatory. And because God is omniscient, he knows what is good and obligatory for reasons other than his command and commendation. And because we do not always have such knowledge, he can inform us as to which actions are good or obligatory for such reasons. And, like human parents, God may command us to do what is obligatory anyway (such as keeping our promises to other humans) and commend us to do what is good anyway. And God's command and commendation can add to the obligation or goodness of the act. But, if what I have written earlier is correct, there are limits to what God can *make* to be good or obligatory. And because of the limits to our obligations, there is scope for "works of supererogation," as the Catholic tradition has maintained in contrast to classical Protestantism.

In Plato's dialogue *Euthyphro*, Socrates asked the famous question: "Is that which is holy loved by the gods because it is holy, or is it holy because it is loved by the gods?"[3] Put in theistic terms (and phrased simply in terms of command and obligation), the Euthyphro dilemma becomes the following: Is that which is obligatory commanded by God because it is obligatory, or is it obligatory because it is commanded by God? Kant gave the simple answer of taking the first horn of this dilemma;[4] other thinkers in the Christian tradition (perhaps William of Ockham, and certainly Gabriel Biel[5]) have taken the second horn; but the view that I am putting forward takes the first horn for some obligations and the second for others. In my view we ought not to rape or to break a just promise (that is, one that we had the right to make), whether or not there is a God; here God can only command us to do what is our duty anyway. But for the latter, only a divine command would make it obligatory to join in communal worship on Sundays rather than Tuesdays. That there are very general principles of morality, including not only the principle of the obligation to please benefactors but other principles as well, was recognized by both Thomas Aquinas and Duns Scotus. Aquinas held that "the first principles of natural law are altogether unalterable."[6] He does not tell us much in the *Summa Theologiae* about which these are, but he does write that they are principles too general to be mentioned in the Ten Commandments, principles such as that no one ought to do evil to anyone, which he says are "inscribed in natural reason as self-evident."[7] Scotus tells us that the only moral obligations from which God could not dispense us are the duties to love and reverence God himself, which Scotus sees as constituted by the first three of the Ten Commandments.[8] So both writers hold—and, I have claimed, are right to hold—that there are necessary moral truths independent of the will of God, but that the will of God makes a very great difference to what are the contingent moral truths.

3. GOD AND THE IMPORTANCE OF MORALITY

The existence and commands of God make acting morally always more important and sometimes very much more important than it would otherwise be.

Apart from the existence and commands of God, it is bad if I do not give a sum of money to some medical charity for research (which may or may not produce results) into how to prevent the spread of a rare disease in China (when the occasion arises and I have money to spare). But it seems doubtful that I have a duty or obligation to give money. One might plausibly say that even if I have some minimum duty to help any sentient being in a crisis, I don't *owe* lots of my spare money to help Chinese in a nonemergency situation; they have given me nothing, and so I cannot *owe* them this kind of nonemergency help. True, I owe my parents much; and perhaps I owe all my ancestors something—since but for their actions (of begetting and nurturing) I would not exist. A debt to a parent can be satisfied by caring for those whom they love, or repaying a debt that they forgot to pay. And if I and the Chinese have common ancestors (as surely somewhere in remote past we do), then that might create an obligation on me to help them. And if my parents benefited by exploitation of Chinese in the past, that too might create an obligation on me to help them now. But the links are somewhat tenuous, and any obligation correspondingly limited. And maybe on some distant planet there may appear rational creatures who have no historical connections with ourselves. Any *obligation* to care for them (at least in nonemergency situations) might be very limited.

But if God made me from nothing, and sustains the laws of nature that allow others to feed, clothe, and educate me, I have an enormous debt to him; and so there is a much greater obligation than there would be otherwise, to care for others whom he has benefited in the same way and which in virtue of his perfect goodness he would want me to do. The mere existence of a perfectly good creator makes it so. Also as I noted, the Christian tradition, like that of Judaism and Islam, holds that God has issued commands; and these commands impose obligations. By his commands, God makes it a duty on all of us to help others in various ways; and he commands many individuals to follow very demanding vocations. What would otherwise be supererogatory often becomes obligatory; and what was obligatory becomes a much greater obligation. And—given the view common to most theistic religions—God wants to take to heaven those who love to do good and so would be happy in heaven. For heaven is a place where people see God as he is, and respond in grateful worship and service (for example, by asking God to help others on earth)—without the obstacles to such activity that are so prevalent on earth (obstacles in the form, for example, of a clouded vision of what is good, and temptations to do what is bad). Only if someone loves the good will they want to see and worship God, and serve him and others. We can make ourselves the sort of people who love to do good by making ourselves do good despite these obstacles, so that doing good becomes natural. And so, not just because it is good in itself and because God commands it, but also for the sake of our own future, it matters greatly that we should do good. God makes morality a much more serious matter than it would be otherwise.

4. GOD AND MORAL KNOWLEDGE

How do we know what is morally good? If there is a God, all knowledge of moral truths that hold apart from those dependent on his command or commendations is clearly due to God, because he made us, gave us moral awareness, and gave us an awareness of many of the nonmoral facts of the world that enable us to apply the necessary moral truths. And he gave us experience of the world and the ability to discuss moral issues with others, so that we could improve our understanding of what are the necessary moral truths—in the way I discussed earlier. God did not give moral awareness to cats and dogs. But we clearly need further help in discovering some of the more specific necessary moral truths—such as those concerning whether abortion or euthanasia are always morally wrong or wrong only under certain conditions. For it looks as if some of us are too stupid or self-deceiving to discover such truths for ourselves. It would help us if God revealed what are the relevant necessary moral truths. As for the contingent moral truths created by divine command or commendation, particular individuals might learn what God has commanded them to do by means of some deep private religious experience (for example, they might learn in this way to which particular vocation God has called them). But for knowledge of God's commands (and commendations) of a general character, as well as for knowledge of the necessary moral truths that we are not capable of discovering by ourselves, we need a more public revelation. Different religions make different claims about what God has revealed. For Christians that revelation is to be found in the Bible (with the qualification added by Orthodox and Catholic Christians "as interpreted [and perhaps amplified] by the Church"). But any claim to revelation needs to be backed up by evidence that it comes from God. Claims about what God has commanded must be consonant with those moral truths that we know to hold independently of the will of God—a command to rape or break a just promise, for instance, could not come from God. But within those limits, the teaching of some prophet about what God has revealed needs to be confirmed by God's signature. A signature is an act that can be done readily only by the person whose signature it is and one that is recognized as a mark of endorsement in the culture in which it was made. A person's name handwritten by himself or herself at the end of a document constitutes a signature in our culture, as the imprint of a signet ring used to. Cultures vary in respect of which acts they recognize as marks of endorsement. Ancient Israel recognized a violation of natural laws by the agency of some prophet that forwarded the work of that prophet as just such a mark of endorsement by God. When Elijah called on God to provide fire from heaven to ignite a water-sodden sacrifice,[9] he was (in modern terminology) calling on God to do an act that would violate laws of nature. God alone who sustains laws of nature has the power to set them aside. When the fire came from heaven, it led to the acceptance by Israel of Elijah's teaching and the elimination of the prophets of Baal. Hence Israel recognized this as God's endorsement of Elijah's teaching. My own Christian view (for which I have argued elsewhere[10]) is that God has endorsed the teaching of Jesus Christ and the church that he founded and so the Bible that it declared to be divinely inspired. He endorsed this by bringing about the resurrection of Jesus (a clear violation of natural laws if it happened in the way recorded in the Gospels), which forwarded the victory of the church and the propagation of its teaching through the blood of its martyrs. No other religion has as its foundation event a miracle for which there is in any way the kind of historical evidence that there is for the resurrection of Jesus. Islam, for example, has usually avoided appealing to miracles in support of its claim that the Qur'an is the word of God. Muhammad claimed to have performed no miracles and seems to appeal to the internal character of the Qur'an as evidence of its divine origin. Muslims have appealed to the "inimitable" nature of the Qur'an,[11] including its content containing information that could not by normal processes have been available to an illiterate prophet, and that can be construed as an appeal to a miracle. But it is far from obvious that laws of nature would not allow an illiterate prophet to have such information; whereas if the resurrection of Jesus occurred in the way for which the different books of the New Testament (treated for this purpose as ordinary historical documents) provide—in my view—good evidence, it was without any doubt a very striking miracle. But it would take us too far away from our main theme to discuss here which if any of these claims that God intervened in history to authenticate a claim to revelation are correct. My only point is that without such evidence of divine intervention, we would have no knowledge of which commands God had issued, and much less knowledge of some of the necessary truths of morality that hold independently of God's command.

5. WHY GOD ISSUES COMMANDS

Although obviously God has good reason to tell us those moral truths that hold independently of his will but that we are not clever enough to discover, what reason would he have for adding to our moral burdens by issuing commands? Four reasons I suggest. First, to give us further motivation to do what is obligatory anyway. As I noted earlier, parents often tell their children to do what they ought to do anyway—sometimes no doubt because children may not realize what they ought to do anyway, but on other occasions, when children do realize this, to reinforce the obligation. Parents care that their children do what they ought to do. So, if there is a God, does God. We do not need God to command us not to murder, but his command may add to our motivation not to do so.

Second, God may issue commands for the purpose of coordination.[12] Often we can only attain good goals that we have some obligation to promote if the actions of each of us are coordinated with those of others. We have an obligation to avoid crashing each other's cars, and to enable us to fulfill this obligation the state lays down a coordinating rule "always drive on the left" or "always drive on the right." I mentioned earlier the obligation to worship on Sundays. Plausibly we have some obligation to join in public prayer, and plausibly too—barring a divine command—there is no particular reason why we should worship publicly weekly rather than daily, or on Sundays rather than Thursdays. A divine command is necessary to ensure coordination. Or consider the New Testament's "Wives, be subject to your husbands."[13] Husbands and wives have certain obligations to each other and their children—for example, to care for each other and educate their children. Clearly any institution needs a system for resolving differences about how the institution should fulfill its obligations. Some sort of "majority vote" system is used by many institutions. But of course that is of no use in a two-member organization, such as marriage. Clearly too, the parties ought to seek agreement on how to fulfill these obligations central to marriage—on where they should live, how their children should be educated, and so on. But if they can't reach agreement by discussion within a limited time, one of them must have a deciding vote. Otherwise the marriage will not last. I can't see any necessary moral truth about which of them, husband or wife, it should be. It is something appropriately laid down by their creator, just as driving on the left (or right) is appropriately laid down by the state that owns the roads.

Third, there are many good things that it is good that humans should do for other humans, but that humans have no obligation to do unless a command is issued by a competent authority. Parents may tell their children to do things that they would otherwise have no obligation to do, because it is good that those things should be done by the children (and not just by the parents) and within narrow limits parents have the right to tell children to do them. For God, as I noted earlier, the limits to his right to command must be far less narrow than for human parents. One example of a possible divine command of this kind might be the command of Jesus forbidding divorce (possibly subject to the qualification "except on the ground of unchastity").[14] Marriage involves a promise to the other party, and clearly—to my mind—it would be wrong anyway (without any divine command being issued) for either spouse to break this promise without the consent of the other spouse. But there is normally no obligation on those who make mutual promises not to release each other from the obligation to keep them. God, however, could forbid such releasing. But why should God do so? Why should God make divorce difficult or impossible—say for a Christian wife to divorce a cruel husband? These instructions have never been seen as forbidding a temporary separation in such circumstances, but why should not the Christian wife marry again? I suggest two connected reasons. The first is to allow great generosity of commitment in the first place; the stronger understanding of what is involved in getting married will mean that the marriage will start on the right foot. And the second reason is that this understanding of the vow will have the consequence that even if one spouse does not keep the vow, the other spouse will have an obligation by his or her example of steadfastness to encourage both the former party and others beyond the marriage to take the vow seriously in the future. If God forbids divorce, he forbids it because he wants us in these ways to promote our own good and the good of others. Otherwise it would be at most supererogatory not to remarry for these reasons. In issuing commands for the second or third reasons, God would give each of us a special place in God's providential plan for the world. For a commander to tell a particular person to perform a particular task makes and shows that person important to the commander. God deals with us on an individual basis, and he wants us so much to play a particular role in his plan and it is so good for us that we should, that he may command us to do so.

One reason why parents command children to do what otherwise would only be supererogatory (to do shopping for a sick neighbor, for instance) is that they want their children to get into the habit of doing what is good beyond obligation. When the children are young, parents command them to do such acts. Commands often have more effect than good advice, but once children get into the habit of doing supererogatory good acts, the need for command diminishes. God rightly want humans to be holy, and so he has this fourth reason of helping the process of our sanctification, for imposing obligations on us (by way of commands) for some or all of our earthly life. (That, of course, still leaves us with the causal freedom to disobey God's commands.)

So there are various reasons why God might choose to issue commands to humans; and if my previous arguments are right, such commands will impose new obligations on us and make the observance of morality a more serious matter than it would be otherwise.

NOTES

1. "Makes a great difference" in the sense that things are very different if there is a God and we exist, compared with the situation when there is no God and we still exist. I ignore the point that most probably if there were no God, we too would not exist.

2. John Rawls, *A Theory of Justice* (Oxford: Oxford University Press, 1972), 20.

3. Plato, *Euthyphro*, 9e. From the Loeb Classical Library edition of the works of Plato, vol. 1, trans. H. N. Fowler (Cambridge, Mass.: Harvard University Press, 1914).

4. See Immanuel Kant, *Lectures on Philosophical Theology*, trans. A. W. Wood and G. M. Clark (Ithaca, N.Y.: Cornell University Press, 1978), 159. Kant writes: "The knowledge of God . . . must not determine whether something is morally good or a duty for me. This I have to judge from the nature of things."

5. See his *Canonis Missae Expositio*, 23E, "The reason why the divine will accepts things as thus or thus, is not a goodness found independently in objects by God, but the reason lies only in the divine will, which accepts things as having such and such a degree of goodness; that is why they are good in that degree and not vice versa" (my translation).

6. St. Thomas Aquinas, *Summa Theologiae*, 1a. 2a. 94.5. From the Blackfriars edition of the *Summa*, vol. 40, trans. T. F. O'Meara and N. J. Duffy (New York: Blackfriars, 1968).

7. St. Thomas Aquinas, *Summa Theologiae*, 1a. 2a. 100.3. From the Blackfriars edition of the *Summa*, vol. 41, trans. T. C. O'Brein (New York: Blackfriars, 1972).

8. Ordinatio III, suppl. dist. 37, text and translation on pages 268–87 and commentary on pages 60–64 of *Duns Scotus on the Will and Morality*, ed. Allan B. Wolter (Washington, D.C.: Catholic University of America Press, 1986).

9. 1 Kings 18:17–40. I am not arguing that this story is true. I am using it merely to illustrate ancient Israel's understanding of how to recognize a divine signature.

10. See my *Resurrection of God Incarnate* (Oxford: Clarendon Press, 2003).

11. For different interpretations of the Qur'an's "inimitability," see J. Wansbrough, *Quranic Studies: Sources and Methods of Scriptural Interpretation* (Oxford: Oxford University Press, 1977), 77–78.

12. I owe this important point to Joseph Shaw.

13. Ephesians 5:22.

14. Mark 10:10–12, possibly qualified in Matthew 5:32.

Part III

CONCLUDING RESPONSES

Chapter Nine

This Most Gruesome of Guests

A Response by William Lane Craig

I am grateful to Michael Murray, Robert Garcia, and Nate King for the opportunity to pursue this most important debate in a published format and to our several respondents who have extended the debate by their thoughtful contributions.

As I said in my closing statement of the debate proper, this is really a debate about moral nihilism. Humanist philosophers like Paul Kurtz tend to assume that if theism is false, then some sort of ethics grounded in the objective value of human beings is true. But such an assumption is too quick. For, as I explained in my opening statement, humanist philosophers are engaged in a war on two fronts: They must defeat not only the theist but also the nihilist. And it is very far from obvious that, given atheism, the nihilist can be successfully repulsed.

Now in the debate I staked out two basic contentions that I proposed to defend:

I. If theism is true, we have a sound foundation for morality.
II. If theism is false, we do not have a sound foundation for morality

In this final response, I want to revisit these contentions in order to see how they fare in light of our respondents' criticisms. I shall not comment on issues, however interesting they may be, raised by our respondents that are not germane to these two contentions.

With respect to each contention, I considered three components of morality requiring a sound foundation: objective moral values, objective moral duties, and moral accountability. Any proffered moral system either lacking these three components or failing to provide an adequate foundation thereof

will be inadequate as a moral system. So far as I can tell, none of our respondents disputes this assumption with respect, at least, to the first two components; nontheist moral philosophers will tend to deny the necessity of the
third component because atheism so obviously fails to provide any ultimate
moral accountability for one's actions.

FIRST CONTENTION: GOD AS
THE FOUNDATION OF MORALITY

The first contention, that if theism is true, we have a sound foundation for
morality, should not really be a point of controversy. Even nihilists will generally concede this conditional claim. The theism of which I speak is traditional Anselmian theism, or perfect being theology, which conceives of God
as the "greatest conceivable being."[1] Any moral objectivist, whether he or she
bases moral values and duties in God or regards them as existing independently of God, will regard this first contention as true, since it states a merely
sufficient, but not a necessary, condition of morality.[2] The atheistic moral objectivist will dispute my identification of moral values and duties with divine
properties and commands respectively, but he or she will not dispute the truth
of contention (I). Rather his or her real bone to pick is with contention (II).

But to consider my three subcontentions in support of (I), I think that Mark
Murphy, whose chapter is a model of lucidity and generosity, is correct in
stating that the sort of grounding I have in mind for moral values and duties
is what he calls "informative identification" (127). Moral values are identified with certain attributes of God, and moral duties with what God commands. As I emphasized in my second speech, my concern here is with moral
ontology, not moral epistemology.[3] Epistemological objections are thus red
herrings that need not detain us. We may therefore dismiss as irrelevant much
of Walter Sinnott-Armstrong's response, which is pervaded by the conflation
of moral epistemology with ontology.[4] Sadly, the same is true of Louise
Antony's paper.[5] To repeat, my concern is with an *ontological* foundation for
morality, not with epistemological foundations. As far as moral epistemology
is concerned, I can appeal to all the same mechanisms, such as moral intuition
and reflection, by means of which Sinnott-Armstrong is confident that he accurately discerns the good and the right. I, too, can affirm with Antony that
human beings have a capacity called a conscience, which enables them to discover for themselves what is right and wrong. In fact, the apostle Paul actually teaches that God's moral law is "written on the hearts" of all men, so that
even those who do not know God's law "do naturally the things of the law"
as "their conscience bears witness to them" (Rom. 2:14–15). If that is the

case, a theist's moral epistemology may not differ broadly from Sinnott-Armstrong or Antony's own moral epistemology. My argument is that theism is necessary for there to be moral goods and duties, not that it is necessary for us to discern the moral goods and duties that there are.

Again, Sinnott-Armstrong's complaints that I have not shown that theistic-based ethics is true is similarly based on misunderstanding.[6] My goal in defending the first contention is to sketch a moral theory according to which objective moral values and duties exist; the intention, at least at this point, is not to prove that that theory is true. Perhaps an analogy will help. In physical science, theorists often formulate quite different accounts of some phenomenon without having any means of adjudicating between them. Quantum mechanics, for example, is susceptible to around ten different physical interpretations that are mathematically consistent and empirically equivalent, and no one yet knows which, if any, is the true theory. Or again, in contemporary cosmology, astrophysicists are exploring two competing theories aimed at explaining the recently discovered cosmic acceleration, one in terms of a positive cosmological constant and the other in terms of energy fields known as quintessence. The jury is still out. Or again, the standard model in particle physics is being sharply challenged by nascent string theory. No one would think to accuse the physicists who are developing their respective theoretical accounts of the phenomena at issue of begging the question. Of course, the hope is that these theories will generate fruitful research programs that will enable us to adjudicate between the competitors. But until that time arrives, a theorist will attempt to defend the conditional claim *that if his or her theory is true, it explains the phenomenon in question.* Moreover, he or she may also attempt to show the explanatory inadequacy of competing theories. In the same way, a defense of my first contention requires at most a coherent account of the three components of morality that I have identified, not a demonstration that that account is true.

Objective Moral Values

With these confusions out of the way, we may ask whether the account I have suggested does provide an adequate basis for moral values, moral duties, and moral accountability. Consider first the question of moral value. On the account I suggest, the Good is determined paradigmatically by God's own character. Just as a meter was once defined paradigmatically by the length of an iridium bar housed in the Bureau des Poids et des Mesures in Paris, so moral values are determined by the paradigm of God's holy and loving character. Fortunately, God's character is not malleable, as is a metal bar; indeed, on classical theism it is essential to him. Moreover, since according to classical theism, God exists necessarily, his nature can serve to ground necessary moral truths.

Perhaps the most important objection to dispatch at this point is the contention by Richard Swinburne and, apparently, Stephen Layman that certain moral principles, being necessarily true, cannot have an explanation of their truth. The assumption here seems to be that necessary truths cannot stand to one another in relations of explanatory priority. Not only do I see no reason to think that assumption true, but it strikes me as obviously false. For example, "States of consciousness exist" is necessarily true, since "God exists" is necessarily true. That is to say, the fact that a personal, metaphysically necessary being like God exists explains why it is necessarily true that states of consciousness exist. To give a nontheological example, the axioms of Peano arithmetic are explanatorily prior to "2 + 2 = 4", as are the axioms of Zermelo-Fraenkel set theory to the theorems thereof. In metaphysics, "No event precedes itself" is necessarily true because it is necessarily true that "Temporal becoming is an objective and essential feature of time." I should regard as utterly implausible the suggestion that the relation of explanatory priority in such cases is symmetric. But if necessary truths can stand to one another in asymmetric relations of explanatory priority, then there is no objection so far to holding that moral values exist because God exists.

I am therefore puzzled by Murphy's assertion that "if the standard for explanation here is logical entailment—*p* explains *q* only if *p* logically entails *q*—then Craig's theistic account fails as well. For *God exists* plainly does not logically entail *moral value exists*. . . ." (126). But most certainly it does! On classical theism there is no possible world in which God fails to exist and, since his character is essential to him, no world in which moral values fail to exist. Perhaps the stumbling block here is the presupposition on Murphy's part that God, if he exists, exists contingently and therefore cannot ground necessary moral truths. That is clearly Swinburne's position. But such a presupposition is out of line with classical theism, which holds God's existence to be metaphysically necessary. The central insight of Anselm's ontological argument, whether one regards it as a successful piece of natural theology or not, is that if God exists, he exists necessarily. God's existence, then, is either necessary or impossible. Layman's personal concern expressed in his ninth endnote that "since I am offering an argument for God's existence, I must of course allow for the possibility that there is no God" is quite misplaced, being based upon a confusion of epistemic possibility and metaphysical possibility. The natural theologian must allow at most the epistemic possibility that there is no God, not the metaphysical possibility. The mathematician seeking to prove Goldbach's Conjecture may allow that for all we know the conjecture is false but nonetheless insist that it is either necessarily true or necessarily false; it is not contingent. So also with God's existence: If he exists, he does so necessarily and therefore an informative identification of moral values and duties with his character and commands is available. In that case, God's existence entails (and is entailed by) the existence of moral values.

I trust that the foregoing puts to rest Antony's astonishing claim that I have not so much as acknowledged, must less endeavored to answer, "the main objection" to my position, namely, "the objection found in the *Euthyphro*" (81). I can assure her that I have, indeed, encountered the argument before, and the very formulation of my position was intended as a direct response to Plato's dilemma.[7] The reason she finds me to be "of two minds about the issue" (71) is that the only alternatives she apparently knows are Platonism or voluntarism, and I affirm neither. I am gratified that none of the other commentators was similarly confused about the formulation of my position. I shake my head in bewilderment at the sort of man Antony must take me to be when she expresses "the dark suspicion that Dr. Craig is not really interested in engaging atheists in rational discussion, but rather is speaking exclusively to his theistic contingency, with the aim of reinforcing for them the vile stereotype of atheists so prevalent in contemporary American society" (81). This, about a debate at a secular college at the invitation of a free thought institute, in which I opened with the statement "Let me just say at the outset, as clearly as I can, that I agree that a person can be moral without having a belief in God" (29), a sentiment reiterated in every one of my speeches in the debate.

So far as I can tell, that pretty much takes care of the criticisms raised by our respondents to my first subcontention, that if theism is true, we have a sound (ontological) foundation for objective moral values.[8] All that remains is Sinnott-Armstrong's complaint: "Even if God does exist and does have qualities with objective moral value, this conclusion about God has nothing directly to do with us humans here on earth" (105). *Au contraire,* it shows us at least what the paradigm of a good person looks like. Since we, too, are persons—in theological language, the *imago Dei*—we are given a model of moral character to emulate. More importantly, perhaps, God's character is the fount of his moral commands to us, which form our moral duties. Thus, on classical theism God's character is of utmost relevance to us humans here on earth. Since the question of moral duty is the subject of my second subcontention, let us now turn to it.

Objective Moral Duties

My second subcontention was that if theism is true, then we have a sound basis for objective moral duties. I take it for granted that there is a difference between moral goods and moral obligations. It is good that I become a wealthy philanthropist and support worthy causes throughout the globe; it is also good that I forgo the pursuit of wealth to become a medical missionary to Chad. But obviously I cannot do both, since they are mutually exclusive. I am not, therefore, morally obligated to do both, though both are good. Goods, then, do not imply moral obligations. Whence, then, arises moral obligation? Why am I morally obliged, duty-bound, so to speak, with respect to certain actions? The theist has a ready answer: God's commands or will lays certain duties upon me. We may give an account of moral requirement, permission, and prohibition as follows, for any agent S and action A:

A is *required* of S if and only if a just and loving God commands S to do A.

A is *permitted* for S if and only if a just and loving God does not command S not to do A.

A is *forbidden* to S if and only if a just and loving God commands S not to do A.

Thus, the theist has a perspicuous account of moral duties.

Sinnott-Armstrong finds such an account "incredible" (106). For "even if God in fact never would or could command us to rape, the divine command theory still implies the counterfactual that, if God did command us to rape, then we would have a moral obligation to rape" (106). Antony makes a similar claim. The difficulty with this claim is that, on the version of divine command theory that I have defended, the counterfactual in question has an impossible antecedent and so, on the customary semantics, has no nonvacuous truth value. Even if we, with Antony, reject the usual semantics and allow that some counterfactuals with impossible antecedents may be nonvacuously true or false, how are we to assess the truth value of a statement like this? It is like wondering whether, if there were a round square, its area would equal the square of one of its sides. And what would it matter how one answered, since what is imagined is logically incoherent? I do not see that the divine command theorist is committed to the nonvacuous truth of the counterfactual in question nor that anything of significance hangs on his thinking it to be nonvacuously true rather than false.

Sinnott-Armstrong, after presenting several arguments said to show the superiority of a secular account of moral duty to a theistic account (the consideration of which we may defer until later, when they are relevant), provides "a cavalcade of devastating objections" (108) to divine command morality. The first of these is again the *Euthyphro* dilemma. I repeat that the particular version of divine command theory that I present was formulated precisely so as to be immune to that dilemma. The arbitrariness horn of the dilemma, which concerns Sinnott-Armstrong, is avoided by rejecting voluntarism in favor of God's commands' being necessary expressions of his nature.

In contrast to Antony, Sinnott-Armstrong knows this, but he attacks straw men while continually backpedaling until he arrives at the theory that I actually defend. He insists that it is still vulnerable to the arbitrariness objection: "Even if it is God's essential nature necessarily to command us not to rape, that command remains arbitrary unless there is some reason for that command, such as that rape is bad on independent grounds" (109). There are a couple of confusions operative here. First, Sinnott-Armstrong confuses arbitrariness with explanatory ultimacy. God's commands are not arbitrary in the sense that he could have commanded the opposite of what he did command. Statements of moral obligation such as we are considering are logically necessary. But his commands *are* explanatorily ultimate. That is not to say that some commands cannot be explanatorily prior to others. For example, the prohibition against rape may be explained by saying, with Sinnott-Armstrong, that God forbids rape because it is wrong, all things being equal, to harm another person. But why is it wrong to harm another person? Here Sinnott-Armstrong reaches his own explanatory ultimate: There is no reason why it is wrong to harm another person. In the sequel, we shall take up the question of the adequacy of this explanatory stopping point in the sequel. For now, we note simply that the difference between the theist and Sinnott-Armstrong is not that one has an explanatory ultimate and the other does not. It is rather that the theist has a different explanatory ultimate: God commands us to love and not to harm one another. Second, Sinnott-Armstrong confuses moral badness with moral wrongness. The morally good/bad is determined by reference to God's nature; the morally right/wrong is determined by reference to his will. The divine will or commands come into play as a source of moral obligation, not moral value. The theist can agree that God forbids rape because it is bad; and it is bad because it is incompatible with God's nature. There is no arbitrariness to be found here.

The second, third, and fourth objections of Sinnott-Armstrong's "devastating" cavalcade are such breathtakingly bad arguments that I shall not spend time on them here.[9] So far as I can tell, our respondents raise no further significant objections to my second subcontention.

Moral Accountability

That takes us, then, to the third subcontention, that if theism is true, we have a sound basis for moral accountability. This is a point emphasized strongly in John Hare's chapter. Classical theism, through its doctrine of human immortality and divine rewards and punishment, secures moral accountability and so escapes moral futility. This point is so obvious that denials could only be based on misunderstandings or misconstruals. True to form, Sinnott-Armstrong disputes the point by protesting that no reason has been given to think that these elements of classical theism are true, which, as explained above, is irrelevant to the adequacy of the theory if true. He does make some gestures toward impugning the biblical God's justice, but such misgivings are based on mistaken generalization of a highly contextual command and the failure to realize that one's deserts come in the afterlife rather than this life. In any case, these critiques of biblical passages do not really undermine theistic ethics but represent at most objections to a doctrine of biblical infallibility.[10] Sinnott-Armstrong also raises irrelevant epistemological issues, which require me only to add that, of course, a just God will not hold people accountable for carrying out injunctions of which they are ignorant.

One of the reasons that moral accountability is important is that we want our moral choices to make a difference. Sinnott-Armstrong opines that "such a view robs us of any incentive to improve this finite world" (114). Nonsense; it is precisely because our moral choices do make a lasting difference that attempts to improve this finite world are not futile. Realization of this fact can increase incentive to better the world. Sinnott-Armstrong objects that were I to refrain from self-sacrificial action, God would forgive me, so that there is no net difference. This objection again confuses moral goodness with moral obligation. It is a great good that Wesley Autrey threw himself onto the New York subway tracks, risking his life to save another person, but he was not morally obligated to do so. His was a supererogatory act, and had he refrained he would have done no wrong. His act not only deserves reward, but by so acting he has morally improved the world and made a lasting difference.

But are such altruistic, self-sacrificial acts really possible, given the moral accountability present in theism? In his carefully crafted article, Don Hubin argues that classical theism is incompatible with "acts of morally laudable, altruistic, *genuine* self-sacrifice" (134). Given the meaning that Hubin packs into "genuine," I should say that such a thesis, far from being the provocative and weighty claim that it at first blush appears to be, turns out to be a conclusion that the theist will find almost obviously true and will, indeed, be eager to affirm. It amounts to saying that we do live in a moral world after all. Hubin recognizes that his thesis in no way suggests that classical theism is incompatible with the virtue of altruism, for altruism has to do with the agent's motivations for action. Even if, on theism, there are no acts of morally laudable, *genuine* self-sacrifice, still there may be the virtue of altruistic behavior, which God may reward.

So why, on theism, can there not be morally laudable acts of *genuine* self-sacrifice? Simply because, as Hubin defines it, genuine self-sacrifice must involve a net, long-term cost to the person undertaking such an act. He explains,

> A personal cost is necessary for self-sacrifice. And, it has to be a *net* cost to the individual. Local costs that are compensated are not sacrifices. We often speak of someone sacrificing to get through law school, medical school, or even a graduate program in philosophy. But if these sacrifices are amply rewarded by a welcomed financial success or, more plausibly in the last case, by some sort of psychic satisfaction, they don't constitute a genuine sacrifice of the self. (139)

A genuine act of self-sacrifice must, then, involve a permanent net loss for the individual involved. But given the justice of God, he will not allow morally laudable local acts of self-sacrifice to go unrewarded. Therefore, no morally laudable acts can be *genuinely* self-sacrificial.

It seems to me that such a claim involves an idiosyncratic understanding of what counts as genuine self-sacrifice and therefore becomes almost trivial. Hubin's own illustrations of ways in which we often speak betray how counterintuitive a conception he has of genuine self-sacrifice. I should say that persons who endure the hardships he mentions do make tremendous, genuine self-sacrifices, even if these sacrifices do not involve permanent net losses for the individuals involved, and if Hubin denies that they are genuine, then he is using "genuine" in an idiosyncratic way, so that his claim that theism is incompatible with morally laudable acts of *genuine* self-sacrifice is evacuated of significance. The strangeness of his conception of genuine self-sacrifice becomes even more evident when we reflect that, given theism, it is people who lead lives of narcissistic self-indulgence who are performing acts of genuine self-sacrifice, since such acts will result in a net loss to those individuals. On any normal understanding of the words, it seems bizarre to say that such selfish persons are leading genuinely self-sacrificing lives. Yet that is the implication of the meaning Hubin attributes to *"genuine* self-sacrifice." Far from being a problem for theism, it is part of the glory of theism that there cannot be morally laudable acts of self-sacrifice that go ultimately uncompensated.[11] "For God is not so unjust as to overlook your work and the love which you showed" (Heb. 6:10).

Classical theism therefore imposes no moral requirement that we should engage in acts of what Hubin idiosyncratically calls *genuine* self-sacrifice. Therefore, Hubin's argument that the theist is in an awkward position to promote an ethic of genuine self-sacrifice falls to the ground. The theist is interested in promoting an ethic of altruistic behavior that looks to the good of others rather than of oneself, and Hubin allows the coherence of such an injunction.

So my first contention stands secure: by furnishing a sound basis for objective moral values, moral duties, and moral accountability, classical theism, if true, provides a sound foundation for morality.

SECOND CONTENTION: ATHEISM
AN INADEQUATE FOUNDATION OF MORALITY

This brings us, then, to my second and more controversial contention, that if theism is false, we do not have a sound foundation for morality. I am persuaded that Friedrich Nietzsche was right when he declared that the end of classical theism means the advent of nihilism. "This most gruesome of guests," wrote Nietzsche, is standing already at the door.[12] The most plausible and popular form of atheism is naturalism, which holds that the only things that exist are the things postulated by our best scientific theories. But science is morally neutral; one cannot find moral values in a test tube. It follows immediately that moral values do not exist but are mere illusions of human beings. Even on a looser characterization of naturalism that would permit realities not required by our best scientific theories, still from a naturalistic perspective we are just animals, relatively advanced primates, and animals are not moral beings. If the atheist insists that some animals, namely human beings, are moral beings after all, then we are entitled to ask for some explanation of this peculiarity, especially in light of how different moral properties, especially prescriptive properties, would be from typical physical properties. That is why I focus (to Murphy's puzzlement) on what he calls the "wrong-headed" sociobiological account of morality, which is the second, illusionist alternative noted by Hare. I do not mean to suggest that naturalistic accounts must be committed to a strong program of sociobiological explanation for every moral behavior and belief, but merely that on naturalism it is plausible that morality is illusory. Here the question is precisely whether in Murphy's words, "a nontheistic alternative that attempts to preserve moral value rather than just the appearance thereof" (122) is viable. I have difficulty understanding how this can be plausibly carried out within the context of naturalism.[13]

Objective Moral Value

So, as my first subpoint, I simply ask: If theism is false, why think that human beings are the basis of objective moral value? Murphy's proposal is that moral value be grounded in prudential value for human beings. Basically, the idea is that moral value is based on or to be identified with whatever contributes to human flourishing. Now before looking at the details, I must confess that such a suggestion, given naturalism, strikes me as implausibly anthropocentric. We can limn prudential value for guinea pigs that will be characterized by objectivity, universality, and normativity, but we shall not therefore imagine that the flourishing of guinea pigs is morally good or that anyone has a moral obligation to abet it. Why is a preferential treatment of human flourishing not a case of speciesism, an unjustified bias in favor of one's own species?[14]

To consider Murphy's proposal more closely, I am inclined to agree that prudential value is independent of God in the sense that, given naturalism, it would be possible to give an accurate account of what it would be for a human being to flourish. Obviously, such an account would be vastly different from the theistic account, which sees the knowledge of God as the key to human fulfillment. But on the supposition of naturalism, it would seem to make sense to speak of what would make human beings well-off, just as it would make sense to speak of what would contribute to the flourishing of other animal species. (On my view, in the absence of God one would not have merely a *different* account of moral values, leaving out all those mentioned by Swinburne, for example, which have reference to God, but rather an account at best of the *appearance* of moral value.)

But I am puzzled by how Murphy accomplishes the second step of grounding moral value in prudential value. The claim here is that "what makes a state of affairs morally valuable (or disvaluable) is grounded in what makes people better- (or worse-) off" (124). What justification is there, on naturalism, for this assertion, which represents the second step of his proposal?

So far as I can see, the only justification Murphy offers for this assertion is that "the kind *human* is obviously a distinct sort of organism, and distinct in ways that are obviously ethically significant. To take one example: human beings possess *reflective* and *objectivizing* intelligence, which enables them to call their inclinations into question and to see themselves as one person among others" (125). This leaves me baffled as to the justification of Murphy's grounding claim. Certainly, if naturalism were true, human beings would still be distinct organisms possessed with reflective and objectivizing intelligence. Such properties could still be said to be ethically significant in the sense that they are necessary conditions of being an agent and, a fortiori, of being a moral agent. But I see no reason to think, without begging the question, that humans are therefore objectively morally valuable or have any moral obligations.

There seems to be an enormous gap in Murphy's argument at this point. How does it follow from *Homo sapiens'* reflective and objectivizing intelligence that what is conducive to human flourishing is morally good? Murphy interprets the attempt to connect moral value with prudential value as the attempt to explain "why one should care about someone else's flourishing, someone else's well-being" (125). But I do not see the connection between humans' being endowed with reflective and objectivizing intelligence and prudential value's being other-directed. As a result of seeing myself as one among many, I may realize that I had better look out for my own interests if I am to get ahead.

If being other-directed means simply caring about someone else's flourishing, then for social animals, at least, be they ants or caribou, it is easy to explain why they should care about one another's well-being: Their own flourishing and survival depend upon the flourishing of the herd. Pure self-interest would justify human creatures' being interested in the well-being of at least some others—for example, those of one's tribe. But while self-interest may be prudent, it is indisputably not always moral. In Murphy's own words: "We have not moved from having reasons to look after our well-being to having reasons to look after others; we are still governed ultimately only by reasons of our own well-being rather than also by reasons of others' welfare" (126). Indeed, we seem to have lapsed back into the herd morality of the sociobiological illusionist.

What this suggests is that Murphy has given an inadequate characterization of morality. He tries to show that prudential value may have all four of the earmarks of moral value, including other-directedness, so that the latter can be plausibly grounded in the former. But the demonstration that prudential value has all four of the earmarks of moral value is insufficient to justify a grounding relation between them because the four earmarks are presented by Murphy as merely *some* of the distinctive marks of morality. Since we are talking about necessary rather than sufficient conditions of moral value, there may be other distinctive marks of moral value not shared by prudential value that preclude a grounding relationship.

Indeed, it seems to be a distinctive property of moral goodness that it is desirable for its own sake. That is the import of Murphy's remark that moral value is what is good *simpliciter:* not that it is other-directed rather than self-directed, but that it is desirable in and of itself. As such, it is utterly distinct from prudential value, which, as Layman emphasizes, is always relative. This mark of moral value would seem to preclude its being grounded in prudential value, since there is nothing in considerations of prudence to account for a state of affairs' being desirable for its own sake.

Murphy's attempt to ground moral value in prudential value thus comes up short on a number of counts. Remarkably, he seems ready to concede that there are possible worlds in which humans have reflective and objectivizing intelligence and prudential value exists and yet moral value does not exist.

But then, surely some explanation is needed for why moral value does exist contingently in our world. The theist faces no such problem, since there is no possible world in which God exists and moral values do not exist, since God is necessarily good and his nature is the paradigm of moral value.

Murphy thinks that if the theist can reasonably hold that moral value is to be informatively identified with theistic states of affairs, then mutatis mutandis, "the nontheist can reasonably enough suggest that moral value can be informatively identified with states of affairs involving prudential value: (e.g.) *to be morally valuable* is *to be or serve someone's well-being*" (127). But I think there are two decisive reasons why such a strategy will fail for the nontheist. First, since Murphy lists only *some* of the distinctive earmarks of moral value, the demonstration that prudential value shares those earmarks, even if successful—which is moot—would not justify us in such an identification, since there may well be other necessary marks of moral value not considered by Murphy that are not characteristic of prudential value. Indeed, we have seen that this is, in fact, plausibly the case, since the morally valuable is to be desired for its own sake. Second, if such an identification were successfully to be made, then it would constitute a reductive or eliminative analysis of moral value in terms of prudential value. On the proposal under consideration, moral value does not supervene on prudentially valuable states; rather moral value is identical to prudential value, which as the ground of moral value, is more basic than moral value. So on this strategy, moral value does not really exist; the palm of victory is awarded to the nihilist. For in the absence of God, only prudential value remains.

So what is the atheist to do at this point? It seems to me that he must simply insist, with Sinnott-Armstrong, that whatever contributes to human flourishing is morally valuable or good and whatever detracts from human flourishing is bad and take that as his explanatory stopping point. But then the problem is that, given naturalism, such an explanatory stopping point seems premature because of its arbitrariness and implausibility. As Michael Ruse has argued, we can well conceive of extraterrestrial rational beings for whom rape would not be immoral.[15] Should they visit Earth, why should they respect the values that have evolved among *Homo sapiens*? Had our own evolutionary history gone differently, creatures with a quite different set of moral values might have existed here. As Murphy says, we can conceive of possible worlds in which moral values do not supervene on states conducive to human flourishing. All this underlines the arbitrariness of Sinnott-Armstrong's explanatory ultimate.

One might meet this objection by holding with Swinburne that moral properties supervene necessarily on certain natural states. That would meet the arbitrariness objection. But then the question as to the plausibility of this explanatory ultimate arises. Swinburne's contention at best gives us reason to think that if moral properties do supervene on certain natural states, then they do so necessarily. But that gives us no reason at all to think that, given a naturalistic worldview, there are any moral properties or that they supervene on natural states. If there is no God, then it is hard to see any ground for thinking that the herd morality evolved by *Homo sapiens* is objectively true or that the property of moral goodness supervenes on certain natural states of such creatures.

If our approach to metaethical theory is to be serious metaphysics rather than just a "shopping list" approach, whereby one simply helps oneself to the supervenient moral properties or principles needed to do the job, then some sort of explanation is required for why moral properties supervene on certain natural states or why such principles are true. It is insufficient for the naturalist to point out that we do, in fact, apprehend the goodness of some feature of human existence, for that only goes to establish the objectivity of moral values and duties, which the theist is ready to affirm. Swinburne's belief that no explanation is needed for the existence of moral properties is rooted in his assumption that necessary truths cannot stand in relations of explanatory priority, an assumption that we have seen to be, not merely gratuitous, but plausibly false.

Objective Moral Duties

We come now to my second subpoint of contention (II): If theism is false, there is no basis for objective moral duties. We are inquiring here, not after moral value, but a source of moral obligation. Even if there were Platonic values, it remains mysterious on naturalism why human beings have moral obligations and prohibitions to obey. Prudential obligation—that is, what we ought to do in order to promote our well-being or even the well-being of our species—is of no help here, for these are mere conditional obligations, not categorical imperatives. We are left wondering why, on naturalism, we have a duty to promote human flourishing and an obligation not to detract from it.

Again, Sinnott-Armstrong just takes as his explanatory stopping point the wrongness of our harming others unjustifiably: "I can't help but believe that it would be morally wrong for someone to cause . . . unjustified harm to me. There is no reason why I would have any more rights than any other person. Hence, it must also be morally wrong for me to cause such unjustified harm to them" (101). It is worth noting in passing that Sinnott-Armstrong's self-styled "harm-based morality," even if adopted, gives us an account only of our moral prohibitions (what we ought not to do), but not a hint as to our moral obligations (what we ought to do). His account must be radically incomplete or else, on his view, human beings have no positive moral duties (there being merely wrong actions to avoid). In any case, the argument cited above, if meant to support his assertion that "what makes it morally wrong to murder, rape, steal, lie, or break promises, for example, is simply that these acts harm other people without any adequate justification" (101), confuses once again moral epistemology and moral ontology. It shows why I cannot help believe that it is morally wrong for me to cause unjustified harm to others. But it does nothing to show that unjustifiably harming others is really wrong. Worse, it does nothing to show that so harming others would be wrong if naturalism were true. The theist may agree that such prohibitions exist and that I cannot help believing that I have such prohibitions, but we are still left wondering why, on an atheistic worldview, I have such prohibitions. Think again of Richard Taylor's illustrations cited in my opening speech. Acts that are physically indistinguishable from murder, theft, and rape go on all the time in the animal kingdom, but are not wrong. So why, on naturalism, are such harmful actions wrong for human animals? Sinnott-Armstrong has self-confessedly no answer to this question. His theory is less simple than nihilism and lacks the explanatory power of theism.

Moral Accountability

We come at last to my third subpoint: If theism is false, then there is no ultimate basis for moral accountability. Again, this point seems indisputable. For, given naturalism, there is no reliable mechanism to apportion desert to virtue or vice. None of our respondents has anything to propose by way of such a mechanism. The only remaining question is whether moral accountability is really all that important to morality.

Hubin objects to my assertion that on an atheistic worldview altruistic behavior is "stupid." Here it will be helpful to recall what I said:

> Acts of self-sacrifice become particularly inept on an atheistic worldview. Such altruistic behavior is merely the result of evolutionary conditioning that helps to perpetuate the species. A firefighter rushing into a burning building to rescue people in danger or a policeman who sacrifices his life to save those of his comrades does nothing more praiseworthy, morally speaking, than an ant that sacrifices itself for the sake of the ant heap. On an atheistic view, this is just stupid. (33)

Now, as Hubin says, the charge of stupidity covers a broad range of disparate errors, and I accept his interpretation that this charge means that on an atheistic worldview altruistic acts do not "make sense." Why? Because on atheism such altruistic behavior is "merely the result of evolutionary conditioning that helps to perpetuate the species," so that a person who sacrifices himself for others "does nothing more praiseworthy, morally speaking, than an ant that sacrifices itself." On such a naturalistic worldview morality is delusory. In Richard Dawkins's memorable words, "There is at bottom no design, no purpose, no evil, no good, nothing but pointless indifference. . . . We are machines for propagating DNA. . . . It is every living object's sole reason for being."[16] On such a view, it does seem stupid to act out of anything but self-interest. Why sacrifice your life for a delusion?

Now Hubin detects here an acceptance on my part of "some form of normative egoism" (146). He recognizes that this cannot be a normative *ethical* egoism, since I am not asserting that on atheism altruistic acts are immoral. But there is some sense in which, on atheism, altruistic acts are not "the thing to do" and ought to be avoided.

But if the normativity is not moral, then what is it? It seems to me prudential. Since I think that prudential value is independent of theism, I think it makes sense to speak of what, on atheism, is in an organism's best interest or conducive to its well-being. If there are no objective moral values and duties, then prudential value clearly trumps moral value, for the latter is a delusion. Even if there were, on atheism, moral values and duties (which is moot), moral value and prudential value fall apart and are often in head-on collision. Acting morally will then not make prudential sense. In the absence of moral accountability, life thus becomes, in the language of the French existentialists, absurd. One has moral value pulling in one direction and prudential value tugging in the opposite and no way to decide rationally which choice to make. By contrast, on classical theism moral value and prudential value may seem temporarily out of joint but are ultimately harmonious, so that adopting the moral point of view makes good prudential sense, even if it involves worldly sacrifice.

Hubin summarizes my view by saying that "*worldly* self-sacrificial behavior makes sense . . . only if it is not *genuinely* self-sacrificial" (147), that is to say, only if it does not involve permanent, net loss to the person making the sacrifice. That seems to me correct: If some action involves permanent, net loss to a person, then it does not make sense, prudentially speaking, to engage in it. Since on atheism, altruistic actions fall under such a description, they do not make sense.

Hubin finds the thought that on atheism altruistic actions do not make sense "morally troubling" (147). But why? Such a view can allow that we still ought *morally* to engage in such actions. Hubin alleges that such a view "is a challenge to any demand made on our actions that is grounded ultimately in the well-being of others" (147). But it is clearly not a challenge to any such *ethical* demand; it therefore leaves the virtue of altruism untarnished. The problem is that there is, on atheism, an irreconcilable conflict between any moral demand that might be upon us (the objectivity of which is moot) and the demands of one's own well-being, and there is no way to decide rationally which to follow. I agree with Layman that on atheism what he calls the Overriding Reasons Thesis (namely, that moral value always trumps prudential value) is not true, for one may have extremely strong prudential reasons for not acting morally and there seems to be no common scale in which to weigh moral against prudential considerations.

What about my claim that even if there were, on atheism, objective moral values and duties, they are irrelevant because there is no moral accountability? Antony asks "what values and duties are supposed to be 'relevant' to" (75). Look at the original context of my remark. The quotation from Professor Kurtz that I cited reveals my meaning: "There is no cosmic prospect for the human species. . . . There is no metaphysical basis for hope."[17] I expanded briefly on this in my second speech: "In the absence of moral accountability, our choices become trivialized because they make no ultimate contribution to either the betterment of the universe or to the moral good in general because everyone ends up the same" (38). On naturalism our destiny, both as individuals and as a species, is ultimately unrelated to moral behavior.

Sinnott-Armstrong asserts that an act of self-sacrifice that aids others "gets meaning from the fact that it does aid others" (114). But even if we grant, for the sake of argument, that there are, on naturalism, objective moral goods and moral duties that I may fulfill, such that an act of supererogation has meaning in the sense that it is good and that I went beyond my duty in doing it, still the point remains that such objective values and duties do not finally matter, since everything winds up the same. As Bertrand Russell lamented in a famous passage:

> That man is the product of causes which had no prevision of the end they were achieving; that his origin, his growth, his hopes and fears, his loves and his beliefs, are but the outcome of accidental collocations of atoms; that no fire, no heroism, no intensity of thought and feeling, can preserve an individual life beyond the grave; that all the labours of the ages, all the devotion, all the inspiration, all the noonday brightness of human genius, are destined to extinction in the vast death of the solar system, and that the whole temple of Man's achievement must inevitably be buried beneath the debris of a universe in ruins—all these things, if not quite beyond dispute, are yet so nearly certain, that no philosophy which rejects them can hope to stand. Only within the scaffolding of these truths, only on the firm foundation of unyielding despair, can the soul's habitation henceforth be safely built.[18]

Given the scaffolding of these truths, it does not really make any difference how one lives. Hubin notwithstanding, on naturalism acts of self-sacrifice are, indeed, empty and ultimately meaningless gestures.

The anguish of the human predicament becomes poignantly evident in Louise Antony's indignation at the idea that her sacrificing her life for the life of her child fails to "have a point" on atheism. She protests, "It would only be pointless if my child's continued existence is itself pointless, and if Dr. Craig were to suggest such a thing to me, he'd see what righteous anger can be summoned by an atheist" (76). Unfortunately, as Russell and Kurtz both see, the tragic, awful truth is that in light of the universe's inevitable fate our children's lives are, indeed, utterly pointless, as pointless as our own. Therefore, as Antony herself acknowledges, her sacrifice is also pointless. At this point she can react only with anger.

> Good men, the last wave by, crying how bright
> Their frail deeds might have danced in a green bay,
> Rage, rage against the dying of the light.[19]

Robert Adams has pointed out that to believe that God does not exist and that there is thus no moral accountability is quite literally de-moralizing, for then we should have to believe that our moral choices are ultimately insignificant, since both our fate and that of the universe will be the same regardless of what we do.[20] By "de-moralization" Adams means a deterioration of moral motivation. It is hard to do the right thing when that means sacrificing one's own self-interest and to resist temptation to do wrong when desire is strong, and the belief that ultimately it does not matter what you choose or do is apt to sap one's moral strength and so undermine one's moral life. Think of Layman's illustration of Ms. Poore. Who could deny that if she were an atheist she would experience tremendous de-moralization under such circumstances? By contrast there is nothing so likely to strengthen the moral life as the beliefs that one will be held accountable for one's actions and that one's choices do make a difference in bringing about the good.

Moral accountability is therefore a vital component for any adequate ethical theory. Atheism fails miserably in this regard, for on naturalism moral values and duties are either illusory and therefore trumped by prudential considerations or else, if real, in irreconcilable conflict with prudential value due to the absence of accountability. Moreover, moral values and duties, even if real, remain irrelevant to one's fate and that of the universe, resulting in an undermining of the moral life.

CONCLUSION

Atheism, then, fails to secure objective moral values, objective moral duties, and moral accountability. It therefore cannot, in contrast to classical theism, furnish a sound foundation for morality.[21]

NOTES

1. In Anselm's famous phrase "*aliquid quo nihil maius cogitari possit.*"

2. So I note that Louise Antony in her criticism of my claim that God's existence is sufficient for morality concurs that "the existence of *any* morally good being . . . is . . . sufficient to establish the existence of objective moral value" (80), which concedes my first contention. Her skepticism concerning the metaphysical possibility of an Anselmian deity is irrelevant to my claim that if such a being exists, then he is sufficient, in Antony's words, "to generate a realm of moral fact" (80). I'm presenting, after all, a moral argument, not an ontological argument.

3. Ironically, this distinction is drawn with wonderful clarity by Sinnott-Armstrong himself in his book *Moral Knowledge?* Moral ontology, he explains, studies the metaphysical status of moral properties and facts; moral epistemology studies the justification and knowledge of normative moral claims, asking whether, when, and how substantive moral beliefs can be justified or known or shown to be true. Accordingly, he distinguishes several types of moral skepticism, such as moral justification skepticism, moral knowledge skepticism, linguistic moral skepticism, and ontological moral skepticism. He recognizes that someone might hold that moral beliefs are true (i.e., reject moral ontological skepticism) and yet deny that anyone is justified in holding them (i.e., embrace moral justification skepticism and, hence, moral knowledge skepticism). See Walter Sinnott-Armstrong, "Moral Skepticism and Justification," in *Moral Knowledge?* ed. Walter Sinnott-Armstrong and Mark Timmons (New York: Oxford University Press, 1996), 4–8. It is perhaps telling that Sinnott-Armstrong focuses solely on moral justification skepticism, leaving ontological moral skepticism, the concern in the present debate, out of account.

4. For example, his objection that "the bare claim that there is some all-good, all-powerful, all-knowing god does not tell us which things are good or bad" (102); his interpretation of my first contention to mean "if theism is true, something makes us justified in believing that certain specifiable acts are morally wrong" (103); his question "How do we even know what God commands?" (108); his objection that "divine command theory makes morality unknowable" since "we have no sound way to determine what God commanded" (109); his concern that "if the divine command theory were correct, then [certain] murderers could not know that it is morally wrong to murder" (113); his conclusion that "we know which acts are wrong by seeing the harm they cause, not by thinking about divine commands" (113); and so on.

5. For example, her assertion that "only the theorist who believes that right and wrong are independent of God's commands could have any basis for thinking she or he knows in advance what God would or would not command" (71–72); her allegation that divine command theory is "an insult to any God worth worshipping" (72) because it excludes "the possibility that human beings can discover for themselves what is right and what is wrong—that they resemble their Creator in having a capacity for making such judgments" (72); her resulting misinterpretation of the story of Abraham and Isaac as teaching, on a divine command reading, that there was "nothing in the *nature* of the command" (77) to kill his son "that in any way signaled to Abraham that it was not really God speaking to him" (77), so that Abraham

would not have "even considered the possibility" (77); her consequent reinterpretation of that story to teach by way of contrast to the divine command reading that "Abraham does possess a moral sense that's independent from God's commands" (78); her subsequent discussion of whether we should trust in God "to know the moral facts of the matter" on the analogy of "the trust that laypersons rationally invest in their doctors" (78) on medical matters; and so on.

6. For example, his construal of the paragraph cited from page 30 as an argument that "is supposed to show that objective values exist" and that therefore "begs the question" (104); his claim that my assumption that God's qualities are objective moral values "again begs the question" (104); his query "Why believe this additional claim?" (105) in response to my assertion that God's nature supplies the absolute standard for moral assessment; his pronouncement "You can't show a sound foundation for morality simply by announcing a theory without any reason to accept that theory" (107); and so forth. Sinnott-Armstrong's chapter is so compromised by such confusions that, though loaded with plenty of red meat for free-thought popularizers, it has little of philosophical substance to long detain us.

7. She need only look at William Alston's fine article, from which I drew inspiration, "What Euthyphro Should Have Said," in *Philosophy of Religion: A Reader and Guide*, ed. William L. Craig (Edinburgh: Edinburgh University Press, 2002; New Brunswick, N. J.: Rutgers University Press, 2002), 283–98.

8. Well, there is Antony's complaint that, if we assume as our departure point the Anselmian definition of "God," the question then becomes, "Is the Creator of the universe God?" (80). This objection, based in her construing my position to be some sort of divine voluntarism, finds no point of contact with my argument. In this debate I have argued neither that there is a Creator of the universe nor that God is good in virtue of his being the Creator of the universe. My taking God to be the *summum bonum* also invalidates her complaint that on my view God is not worthy of worship but is guilty of a kind of vanity.

9. His second objection (that divine command morality is childish) is either a thinly veiled *ad hominem* argument or else, if taken as an inductive argument against the truth of divine command theory, irrelevant, massively undersupported by the evidence, and a textbook example of the fallacy of *consensus gentium*. His third objection (that divine command morality is unknowable) conflates epistemology and ontology, as explained above, and involves incidentally an exegetically naive interpretation of biblical passages with no attempt whatsoever to understand them in their theocratic and historical context. His fourth objection (that divine command morality is hard-hearted) is an absurd caricature, blending *ad hominem* attack with *ad populum* appeals and confusing questions of moral obligation with questions of moral motivation. I also leave aside as a mere cavil his complaint that on my view moral duties are subjective because they are not independent of what anyone thinks, since "anyone" includes God—as if to say, when I ask, "Has anyone seen my wife?" an appropriate answer would be "Well, surely she, at least, has seen herself!"

10. This same point needs to be made in response to Antony's unnecessary polemic against the "vengeful, despotic god depicted in the pages of the Hebrew Bible" (80). Her excursus is meant merely to motivate the question (which hardly needs motivat-

ing) as to whether a Creator of the universe must be good and so must be obeyed. Actually, the demonstration that God is depicted in the Hebrew Bible as both the Creator of the universe and as morally deficient does nothing to suggest that these two notions are compossible. It would show no more than that some of the biblical writers failed to depict God consistently—compare Antony's own remark that had she written the story of Abraham and Isaac, she would have done so differently. Criticisms of the moral portrait of God painted in the Bible are thus philosophically irrelevant, since at most the moral inadequacy of such portrayals only calls into question a doctrine of biblical infallibility, not God's goodness or divine command moral theory.

Nevertheless, in the interests of polemics I cannot resist saying that Antony's exegesis is naive and tendentious. "What part of 'chosen people' do you not understand?" (79) she asks, oblivious to the fact that Yahweh chose Israel as the means by which he might bless the world: the promise to Abraham was that "in you all the families of the earth shall be blessed" (Gen. 12:3). So we find in the Hebrew Bible the remarkable story of an Israelite prophet being sent to the Assyrian capital of Nineveh because God pitied Nineveh, "that great city, in which there are more than 120,000 persons who do not know their right hand from their left" (Jon. 4:11). Contrary to Antony, the Bible is not full of accounts of God's killing, smiting, or displacing presumably innocent people. These narratives cluster primarily around the Israelite conquest of Canaan. Moreover, it is not the case that "the only 'crime' committed by the Canaanites was living in a land that God wanted for *his* people" (79). Rather God stays his judgment of the Canaanite clans four hundred years because their iniquity "is not yet complete" (Gen. 15:13–16). By the time of their destruction, their culture was debauched and cruel, embracing such practices as ritual prostitution and child sacrifice. Of course, Antony is right that among the dead in Egypt and Canaan were innocent children. But on any moral theory God, not being a human being, is not bound by the same moral obligations that humans have toward one another. God has the right to give and take human life as he pleases and is under no obligation to prolong anyone's life indefinitely. When God takes a child's life, he does not do so capriciously but has morally sufficient reasons for doing so. As for slavery, Wilberforce argued correctly that the Bible never gives moral approbation to slavery but merely recognizes it as a fact of life in the Ancient Near East to be reckoned with. This whole discussion concerns isolated biblical narratives and ignores the larger portrait of God in the Hebrew Bible, which is morally magnificent, especially when contrasted with the deities worshiped by other peoples of the Ancient Near East.

Curiously, apart from Abraham's call none of these instances is relevant to Antony's main question concerning the story of Abraham and Isaac: "*Does* [Abraham] have good reason to think that God knows better what is moral than he does?" (79), since they all take place hundreds of years *after* the life of Abraham! It is interesting to note that God had promised Abraham that it was through Isaac that his descendants would come (Gen. 21:12), so that the command to sacrifice Isaac was actually a test of Abraham's faith in God's promise—a test that Abraham would have failed had Antony written the story.

For more on these issues see Paul Copan, *That's Just Your Interpretation* (Grand Rapids, Mich.: Baker, 2001); Copan, *How Do You Know You're Not Wrong?* (Grand Rapids, Mich.: Baker, 2005); www.christian-thinktank.com/qamorite.html.

11. Actually the situation is much more subtle. For on Christian theism, if God were to give us our moral deserts, we should all find ourselves condemned. It is only through the imputed righteousness of Christ that salvation and eternal life are achieved. In that light morally laudable acts of genuine self-sacrifice do, tragically, seem to occur all the time in the lives of unregenerate persons and apostate believers. Because such persons reject God's offer of forgiveness on the basis of Christ's expiatory death, their morally laudable acts of local self-sacrifice are ultimately unavailing and so uncompensated and thus involve net loss for them—unless in such cases, such acts perhaps serve to mitigate the severity of their punishment. For present purposes we may leave such theological subtleties aside.

12. Friedrich Nietzsche, *The Will to Power: An Attempted Transvaluation of All Values*, vol. 1, trans. Anthony M. Ludovici (New York: Russell & Russell, 1964), 5.

13. It was intriguing to me to note that none of our respondents cared to defend Kurtz's own so-called objective relativism, which collapses so quickly to nihilism. Indeed, Professor Kurtz seems to have all but dropped out of the debate.

14. Our editors suggest that Murphy could avoid the charge of speciesism by claiming that the moral value of all animals is grounded in what is prudentially valuable for them. But such a move would be desperately implausible, lest animals be convicted of moral crimes like murder, rape, theft, greed, and so on, and animals be of equal value to people.

15. Michael Ruse, "Is Rape Wrong on Andromeda? An Introduction to Extraterrestrial Evolution, Science, and Morality," in *Extraterrestrials: Science and Alien Intelligence*, ed. Edward Regis Jr. (Cambridge: Cambridge University Press, 1985), 43–78.

16. Richard Dawkins, *Unweaving the Rainbow* (London: Allen Lane, 1998), cited in Lewis Wolpert, *Six Impossible Things before Breakfast* (London: Faber and Faber, 2006), 215. Unfortunately, Wolpert's reference is mistaken. The quotation seems to be a pastiche from several sources, including Richard Dawkins, *River out of Eden: A Darwinian View of Life* (New York: Basic Books, 1996), 133; Richard Dawkins, "The Ultraviolet Garden," Lecture 4 of 7, Royal Institution Christmas Lectures (1992), available online at physicshead.blogspot.com/2007/01/richard-dawkins-lecture-4-ultraviolet.html.

Thanks to my assistant Joe Gorra for tracking down the reference.

17. Paul Kurtz, *The Courage to Become* (Westport, Conn.: Praeger, 1997), 27–28.

18. Bertrand Russell, "A Free Man's Worship," in *The Basic Writings of Bertrand Russell*, ed. Robert E. Egner and Lester E. Denonn (New York: Simon & Schuster, 1961), 67.

19. Dylan Thomas, "Do Not Go Gentle into that Good Night."

20. Robert Adams, "Moral Arguments for Theistic Belief," in *Rationality and Religious Belief*, ed. C. F. Delaney (Notre Dame, Ind.: University of Notre Dame Press, 1979), 125–27.

21. My thanks to Mark Linville, Robert Garcia, and Nate King for their comments on this chapter.

Chapter Ten

Ethics without God: Theism versus Secular Humanism

A Response by Paul Kurtz

1.

The point of view that I sought to defend in the original debate was humanism—more precisely, secular humanism, a widely held viewpoint today. This is continuous with the ideals of the Enlightenment, an effort to ameliorate the human condition. Secular humanists maintain that goodness without God is "good enough." As a nonreligious secular humanist, I am skeptical about religious claims for the existence of God, for which I find insufficient evidence. I am not inferring the nonexistence of God from the lack of evidence. I am simply saying that the burden of proof rests with claimants and I find the case for God totally inconclusive. Thus I am a nontheist or atheist, but I do not consider that atheism by itself defines my position, for I affirm a whole set of ethical humanist values. Life presents us with manifold opportunities to achieve our goals and lead the good life, depending on the cultural milieu. We can be a person of good will, a good citizen in the community, and contribute to the well-being of others. We can lead a morally significant and rewarding life without belief in God. Moreover, we can develop reliable ethical knowledge in our practical choices and actions.

Craig concedes in this debate that "a person can be moral without having a belief in God" (29). Later in the debate he said, "We all believe in the intrinsic value of human beings, and in love for one another, and cooperative behavior" (42), with which, of course, I concur. But Craig maintains that "this is not good enough" for him and his fellow theists, for it does not provide "a solid foundation for morality." He is seeking ontological roots for "objective moral values," "moral duties," and "moral accountability." Craig indicts both atheists and humanists for lacking ontological foundations for their positions.

I am skeptical about the demand for ontology to resolve moral disagreements—I have difficulty in understanding what he means by ontological foundations, though I have studied and written on metaphysics.

If, for example, a person is trapped in an unhappy marriage and is faced with the option of a divorce, or if a society is embroiled in a heated debate of going to war—let's say with Iraq—how does it help the participants to solve these quandaries by locating "the ontological grounds"? How is the appeal to God going to resolve the dispute between Muslims (whether Sunni or Shiite), Jews, and Christians in the Middle East? The appeal to the ontology of theism—differently interpreted—only seems to exacerbate the conflict. I submit that in general there is a kind of autonomy of moral choices, and that there are many relevant considerations in defining what to do, without the need to plumb the hidden depths of Being. The history of ethics clearly demonstrates that there are rational deliberations that can help us formulate judgments of practice. This is separate and distinct from theology and not dependent on it; and philosophers have devoted much energy to exploring on the metaethical level various criteria—such as utilitarianism, deontology, and virtue ethics.

The philosophers who have contributed to this book apparently agree about the integrity of philosophical analysis. Atheists Walter Sinnott-Armstrong, Louise Antony, and Donald Hubin share this view and theists such as Mark Murphy and Richard Swinburne concur. Steven Layman and John Hare use philosophical analysis, though like other theists invoke God at times, mistakenly I submit. Indeed, it would be outrageous to ignore the history of ethics from Socrates and Aristotle to Spinoza, Mill, Rawls, and Dewey, all of whom attempt to work out principles, values, and methods of resolving ethical quandaries without going outside to theology. Although Kant attempted to overcome the antinomy between virtue and happiness, he distinctively emphasized the autonomy of reason and the possibility of developing categorical imperatives solely by means of reason, not theology.

Thus the issue of autonomy is crucial, not only in ethical discourse, but also in other fields, such as the sciences. Surely one can use physics and mathematics to work out testable hypotheses and theories without invoking occult foundations. The laws of physics are not deductive principles abstract in form, but tested by their experimental predictions, the coherence of theories, and they are open to revision in light of new evidence. Science makes progress but its principles are nonetheless fallible in the sense that they're always amenable to possible change in the light of new theories and new evidence.

This is similar for political controversies in democratic societies where a body of laws or a constitutional framework enables judges to make decisions and where the civic virtues of democracy, such as tolerance, respect for majority rule, negotiation, and compromise apply to everyone in the political community, believers and unbelievers alike, without reference to their theological premises or lack of them. John F. Kennedy, in running for the presidency of the United States, said that he was seeking the office, and happened to be a Roman Catholic, but that his religious faith would not determine his decisions. The separation of religion and the state is thus important. The same considerations apply to virtually all specialties from history and the social sciences to the arts and humanities.

Thus, I submit that Craig's demand for foundations for ethics—theological in his case—commits an egregious error and rests upon a mistake, as Henry Prichard[1] argued in an earlier period. The quest for an "ultimate justification" for moral principles grounded in ontology is an illegitimate demand. The search for "occult" causes to bridge the "moral gap" is profoundly askew. If we had to convince others in a democratic society, for example, that unless they accept an ontology or theology then they are immoral nihilists, we might never resolve moral disagreements or find common ground. Similar considerations apply to economics, where internal principles within the field count, without occult causes intervening. If anyone sought to burden the economics of the marketplace with occult foundations, he or she would be laughed out of court—a good case in point is a prohibition on interest in Islamic countries as required by Quranic law (Sharia) and the somersaults that have to be done to get around it.

I would argue that the best solution for moral quandaries is a function of the methodological and epistemological criteria that arise in concrete cases as we seek to clarify and define key concepts and seek to justify judgments about practices. We begin moral inquiries in the midst of life, not by searching first for ontological principles upon which everyone must first agree, and deducing imperatives from them.

If the question, "Is goodness without God good enough?" is interpreted to mean that everyone *must* believe in God or that God is essential in some way to be fully good, then that clearly is false, for as most contributors to this volume recognize we often encounter virtuous and bad people on all sides of most questions. Experience has demonstrated that not all the moral saints are inside the churches and the sinners outside.

Another issue that is crucial in ethical deliberation is the role of *deductive* inference. Is it the case, as Craig seems to imply, that "God's own holy and loving nature supplies the absolute standard against which all actions are measured" (30)? Come on, now. How can that be accepted in the Congress where one is debating legislation about stem-cell research; or at a convention of educators where the discussion is about the Head Start program; or a meeting of cardiologists determining how to cope with heart disease; or psychologists dealing with disturbed patients? As I said in the debate, it is hazardous to deduce a set of moral commandments from that premise or from any other premise about God's nature.

To further illustrate the point, what can we deduce about homosexuality from the existence of God? Does it follow that homosexuality is sinful and that same-sex marriage is a violation of divine law? That has been the position of the Roman Catholic Church, though paradoxically a significant percentage of priests have been gay. What is the basis of that claim? Is this a deduction from God himself? Interestingly, many Protestant denominations, Episcopal, Presbyterian, and Jewish and Unitarian congregations, believe that homosexuality and same-sex marriage is morally permissible, and indeed, if there are loving relations of sincerity and trust it can be praiseworthy. Protestant fundamentalists and Muslims of course deny that. Is the prohibition against homosexuality in Judaism and Christianity based on quotations from the Hebrew Bible and the views of St. Paul in the New Testament?[2] Does that depend on revelation? *Whose* revelation? The Jews do not accept the New Testament, nor do the Muslims, who draw inspiration from the Qur'an and accept without question the alleged revelations of Muhammad as received from God; or, again, Joseph Smith and his revelations as recorded in the Book of Mormon differ with other religious traditions. So is one doing ethics or is the suppressed premise rooted in faith, with an incestuous relationship between one's moral bias (pro or con) and one's concept of God?

Another illustration of the problem is the treatment of women by patriarchical religions, such as Islam, Roman Catholicism, and Orthodox Judaism. Women in many cultures today are still held in bondage to men, and the Qur'an or Bible is used to justify inequality of the sexes. So if God is holy, why are different injunctions deduced by theists from his nature? Given this, reference to God is hardly a reliable foundation for moral judgments.

The second main charge against humanism that Craig levels in the debate is that since humanism "is without foundation," it immediately leads to nihilism. Why is it the case that God is a necessary and sufficient condition for morality and that anyone who does not accept this must *ipso facto* be a wicked nihilist! *Nihilism* derives from the Latin *nihil*, meaning "nothing"; it is the doctrine that maintains that moral values and beliefs are unfounded, that existence is meaningless, and that there are no reliable standards of truth or value. This belief became prominent in Russia before the Russian Revolution when some people were so turned off by the system they rejected everything and turned to violent anarchism and revolution in order to destroy it. I must confess that I do not know any genuine nihilists myself. I have had scores of students over the years in quandaries about what they ought to believe in, and many of them became subjectivists. Some even flirt with leading promiscuous lives, for they generally find life enjoyable and hedonism satisfying—hardly a nihilist option. At least they expressed an ethic of naked egoism, though not to the liking of Craig or even me. It is true that some people suf-

fer depression—all is black and in despair—but this is not the same as nihilism, for severe depression may have physiological causes, which can often
be treated by medication and cognitive-emotive-behavioral therapy. It is libelous to insist that without God there are no objective norms and that one
must be a nihilist if one lacks foundations. Why not a libertarian or Marxist,
a Buddhist or Confucian, or any other number of alternative life stances?

2.

I agree with fellow atheist philosophers Walter Sinnott-Armstrong, Donald
Hubin, and Louise Antony's criticisms of Craig. Craig insists that without God
it is impossible to declare that it is morally wrong to rape, murder, steal, or lie.
Walter Sinnott-Armstrong correctly points out that an important reason that we
should not commit these acts is that they "harm other people without any adequate justification" (101). There is no need to invoke God to reject these acts.
For Sinnott-Armstrong a key question to ask Craig is, If morality depends
upon God, how do we define the deity—is he Zeus, or Jehovah, Jesus, or Allah? Craig begs the question, for he masks the values that he cherishes in his
very definition of God as "loving, generous, just, faithful, kind, and so forth"
(30). Why not the jealous and vindictive God of the Old Testament or the
Qur'an? Craig's conception of God already assumes a set of values packed
into its definition, and hence it begs the question; and thus it does not provide
adequate foundations for moral values, duties, and accountability.

Donald Hubin adds still another justification for acting morally without
God, namely that human beings are capable of genuinely altruistic actions that
at times involve self-sacrifice contrary to a person's own self-interest. Hubin
makes a move that I agree with, namely that people may be motivated altruistically even if they do not believe in God. They make sacrifices for their parents, children, friends or colleagues, even strangers in their midst. Theism has
been burdened with the doctrine of original sin. We need to leave room for
beneficence, empathy, and caring in human motivation. The evidence for altruistic deeds is abundant—contrary to Ayn Rand—and can be found not only
in the helping professions (teachers, nurses, doctors), but in everyday life. And
this is not simply reducible to self-interest or egoism. Hubin points out that if
a person "values the well-being of the others more than he or she values his
own well-being, he or she is acting sensibly and rationally. And to have such
values is not to be stupid; it is to love others as oneself" (148).

I agree with Louise Antony that not only is God *not* necessary and sufficient
for the existence of objective moral truth, but an impediment to it. Thus, to base
morality on God "is not enough." She agrees with Socrates in the *Euthypro* that

something is right not because the gods command it, but they command it because it is right. Thus morality is independent of God, and human beings can discover themselves what is right and wrong. Those who defend the divine command theory undermine the very basis of morality. Nor do we need the contrived rationalization that divine accountability will provide ultimate justification for moral deeds. One should act morally for its own sake, not because of hope for reward or fear of punishment. In any case the problem of evil is the Achilles heel of monotheism. Why would a beneficent God permit evil in the world, if he is omnipotent and just?

Inasmuch as I agree substantially with the above three chapters, let me move on to the articles by the theists. I found the chapter by Mark Murphy particularly challenging. First, he criticizes my interpretation of the question, whether one can be morally good without believing that God exists by saying that this "is not a particularly interesting, live question" (118). He responds, "*of course*, atheists can live lives that are in large measure morally upright, even extraordinarily admirable or heroic" (118). However, his view is surely a minority viewpoint in America today where a majority of the population (in 2007) consider atheists the least desirable minority of citizens, and only one member of Congress (Rep. Pete Stark [D-Calif.]) has had the courage to publicly announce that he is an atheist. Although moral philosophers are familiar with the history of ethics, the general public is not; so it is important to establish that fact. I should point out that there are different kinds of unbelievers. One can be an atheist and uncaring about human suffering (e.g., Stalin and Pol Pot); so I wish to focus on atheistic humanism, namely secular humanism.

Murphy, however, maintains that he and other theists deny that atheists can live *fully* admirable lives. He says that this is because theists "take God as their intentional object" (118), whereas atheists do not. *Au contraire*, I deny that we need to take God as the "intentional object." Murphy also says that I offer no evidence in the debate for the claim that God does not exist; of course I do in my writings and have spent a good deal of time examining the case for God, pro and con.[3] I think that the God idea is a delusion with insufficient support by reason or evidence. Hence, we do not have any moral duty toward this fictitious being, a construct of human wish-fulfillment.

Murphy asks, Can a nontheist lead a *fully* admirable life? I respond, Yes, but it depends on what you mean by *full*.[4] This life can be overflowing with adventure and exploration, exhilaration and enrichment; it can be a life of creative fulfillment and joy. The fullness of life includes the capacity for sexual satisfaction and orgasmic love. It also includes moral deeds, shared experiences, intellectual discoveries, and aesthetic enjoyment. Secular humanists consider many "spiritual" values crippling and out of touch with the *lebenswelt*. For example, I consider enforced celibacy a crime against nature—as repressive "spiritual devotion." I do not know what Murphy means by "perfect goodness" and would be wary of someone who claims that form of spiritual virtue. I should add that on my view, humanists can be morality inspired, not only by personal creative endeavors, but also by altruism, empathy, and caring for others, and in working for social justice on the larger social or planetary scale.

I do appreciate Murphy's effort in the rest of the chapter to show that atheists—I prefer "secular humanists"—can be morally responsible persons. Let me add that I believe that although we can develop reliable ethical knowledge, this should be salted with a dose of skepticism about reaching ultimate certainty. I also think that moral principles are at best general, if not universal, for we recognize that there may be exceptions to them. Moral judgments are *prudential*, yes indeed, as are recommendations in economics, education, social psychology, engineering, medicine, dentistry, and other applied sciences; yet they can contribute significantly to the fullness of life. Thus I submit that the *flourishing* of life is an important criterion of its adequacy, and that moral judgments have a kind of internal credibility and coherence without reference to a divine ground. I also hold that humanists recognize their obligations to others, but this is related in part to a person's station and duties and his or her commitments in society (as a father or mother, teacher or employer, coworker or citizen). Secular humanists are thus able to act responsibly without benefit of dogma or clergy.

The salient point of humanist ethics is that since God is dead, humans are alive, and that as such we are—in large part—responsible for our own destinies. This includes the achievement of our plans and projects (individually and socially), and the discovery that life can be intrinsically worthwhile. This requires a degree of courage, the willingness to enter into the world and take some responsibility for our common future. I think that we not only need to eat of the fruit of "the tree of knowledge of good and evil" but of "the tree of life" itself. Human life is intrinsically good for its own sake and needs no further justification. It was fitting that humankind was expelled from Eden, so that men and women can build their own habitats. The Promethean myth is the inspiration for heroic deeds. Humans are not obedient sheep who need to prostrate themselves before God in prayer and supplication, but free persons capable of controlling their own lives.

John Hare correctly observes in his article that there are many types of goodness besides moral goodness, though he confines his remarks to the moral domain. Such language confers a kind of mystique to morality. Actually, many naturalists prefer the term "value" and "valuation," for this enables them to deal with the wider range of goods and values that people experience. To restrict good or value to "morality," as religious thinkers are wont to do, unnecessarily ties it to the language of "spirituality," "sin," and "sacrifice." Hare declares that moral goodness without belief in God is not good enough, for this he thinks is "rationally unstable." People who do not believe in God (such as Spinoza) may lead a conspicuously good life, but they are lacking something, he says. All too many people think about their own advantage and not the happiness of others. "What is required," says Hare, is "the agency of providence, which has powers not merely human" (88). Drawing on Kant, he states that there is a propensity to prefer one's own happiness over one's duty to others; this "moral gap," he opines, can only be bridged by God. As I read Kant, God, freedom, and immortality are postulates that enable us to overcome the antinomy between virtue and happiness, but our ethical deliberations are nonetheless based on rational considerations, and divine providence does not intervene. What is the difference between an illegitimate deus ex machina interposed in astronomy to fill a gap in our explanations of the natural universe and the resort to divine immortality to fill in the so-called moral gap? Thus I fail to see why it is rationally "unstable" and why humans cannot be interested in their own welfare at the same time that they have an altruistic interest in others. Moreover, I accept both the deontological obligatory character of key ethical principles and their prudential reasons for justification. I should add the disclaimer that there is no guarantee in human life that the conflict between a person's own happiness and the happiness of others can always be resolved. A bit of humility is called for. There are profound paradoxes in life: Often our choices are between two goods or rights—both of which we cannot have—or the lesser of two evils. Thus many dilemmas do not have easy solutions. Perhaps in an ideal world where God is the divine judge and all the furniture in heaven is in place everything will turn out right in the end. But as I have said, the salvation fantasy is a form of collective self-delusion. I am here implying that the demand that ultimate moral judgments be *universally* or *essentially* or *absolutely* true is a straightjacket imposed on life, which is apt to be messy, with loose ends flapping in the breeze. The alternative for secular humanists is what I call *objective relativism*. It is not based on God's absolute commandments, which are apt to be a ballet of bloodless categories that do not deal with real life. For example, the Ten Commandments state "thou shalt not kill," but this doesn't leave room for killing in self-defense or in time of war, euthanasia, or assisted suicide—all justifiable in certain circumstances.

C. Stephen Layman proposes a moral argument for the existence of God, but I submit that his heroic effort fails. He begins with the "overriding reasons thesis" (ORT)—that is, that the strongest reason always favors what is morally required. Surely the quest for reasons is favored by philosophers—nontheists and theists alike—with varying degrees of agreement about what this entails. How prove the ORT thesis, he asks? This is not a necessary truth. Alas, ordinary men and women in the moral agora do not necessarily accept the appeal to reason, and they draw upon faith, custom, emotion, or authority for their moral justifications. Often the reasons we offer are tentative, hypothetical, and comparative.

Layman, like everyone else, recognizes that there are exceptions to every rule, for example, "the conditional thesis" that sometimes we need to override the overriding thesis. The point is, of course, that in moral dilemmas there may be a clash of conflicting principles, virtues, and values, and they need to be weighed in balance. The meliorist evaluates better or worse, not absolute good or bad, for often our choices need to be weighed on a comparative scale.

Layman's proof fails—for he begins with universal principles, and since he cannot reconcile them with self-interest, resorts to God to rescue him. Moral choices are far more nuanced in life, they are relevant to concrete contexts where there are competing demands made on us, differing values and norms, goods and bads, rights and obligations, responsibilities and duties. Moral choices are often problematic, though there are degrees of objectivity in concrete situations of living.

I have left Richard Swinburne's chapter last to comment on because it is both insightful and, in my view, patently false. In the first instance Swinburne concedes my argument that the actions of God make no difference because there are "moral truths," and in the second instance he thinks that God makes a difference about the "content," "seriousness," and "knowledge of morality"—but this only compounds the confusion.

Swinburne states that some moral judgments about particular cases or kinds of actions are true or false as a result of experience and reflection. With this I agree. What I find questionable is his claim that these are "logically necessary truths." I differ with him because although I think that there are general truths in morality (I call them prima facie *general* rather than *universal* principles as deontologists such as W. D. Ross did[5]), they are *not* logically necessary per se, but empirical generalizations based on the long evolutionary history of the human species and developed because of their adaptive value. In other words I think that the human animal is a *moral animal*, at least potentially, but how this is exemplified is culturally conditioned. I call these general principles, which both humanists and atheists, theists and nonbelievers share, the "common moral decencies." They are obligatory if the social group is to survive. What I find puzzling is why Swinburne abandons experience and reflection by his leap of faith, based on his acceptance of Christian revelation. Aquinas's distinction between natural and revealed theology can no longer be accepted today; although Aquinas attempted to demonstrate the existence of God by means of the famous Five Ways, revelation, he said, was itself based on faith. Aquinas did not have the benefit, as we do today, of biblical criticism, which has submitted claims of revelation to careful scholarly and scientific examination.[6]

Today we are in a post–biblical criticisms period that has taken over two centuries to develop. I am referring to the effort to examine biblical claims meticulously to see if they can be corroborated by careful historical, linguistic, archaeological, and scientific investigation. Suffice it to say that I find the supposedly inerrant and sweeping claims of the New Testament about Jesus' divinity to be highly doubtful. The New Testament evidence for Jesus' birth, ministry, and resurrection is not corroborated by a sufficient number of reliable witnesses. None of the authors of the four canonical Gospels (Matthew, Mark, Luke, and John) knew Jesus directly. Indeed if you read the four Gospels side-by-side you find contradictory accounts of the story. Similarly, Paul did not know Jesus directly, except for an alleged encounter on the road to Damascus (which, if true, can be read today as a kind of epileptic seizure). In any case, the New Testament is based on second- and third-hand testimony. There is no independent historical confirmation of its account of the life of Jesus. The resurrection of Jesus, which Swinburne accepts at face value, is a crucial claim for the special divinity of Christ. But it is highly doubtful on evidential grounds. The Gospels are tales of fiction written by propagandists for a faith after the alleged "miracles" occurred; and there is no independent corroboration by external literature, which would be required in any historical study—all the more so for the Jesus story, for extraordinary claims require strong proof, and we hardly have that for Jesus. This is compounded if we investigate how the Bible was collected.[7] There are many apocryphal books that were excluded from the original Gospels by the Nicene Council in the fourth century, largely for political reasons. Similarly the historical accounts in the Hebrew Bible are highly questionable, to say the least; they are buried by the sands of time, written by political ideological authors much later for their own purposes.

The same thing can be said of the Qur'an. The claim that Mohammad received revelations from Gabriel is likewise doubtful. Quranic scholars have examined how the Qur'an was written and they have discovered that there were many versions of the Qur'an. Moreover, the historical testimony of Muhammad's companions as recorded in the Hadith is exaggerated, extrapolated, and dubious. Thus Islamic revelation does not provide a credible case that Allah or Gabriel proclaimed moral truths for mankind.[8]

The three classical Abrahamic religions are not so much "the word of God" as the words of humans later contrived to justify the articles of faith. The spiritual-political-moral yearnings of ancient nomadic-rural peoples can no longer be accepted simply on the basis of faith. The fact that messages from on high appear in the Bible or Qur'an is no evidence that divine moral commandment had been received nor that they should be obeyed in every epoch.

I should add that we have had ample opportunity to examine the emergence of the new religions of the nineteenth century, such as those expressed in the Book of Mormon and the "revelations" of Mary Baker Eddy (Christian Science) or Mary Ellen White (Seventh-Day Adventists) and other alleged prophets — similarly for the appearance of new religious cults in the twentieth century, many of which draw upon popular urban legend and are derived from paranormal, space-age, and psychic claims. What we have learned is the fallibility of so-called eyewitness testimony, especially when transmitted second-and third-hand. Many revelatory claims are accepted because charismatic individuals possessing powers of persuasion and suggestion and artificially using trickery and deception have recruited gullible believers to swallow the new creed as true. I have called this "nincompoopery," and it applies to new faiths as well as the old. Magical thinking was widespread before the dawn of science and continues today.[9]

In the light of this I find Richard Swinburne's acceptance of the specific commandments of Jesus, for example, on divorce and other alleged quotations from the New Testament highly questionable.[10] Likewise for St. Paul's statement that the duty of wives is to "obey their husbands."[11] How can the views that were held in a prescientific, patriarchal society be appealed to in order to justify moral positions today? References to the ancient sacred literature do not respond to the basic humanist principles that women are equal in dignity and value and should enjoy the same rights of self-determination as men, nor do they overthrow the civic virtues of democracy, widely accepted today, or the Universal Declaration of Human Rights.

What I find contradictory is that Swinburne is willing to go beyond moral experience and reflection used to establish what he considers to be essential universal truths, by his acceptance of biblical injunctions. I find this resort to revelation especially disconcerting. Swinburne recognizes that many religions — Christianity, Judaism, and Islam — draw on revelation from on high either by God himself or his prophets. For the long history of the three Abrahamic religions, the original claims were beyond scrutiny. These were indeed accepted on the basis of faith; an examination of their roots was inaccessible for millennia. They cannot be assumed today at face value; and that is why I find the effort to invoke God to justify certain moral commandments highly questionable. Swinburne accepts the New Testament because he considers the resurrection a miracle. In my view, it is indeed based on a miracle. To paraphrase Hume, the willingness of believers to accept miracles without adequate evidence or in spite of evidence to the contrary, is *indeed* a miracle, since it subverts all of our faculties of understanding.[12]

3.

I have attempted thus far in my response to show why I think theists are mistaken in the belief that God provides adequate foundation for morality. The main reason for this, of course, is that I am skeptical of the counterfactual claim that *if* God exists, *then* these necessary moral truths may be deduced from him. So I begin with the antecedent, for we do not have sufficient evidence or reason to believe that God exists.

Indeed, I submit that the entire system of theist faith is a human construction—woven out of credulous human imagination, institutionalized historically, its beliefs indoctrinated and dissent suppressed. Belief in God and God himself are *human*, not divine, and so we have basically two human value systems competing. It is not God versus Man, as we are so often admonished by theists, but two human systems at loggerheads. The difference is that theists have claimed that theirs was different because it was divinely inspired—whereas I submit that this is the great deception, and that both are human, all too human!

It is difficult to see how religious traditions today, which focus on a God whose prophets or emissaries are confined to the planet Earth, can ignore the discoveries of Edwin P. Hubble (1889–1953) and other astronomers, that the distances of nebulae are far greater than heretofore conceived. The universe as viewed by contemporary science is expanding, with billions of galaxies and star systems and billions more planets beyond our solar system. How puny the classical religions of the past are, given their grounding in pre-Copernican, pre-Darwinian, and pre-Hubbleian revolutions. The cosmic scene we are exploring is a magnificent spectacle to behold, far greater in grandeur than Moses on Mount Sinai, Jesus on Calvary, or Muhammad in the caves and mountains near Mecca. The appropriate response is one of awe and astonishment at the vastness of the cosmos. The effort to read in God as an anthropomorphic person (theism) who takes on human form and communicates with selected prophets in the past is the height of conceit, one that is partial to the human species on the planet Earth. This only magnifies the anthropocentric bias of the ancient religions that still persists—fantasies based on the limited cosmologies of their day.

Where do we then start in the dispute between theism and atheism? I do not accept the agenda of the supernaturalists that the starting point is God. The classical philosophical arguments of Aristotle (or Aquinas) for the existence of God were based on the science of an earlier period and are inconclusive today. They were introduced before the growth of modern science, which is able to develop hypotheses and theories about the world and test them experimentally. What seemed inscrutable to the ancient mind were natural disasters, comets, eclipses, volcanic eruptions, famine, and disease. All these phenomena now can be accounted for by the discovery of causal explanations. This is the starting point for the *naturalist,* a *methodological* commitment to the use of the hypothetical inductive-deductive method of inquiry. A controversial issue today contrasts the difference between the Darwinian theory of natural selection and that of intelligent design. The former presents empirically testable hypotheses, the latter does not. The naturalistic account begins with nature, the experienced world as we find it, and it seeks to work out explanatory theories that account for the diversity of the species and their extinction. In scientific research, if we cannot find testable hypotheses, we need to suspend judgment, the position of the skeptic.

Now the question we are discussing in this volume is whether atheists who reject the traditional God of monotheism can be good. The answer, of course, depends on which kind of atheism you're talking about. There are varieties of unbelief and many of them have not focused on ethical questions, much the same as there are varieties of theism and different conceptions of morality. Accordingly, I begin with secular humanism, not atheism. It is secular because it is nonreligious, and *it is humanist because of its focus on ethics*.

4.

In the remaining pages of this section I wish to sketch a modified naturalistic ethical theory, which I could not do in the debate, given the limits of time. Much of this of course will be without elaboration. I should point out that not all secular humanists will agree with the views herein outlined. Secular humanism is not an ipse dixit ("thus saith the secular humanist") and there is some diversity of views, though we generally agree that one can be good without God.

The first point that I wish to emphasize is that we need to begin with *value as the broader category, not simply moral value*. Ever since the nineteenth century, philosophers, economists, social scientists, biologists, and psychologists have focused on the problem of value. The term "value" refers to the objects that humans (and other sentient beings) prefer. The bone has value for the puppy, the worm for the bird, the commodity for the human being. Value is "the object of any interest," according to Ralph Barton Perry.[13] This is a naturalistic account relative to human interests, needs, and wants. The fact that someone wants or desires something does not necessarily make it good or right. Nevertheless, preferential behavior is the bedrock of human value, which we later can and do evaluate critically.

Second, closely related to value is *valuing, a selective behavioral process* whereby a person (or organism) strives to appropriate goals. Humans like or desire, prize or cherish, many objectives; we prefer some and shun others. We engage in conative processes of acquiring, using, and consuming them. The full range of values includes *instrumental values* (desired because of what they lead to, e.g., vitamins are for good health) and *intrinsic values* (good for their own sake, e.g., orgasmic pleasure). There are *economic values* sought after in the marketplace (produced, distributed, advertised, consumed), *aesthetic values* (prized because of their beauty, tone, color, shape, form), and *moral values* (e.g., decency, honesty, integrity, etc.). Human beings value a wide range of objects and activities. These often are idiosyncratic (e.g., I like potatoes, you like tomatoes, etc.). Morality seeks to grade or rank values for the individual person on a scale of desirability. Competing value systems in the community lead to a quest for adjudication of differences, finding some better or worse and defining general principles to decide between them.

Third, here we enter into a process of *valuation* and *evaluation*, in which cognition plays a role. Human beings need to make selections between different options. How to choose among alternative values is an ongoing daily exercise. Thus, *decision making is involved in virtually all human endeavors*. Often it is a problem of better or worse on a comparative scale rather than simply good, bad, right, or wrong, and we make prudential choices.

Fourth, e*motion, passion, and feeling enters into virtually all decision-making valuation processes*, though of special significance is the relationship to cognition, thought, and reason. We need to deal with the whole person in whom reason and emotion are intertwined; for what the person likes or dislikes is an essential component of his or her selective process of choosing. In one sense his or her personality traits or states of character define who or what is preferred (e.g., some people are addicted to alcohol, others like sports, religious rituals, musical concerts, or intellectual pursuits). Human societies come to emphasize and encourage some values, which take on higher moral significance, and they discourage, forbid, or enjoin others as demeaning or ignoble.

All of the above aspects of human behavior can be studied empirically. It takes "moral values" out of the abstract clouds and provides some natural bio-somatic, psychosocio-genic phenomena capable of being studied scientifically. Moral values clothed in God-talk are twice removed from flesh-and-bones, blood-and-guts human experience and behavior.

Fifth, there is a good deal of evidence from science that human beings and the social groups in which they live tend to *develop moral standards* whereby certain forms are praised and encouraged, and others denigrated and rejected. Sharing similar basic needs, humans come to reject those forms of behavior that are destructive of the social fabric and they tend to esteem those that enable the group to survive, function, and even flourish. Over the long stretch of the history of *Homo sapiens*, humans have evolved moral tendencies or potentialities that motivate them to value certain forms of conduct and to condemn those they deem harmful. These concern common human problems: the relationship between the sexes, the caring and education of children, the gathering and distribution of food and water, the search for shelter, the treatment of the sick and elderly, the relationship to other groups that are encountered, the need to defend themselves from threats from wild animals or from marauding individuals or tribes, and so forth. Thus many claim that there are similar cross-cultural patterns that function to satisfy basic biogenic and sociogenic needs of individuals and their social groups. We of course recognize that there is cultural relativity in the types of dress preferred, food consumed, and other cultural artifacts; nonetheless there is a core of moral standards or virtues, which I have called "the common moral decencies." These denote universal (or general) principles that people recognize that they ought to abide by, though there may be exceptions. Many thinkers have postulated a common human nature (Aristotle) and stages of moral growth and development (Piaget, Kohlberg[14]). I am here referring to empirical data. Is this the "ontology" that Craig demands? No, as I said, I am dubious of such language since I find it to be speculative. I am simply presenting a naturalistic interpretation of the human species functioning in the world, and it is based on the empirical sciences of biology, genetics, neuroscience, psychology, and the social sciences.

Sixth, general moral principles are enculturated by education, conditioned by custom, and passed on from generation to generation (in the form of *memes*). They are codified by law and sanctified by religion. Every effort is made to educate character in the young so that they express socially approved virtuous conduct. These have, I submit, both biogenic and sociogenic sources.

A brief catalogue of the *common moral decencies* follows. There are no doubt still others that can be added.

- *Integrity*. We ought to tell the truth, keep promises, be sincere and honest.
- *Trustworthiness*. We should show fidelity to our friends, relatives, and neighbors in the community at large; we should be dependable, reliable, and responsible toward others who depend on us.
- *Benevolence*. We should manifest a good will toward other persons. We should avoid malfeasance, harming or injuring others (do not kill, torture, or abuse others). We should avoid malfeasance to public or private property (do not steal or destroy property that is not yours). Sexual relations should be based on mutual consent between adults (do not coerce or rape, do not abuse children). We should strive for a beneficent attitude (kindness, sympathy, compassion). We should assist where we can in alleviating another person's pain and suffering. We should help increase where we can the sum of goods for others to share.
- *Fairness*. We ought to show gratitude to others and hold them accountable for their conduct. We should seek justice and equity. We should manifest tolerance, be cooperative, seek to negotiate any differences peacefully, and work out compromises wherever possible.

Deontological intuitionists think that ethical principles are self-evident to a rational person and that they do not need be proved. Some scientists say that our capacity to recognize them is instinctive.[15] This would be similar to the human capacity for languages. Perhaps this is an oversimplification, for they are not recognized without some measure of education and enculturation. They are tested pragmatically by their consequences (a society that flouts them cannot function very well); they may be discovered by our cognitive faculties, but they are deeply infused by emotions—such as empathy and caring for others—and this means the capacity for altruistic acts.[16] They become in time so important that one cannot ignore them easily, so there is some sense of their obligatory appeal. Although not absolute, they are general and we have a responsibility in principle to follow them except when they conflict with other prima facie general moral principles and values. In any case, I submit that they are not God-given, but are rooted in both our biogenetic evolution and social-cultural civilizing processes. On the contrary, they are considered "sacred" because they are deemed so important. Perhaps they have their genesis in the mothering or parenting care needed to nurture the young. This distinctive behavior is found in other species: Even the most ferocious wolves and lions care for their young. In humans it is extended during the long period of tutelage.[17] Granted that some individuals may lack a moral sense, they may become sociopaths or psychopaths, indifferent to the feelings of others. They have a very low MQ (moral quotient). Hence, every community needs to hold offenders of its cherished principles accountable, and they are punished and/or rehabilitated. The problem with the moral sense by itself is that it competes with other powerful impulses in the human breast: the competition for sexual partners, the lust for personal power, wealth, ambition, glory. There is thus a conflict between decency (the social virtues) and self-interest. Konrad Lorenz postulates the instinct for aggression, particularly among males, and ways to overcome it by sports, the arts, and other forms of substitution and sublimation.

Secular philosophers generally developed ethical ideals for the individual, and they concentrate on maximizing good—which is related to happiness. Some have defended self-interest theories (e.g., libertarians); others hedonism (maximizing of pleasure and the avoidance of pain), and still others self-realization theories (in which the fulfillment of a person's talents are sources of the highest satisfaction).

Generally, secular naturalists have focused on improving human life by seeking to actualize happiness both for the individual and the social good. In regard to the individual, humanists have combined hedonism and self-realization: The good life we seek is concerned with creative fulfillment and joyful satisfaction throughout a complete life. In contemporary affluent societies this leads to *exuberance*, in which the widest range of pleasurable activities is sought. To use John Stuart Mill's language, both the higher and lower plea-sures are desirable—both the biological pleasures of food, drink, sex, *and* the pleasures of intellect, art, and moral deeds. Both self-interest and altruism are essential to a fully developed person. Here the *fullness of life* is the model.

To achieve a full life the individual needs to develop certain *excellences*.[18] These include

- good health (adequate nutrition and exercise)
- self-control and moderation
- self-respect and self-esteem
- high motivation
- the capacity for love (orgasmic, filial, friendship, collegiality)
- caring for other sentient beings
- commitment to a beloved cause(s)
- a sense of joie de vivre
- the achievement motive
- creativity, exuberance

One needs to balance one's commitment to others (family, children, par-ents, lovers, friends) in the community of face-to-face social interaction *and* the community of humankind (on the planetary scale) with one's commitment to oneself to lead a satisfying and fulfilling life. The basic principles that hu-manists find compelling are a generalized *good will* to others and oneself (i.e., to do the best we can), the use of *reason* (to solve problems, to overcome ob-stacles), the *courage* to do so without fear and trembling (the Promethean au-dacity to succeed), and *caring* for other human beings.

In this regard, *altruism* is essential for moral development.

- An altruistic act is carried out for the benefit of other person(s), without any primary expectation of reward and perhaps at some expense or sacrifice to oneself.
- A basic rule of ethical rationality is that we ought to mitigate human suf-fering and sorrow, and to increase the sum of human good and happiness, providing it is possible to do so. An impartial ethical rationality should thus apply to all human beings, who have equal dignity and value.
- Some feelings of empathy seem essential for altruism to flower.

It is apparent that we cannot reduce morality to pure rationality alone— much as philosophers tend to do—for human beings are more than rational animals. This caveat is similar to objections voiced about "economic man," that is, the view that a rational person in the marketplace makes decisions on the basis of self-interest in order to maximize economic gain. The "hidden hand" of the free market, according to Adam Smith,[19] is a dynamic model that engenders profit, productivity, and growth. Unfortunately, consumers and entrepreneurs do not always behave in this way, for advertisers can condition consumers to buy what they want but do not need, and an individual entrepreneur's quest for power and glory may outweigh the desire for gain.

The economic model surely has some explanatory value, but it is not infallible, and there are many deviations from it. Similarly, the ideal "moral person" is not perfectly rational, making choices based on the overriding or strongest reason, for passions, desires, feelings, attractions, revulsions, antipathies, and lusts intervene. I know of enough cases of married philosophers, family men with children and well-established careers, who fell in love with a student and abandoned everything for passion, accepting the scandal that it often provoked. (Similarly for theologians who bugger young lads.) So, where is the perfectly rational person in decision making? I am not of course condoning such behavior, only pointing out the difficulty of acting with pure rationality.

That is why we need to leave room for both cognitive thoughts *and* emotional attitudes in dealing with how human beings actually function. Daniel Goleman has called this emotional intelligence—the capacity to express, but also to moderate, our competing attitudes and desires.[20] This involves both self-control and compassion. I think that some measure of objectivity is still possible within a person's emotional life, given who and what we actually are as blood-and-guts humans throbbing with feelings. I call this *objective relativism* (not objective subjectivism), for our choices are relative to the values that an individual or society cherishes. Nevertheless, they are amenable to some weighing of rational interests and passionate desires and testing them by their consequences. I think that Plato's depiction of three horses pulling the chariot of the soul is rather insightful, since we need to balance desire, pleasure, and reason and it is not the case that pure reason is always the lead horse able to control the other two. Some individuals are able to express their emotions and satisfy them yet balance them rationally with other desires and needs, especially in relationship with other human beings.

One thing that is intriguing about the theists who have contributed to this volume is that I detect a strong whiff of Platonism, for God functions as "the idea of the Good," providing a model for an allegedly higher plane of an abstract Form. Packed into the idea of God are their own moral predilections. The idea of a most holy, omniscient, omnipotent, beneficent, and just being is infused with moral qualities. That is why philosophers such as Dewey[21] have recommended that we need to take account of the immediacies of experience and the things that individuals prize, praise, enjoy, like, want, cherish—or, if you will, the prima facie *given* values that we bring into a situation of choice. Values are based on our interests and desires, but valuations can modify and balance them in the light of reason. What you should decide depends on who you are, how the socio-cultural climate has conditioned your likes and dislikes—and these need to be taken into account and transformed into appraisals by cognitive inquiry. Prizing can be modified by reflective evaluation and perhaps reconstructed, although this may be difficult for many individuals who are steadfast in their proclivities and attitudes and refuse to budge. Something similar is true of the social-moral patterns of a society, its customs, habits, traditions, and laws—to which children have been conditioned. If we are going to get anywhere, particularly in pluralist societies where many value systems compete, we need to find common ground, and the cognitive reconstruction of our values is very important. This is often difficult to achieve. But it can be and has been done by persistent argument and persuasion.

One way to overturn these ancient creeds is by an appeal to reason and/or the lure of enticing new ideals and values. Thus we must in any society confront the old with the new; established moral principles are challenged by daring new ones that may be reformist or even revolutionary in strength. The campaign against slavery was considered radical in its day, as was the suffragist movement for equal rights for women. Today, many conservatives consider "the right of privacy" a shock. It has suddenly emerged to compete with orthodox prohibitions about so many things, such as the right to euthanasia, abortion, and same-sex marriage, all of which horrify traditionalists.

5.

I have introduced the concept of a *valuation base,*[22] which I submit is relevant in any process of decision making and can help us to decide. The valuation base is relative to an existing individual or actual society. It includes both prescriptive values, norms, standards, and principles *and* value-neutral facts, means, conditions, and consequences. What is in the base?

First, the *preexisting prizings*, the immediacies of feelings, desires, attitudes, the well-established values, whether idiosyncratic or common, that we bring with us in any situation, which may either be reinstated or modified by a process of inquiry.

Second, the *rules, norms,* customs, or standards of the social milieu, which have been institutionalized by education, reinforced by law, sanctified by religion, and encouraged by social approbation or disapprobation.

Third, the prima facie *general principles* or rules to which we are committed—the common moral decencies—which compete with new principles, such as the "civic virtues of democracy," "the right of privacy," and "human dignity," which today are being extended on a planetary scale to all members of the human family. It is when there is a conflict that the common moral decencies may need to be balanced with new radicalized or revolutionary principles of ethics, such as in the battle for equal rights, which we are currently experiencing. Here we need to negotiate compromises.

Fourth, of crucial significance is the need to consider the *facts of the case*, the circumstances before us. The individual or social group needs to investigate these in order to make a wise choice.

Fifth, factual knowledge includes an exploration of scientific knowledge, not only about what is the case but what are *the causes* that are relevant to the conditions that we face.

Sixth, we need to take into consideration the *goals* that we wish to achieve, as well as *the means to fulfill them*. We need to ask what is possible and feasible as ways of realizing our ends—the expansion of technological means at our disposal in the modern world (improved travel, communications, health, longevity, etc.) has transformed human life from repeating ancient homilies to adopting dynamic new styles to fulfill new opportunities for achieving a better life.

Seventh is the importance of *moral education for children*, the need to expand their horizons, to develop and cultivate the capacities for moral thinking.[23] Every society needs to enculturate desirable traits of character and instruct children to appreciate virtue and empathy, but it also needs to teach them how to be self-reliant and how to think clearly.

Eighth, an important criterion of adequacy is the *consequences* of our actions, which spill out into the real world once our choices are implemented. This enables us to modify our decisions by seeing their results, and we may generalize what we have learned for similar situations in the future.

Ninth, one further criterion that we use in appraising principles and values is their *consistency* with values and standards we already accept, particularly when we wish to extend human rights and reform inconsistency in treatment by putting it under a common principle.

Undoubtedly, there are other considerations besides those enumerated that may be relevant to a valuational base. For example, in society we need to take into account other people's attitudes in the community and recognize the difficulty often of persuading them to change. We need also to confront economic and political realities.

The choices people make are about conduct and action, not about propositions about practice on the meta-level. They concern real behavior in the world. The key point that I want to suggest here is what I have called the role of *act-duction* in such reasoning. Ethical choices are a function of the unique, deeply private tastes and desires, preferences and wishes of each person. The choices we make are also related to the actual historical, social, and cultural framework in which we exist, including the social mores and laws of our society. Thus life in ancient Egypt, Palestine, Greece, or Rome differs from life in China and Japan, Europe and the Americas. And modern cultures are far different from their ancient precursors.

Ethical knowledge has a degree of probabilism and fallibilism attached to it. We need to recognize that there are alternative lifestyles and a wide variety of human values and norms. This presupposes some comprehension of the fragility of the human condition and some skepticism about our ultimate perfectibility. Thus, ethical wisdom recognizes that life is full of uncertainties. In one sense, it is permeated by indeterminacies.

All of the contingent differences must be put into the valuational base, and they influence the decisions we make. The choice we select is accordingly relative to the given de facto prizings and valuations, customs and laws, institutional constraints and demands of the times. Accordingly there is an intrinsic contextuality and relativity of all choices, for they are always related to specific individuals and civilizations. The relativity of choice is *endemic* to the ethical life. Let me reiterate that there is a difference between totally subjective and capricious choices (as let us say Nero was wont to make) and those *that are informed by knowledge and selected after a careful process of reflective inquiry*. There are ethical qualities that stand out and from which we may learn and generalize. That is why we can empathize with Othello being overtaken by jealousy and anger or Macbeth by the lust for power. There is a kind of eloquent reflection on the human condition as people wrestle with moral dilemmas. And there are certain courses of action that seem appropriate and others that are profoundly flawed, even tragic. It is not simply a deductive or inductive model that we use, or even abduction (used to formulate new hypotheses, according to Peirce). Undoubtedly deduction, induction, and abduction each have a role to play in the process of inquiry. But what is preeminently vital in formulating judgments and practice upon which we act is *act-duction*—namely, *the course of action that I will embark upon at the conclusion of a process of inquiry*. The act plays itself out in the real world for everyone to see; it has an impact on behavioral conduct. The process of evaluation and appraisal is about the appropriateness of particular actions in a specific context or case, and in similar situations like that.

The salient point is that ethics is relative to life as lived by specific persons or societies, and it is rooted in historical-social conditions and concrete behavior. Ethical principles are thus in the mid-range; they are proximate, not ultimate. We do not reason about the moral life *in abstracto* and hope to make sense of it; we always begin *here* and *now*, with *this* individual in *this* society faced with *these* choices. The basic subject matter of ethics is action and conduct.

Rarely when we engage in ethical inquiry do we begin at the beginning—except perhaps in crisis/existential situations where we are forced to examine our root values. Rather, we find ourselves in the midst of practical demands and conflicts, trying to make sense of the web of decisions and behavior in which we are entangled. And included in our nexus is the considerable fund of normative data that we bring with us—the things we cherish or esteem, or conversely detest or reject, and the principles to which we are committed. Ethical inquiry is initiated when there is some puzzle about what we should do or some conflict between competing values and norms. It is here that skeptical inquiry is vital, for it is the open mind in operation that is willing to examine our values and principles and to select those that seem approximate. The ethical inquirer in the best sense is committed to the use of reflective intelligence, in which one is able to define and clarify one's values and principles and to search for alternative courses of action that seem most fitting within the context of inquiry.

I am afraid that the deductive model does not suffice in the real world—that is, simply deducing obligations and therefore actions from universal principles or inflexible moral values. Nor is the inductive model adequate. We cannot generalize principles from the facts of the case, nor deduce what ought to be the case from a set of facts, though the facts are relevant in formulating valuations and actions. The position that I am here defending is a *modified form of ethical naturalism*. I do not think that this reduces us to subjective caprice, where there are no standards for evaluation. There surely are, but these need to deal with the sticky factors in the complex situations we face—the contingent, pluralistic, and bizarre facts in real life that often are stranger than fiction. What I am pointing to is the need to consider a wide range of factors in formulating a decision: values, norms, rights, means-ends, facts, causes, and effects.

This is sometimes criticized as "situation ethics," and people complain that therefore "anything goes." Although what we do always has a frame of reference, we nonetheless can generalize and we can and do develop reliable guides for action in similar situations. We need to make wise choices and develop knowledge relative to the situations in which we find ourselves. I have come to the realization that philosophers are often little help in concrete cases of disagreement, and that metaphilosophy, though useful to professors of philosophy, hardly helps ordinary folks to resolve moral dilemmas.

What I conclude from this is that we either need to transform philosophy from "the love of wisdom" (read to mean "the love of metawisdom" in ethics)—once removed from the life of action or conduct—to the *practice* of wisdom, not simply practical wisdom. I have introduced a new term to designate philosophical practitioners, or if you will, *eupraxsophers*, namely those who are skilled in the "*practice* of good wisdom" and can offer competent advice.[24] This is like competent medical practice or effective psychological therapy in clinical psychology, or a skilled teacher actually challenging students to learn in the classroom. Therefore philosophers in the public square who know about the issues firsthand, and are aware of competing values and principles, need to enter the public square and get their hands messy in concrete cases—and they must be willing to make actual recommendations. Unfortunately, philosophers in the classroom today more often than not present students with all sides of a question and leave it to the students to make up their own minds. So they often revert to their prejudices.

Yet if so, philosophy is deficient, and what we need is a new craft, practiced by *eupraxsophers*, practitioners in the art and science of decision making, men and women with some expertise and reflective experience, able to shed light on alternative courses of action and also able to recommend (not demand, legislate, or dictate) courses of action. Thus, *act-duction* has the inquirer examine all the features of a case to recommend what appears most reasonable and attractive, and it is this kind of practical valuational wisdom that enables individuals in society to make wise choices. Again, it is not simply on the meta-level, but in the normative domain of actual values and principles.

In this sense there are degrees of objectivity, and our values and principles that are submitted to scrutiny in the light of inquiry are comparatively better than those that have not passed the test of both rationality and practical experience. Thus one can be good without belief in God. And such objective inquiry, I submit, is more reasonable than appealing to the premise of the theist, grounded in the final analysis in faith.

Some degree of skepticism is a necessary antidote to all forms of moral dogmatism. We are continually surrounded by self-righteous moralists who claim that they have the Absolute Truth or Moral Virtue or Piety, and they wish to impose their convictions on all others. The best antidote for this is some skepticism and a willingness to engage in ethical inquiry, not only about the moral zeal of others, but about *our own*, especially if we are tempted to translate the results of our own ethical inquiries into commandments. The epistemological theory presented here, and the methodological principles of skeptical inquiry, have important moral implications. For in recognizing our own fallibility we thereby can learn to *tolerate* other human beings and to appreciate a plurality of lifestyles. If we are prepared to engage in cooperative ethical inquiry, then perhaps we are better prepared to allow other individuals and groups some measure of liberty to pursue their own preferred lifestyles. If we are able to live and let live, then this can best be achieved in a free and open democratic society. Where we differ, we should try to negotiate our divergent views and perhaps reach common ground, and if this is impractical, we should at least attempt to compromise for the sake of our common interests. The method of ethical inquiry requires some intelligent and informed examination of our own values, as well as the values of others. Here we can attempt to modify attitudes by the appeal to cognitive beliefs and to reconstruct them by an examination of the relevant evidence. Such a give-and-take of constructive criticism is essential for a harmonious society. In learning to appreciate different conceptions of the good life, we are able to expand our own dimensions of moral awareness.

We might live in a better world if *inquiry* were to replace faith; *delibera-tion*, passionate commitment; and *education and persuasion*, violence and force. We should be aware of the powers of intelligent behavior, but also the limitations of human beings and of the need to mitigate the cold and indiffer-ent intellect with the empathic heart. Thus I conclude that within the ethical life we are capable of developing a body of melioristic principles and values and a method of coping with problems intelligently. There is a form of *eu-praxia*, or good practice, that we can learn to appreciate and live by, and this can be infused with *sophia*. When our ethical judgments are based on ethical inquiry, they are more apt to express the highest reaches of excellence and no-bility, and of civilized human conduct. Although the ethics of secular human-ism developed in this chapter may not satisfy those who hunger for salvation, it nonetheless has much to commend for those seeking the good life for them-selves and their fellow human beings.

NOTES

Author's note. The division of the book into three parts deserves some comment. The first part is a transcript of a debate between William Lane Craig and me. This debate was sponsored by the Bonchek Institute for Rational Thought and Inquiry, since re-named the Bonchek Institute for Reason and Science in a Liberal Democracy. It was held at Franklin and Marshall College in Lancaster, Pennsylvania, on October 24, 2001, before some 1,700 students, faculty, and laypeople from the community, only a short time after the September 11, 2001, Twin Towers tragedy. There was consider-able emotional response from the audience in attendance—much of the debate, at least for my part, was extemporaneous, especially in response to Mr. Craig's argu-ments and rebuttals. I should point out that I did not formulate the question of the de-bate, "Is goodness without God good enough?" I thought that it was vague and am-biguous and I stated from the start that my interpretation of the question was, "Can those who do not believe in God be good?" I, of course, argued affirmatively.

The debate was not intended for professional philosophers, but for the general pub-lic. Sometime after the debate, I was asked by members of the faculty at Franklin and Marshall College whether I would agree to its publication, and I accepted. The plan was to invite several prominent philosophers to comment. I was informed that Mr. Craig and I could edit the language for publication, which I did. I was glad to participate in the second round because it has given me the opportunity to respond to Mr. Craig's argu-ments and to those of the philosophers and theologians who contributed to this volume and also, I might add, elaborate on my own case for secular humanism.

The editors of this book apparently were not involved in the original plan of the de-bate, and so what follows is after the fact. It is seven years since the original debate was held! I am intrigued that of the new essays included in this volume, four are by theists and three by nontheists, and that the two editors are theists, so the match is rather unbalanced. Nevertheless, I agreed to take part in the follow-up dialogue in order to clarify my position.

1. See H. A. Prichard, "Does Moral Philosophy Rest on a Mistake?" *Mind* 21 (1921): 21–37.

2. Leviticus 18:22: "Do not lie with a man as one lies with a woman; that is detestable." Leviticus 20:13: "If a man lies with a man as one lies with a woman, both of them have done what is detestable. They must be put to death; their blood will be on their own heads." Romans 1:27: "And likewise also the men, leaving the natural use of the woman, burned in their lust one toward another; men with men working that which is unseemly, and receiving in themselves that recompense of their error which was meet."

3. See my books *The Transcendental Temptation* (Amherst, N.Y.: Prometheus Books, 1986); *The New Skepticism* (Buffalo, N.Y.: Prometheus Books, 1992); *Forbidden Fruit* (Amherst, N.Y.: Prometheus Books, 1988).

4. Please see my book *The Fullness of Life* (New York: Horizon Press, 1973).

5. W. D. Ross, *The Right and the Good* (New York: Oxford University Press, 1930). W. D. Ross called them "prima facie duties," as distinct from "actual" or "concrete duties."

6. Among some of the key figures here are John Dominic Crossan, Gerd Ludemann, Elaine Pagels, David Friedrich Strauss, Rudolph Bultmann, Ernest Renan, and Albert Schweitzer.

7. See the work of the Jesus Seminar, which claims that there are very few quotations from Jesus that can be authenticated, and of the Jesus Project, which thinks that serious questions can be raised about the existence of Jesus.

8. See the works of Ibn Warraq: *Why I Am Not a Muslim* (Amherst, N.Y.: Prometheus Books, 1995); *What the Qur'an Really Says* (Amherst, N.Y.: Prometheus Books, 2002); *The Quest for the Historical Muhammad* (Amherst, N.Y.: Prometheus Books, 2000); *The Origins of the Qur'an* (Amherst, N.Y.: Prometheus Books, 1998); *Which Qur'an?* (Amherst, N.Y.: Prometheus Books, 2007). See also Robert Spencer, *The Myth of Islamic Tolerance* (Amherst, N.Y.: Prometheus Books, 2005); Andrew G. Boston, *The Legacy of Jihad* (Amherst, N.Y.: Prometheus Books, 2005); John Wansbrough, *The Sectarian Milieu* (Amherst, N.Y.: Prometheus Books, 2006) and *Quranic Studies* (Amherst, N.Y.: Prometheus Books, 2004).

9. See the work of the Committee for the Scientific Investigation of Claims of the Paranormal; Paul Kurtz, ed., *Skeptical Odysseys* (Amherst, N.Y.: Prometheus Books, 2001); Kurtz, *Transcendental Temptation*.

10. Mark 10:9–12 records Jesus' teaching about divorce: "'What therefore God has joined together, let no man separate.' In the house the disciples began questioning Him about this again. And He said to them, 'Whoever divorces his wife and marries another woman commits adultery against her; and if she herself divorces her husband and marries another man, she is committing adultery.'" Matthew 5:32 says, "'But I say to you that everyone who divorces his wife, except for the reason of unchastity, makes her commit adultery; and whoever marries a divorced woman commits adultery.'"

11. Colossians 3:18 says, "Wives, be subject to your husbands, as is fitting in the Lord." 1 Peter 3:1 says, "In the same way, you wives, be submissive to your own husbands so that even if any of them are disobedient to the word, they may be won without a word by the behavior of their wives."

12. "Mere reason is insufficient to convince us of the veracity of a miracle. Whoever is moved by *faith* to assent to it, is conscious of a continued miracle in his own person, which subverts all the principles of his understanding, and gives him a determination to believe what is most contrary to custom and experience." David Hume, *An Enquiry concerning Human Understanding*, Section 10, "Of Miracles."

13. Ralph Barton Perry, *General Theory of Value* (New York: Longmans and Green, 1950).

14. Jean Piaget, *The Moral Judgment of the Child* (London: Kegan Paul, 1932); Lawrence Kohlberg, *The Psychology of Moral Development* (New York: Harper and Row, 1982).

15. For example, see Mark D. Hauser, *Moral Minds: How Nature Designed Our Universal Sense of Right and Wrong* (New York: HarperCollins, 2006).

16. There is a growing scientific literature that postulates that altruism has biological-genetic roots. See Elliott Sober and David Wilson, *Unto Others: The Evolution and Psychology of Unselfish Behavior* (Cambridge, Mass.: Harvard University Press, 1998).

17. E. O. Wilson has attempted to show these kinds of behavior in other species and the human species. See *Consilience: The Unity of Knowledge* (New York: Alfred Knopf, 1988).

18. For a discussion of these, see Paul Kurtz, *Embracing the Power of Humanism* (Lanham, Md.: Rowman & Littlefield, 2000).

19. Adam Smith, *The Wealth of Nations* (New York: Modern Library, 2000).

20. Daniel P. Goleman, *Emotional Intelligence* (New York: Bantam, 1995).

21. John Dewey, *Theory of Valuation* (Chicago: University of Chicago Press, 1939).

22. Kurtz, *New Skepticism*, chap. 9.

23. See the book by Stephen Law, *The War for Children's Minds* (London: Routledge, 2006).

24. Paul Kurtz, *Living without Religion: Eupraxsophy* (Amherst, N.Y.: Prometheus Books, 1989).

Further Reading

Adams, Robert Merrihew. *Finite and Infinite Goods*. New York: Oxford University Press, 1999.

——. *The Virtue of Faith and Other Essays in Philosophical Theology*. New York: Oxford University Press, 1987.

Antony, Louise M., ed. *Philosophers without Gods: Meditations on Atheism and the Secular Life*. New York: Oxford University Press, 2007.

Audi, Robert. *Religious Commitment and Secular Reason*. New York: Cambridge University Press, 2000.

Audi, Robert, and Nicholas Wolterstorff. *Religion in the Public Square*. Lanham, Md.: Rowman & Littlefield, 1996.

Beaty, Michael, Carlton Fisher, and Mark Nelson, eds. *Christian Theism and Moral Philosophy*. Macon, Ga.: Mercer University Press, 1998.

Cuneo, Terence, ed. *Religion in the Liberal Polity*. Notre Dame, Ind.: University of Notre Dame Press, 2005.

Hare, John. *God and Morality: A Philosophical History*. Malden, Mass.: Blackwell, 2007.

——. *God's Call: Moral Realism, God's Commands, and Human Autonomy*. Grand Rapids, Mich.: Eerdmans, 2000.

——. *The Moral Gap: Kantian Ethics, Human Limits, and God's Assistance*. New York: Oxford University Press, 1997.

——. *Why Bother Being Good? The Place of God in the Moral Life*. Downers Grove, Ill.: Intervarsity Press, 2002.

Helm, Paul, ed. *Divine Commands and Morality*. New York: Oxford University Press, 1981.

Kurtz, Paul. *Forbidden Fruit: The Ethics of Humanism*. Amherst, N.Y.: Prometheus, 1988.

——. *In Defense of Secular Humanism*. Amherst, N.Y.: Prometheus, 1983.

——. *Living without Religion: Eupraxophy*. Amherst, N.Y.: Prometheus, 1994.

Layman, C. Stephen. *The Shape of the Good: Christian Reflections on the Foundation of Ethics*. Notre Dame, Ind.: University of Notre Dame Press, 1991.

Martin, Michael. *Atheism, Morality, and Meaning*. Amherst, N.Y.: Prometheus, 2002.

Murphy, Mark C. *An Essay on Divine Authority*. Ithaca, N.Y.: Cornell University Press, 2002.

Nielsen, Kai. *Ethics without God*, rev. ed. Amherst, N.Y.: Prometheus Books, 1990.

Quinn, Philip. *Divine Commands and Moral Requirements*. New York: Oxford University Press, 1978.

———. *Essays in the Philosophy of Religion*, edited by Christian B. Miller. New York: Oxford University Press, 2006.

Rice, Hugh. *God and Goodness*. New York: Oxford University Press, 2000.

Rist, John. *Real Ethics: Rethinking the Foundations of Morality*. New York: Cambridge University Press, 2002.

Wainwright, William J. *Religion and Morality*. Burlington, Vt.: Ashgate, 2005.

Weithman, Paul J. *Religion and Contemporary Liberalism*. Notre Dame, Ind.: University of Notre Dame Press, 1997.

———, ed. *Religion and the Obligations of Citizenship*. New York: Cambridge University Press, 2002.

Wielenberg, Erik. *Value and Virtue in a Godless Universe*. New York: Cambridge University Press, 2005.

Zagzebski, Linda. *Divine Motivation Theory*. New York: Cambridge University Press, 2004.

About the Contributors

Louise Antony is professor of philosophy at the University of Massachusetts, Amherst. Her research interests include epistemology, the philosophy of mind, feminist theory, and the philosophy of language. Her numerous articles have appeared in such journals as *Ethics*, *Philosophical Review*, *Philosophical Studies*, *Philosophy and Phenomenological Research*, *Australasian Journal of Philosophy*, *Philosophical Issues*, *American Philosophical Quarterly*, *Metaphilosophy*, and *Hypatia*. She is coeditor of *Chomsky and His Critics* (with Norbert Hornstein, 2003), coeditor of *A Mind of One's Own: Feminist Essays on Reason and Objectivity* (with Charlotte Witt, 1993; second edition 2002), and, most recently, editor of *Philosophers without Gods* (2007).

William Lane Craig is research professor of philosophy at Talbot School of Theology, Biola University. His research interests include natural theology, the divine attributes, the philosophy of time, science and religion, ethical theory, the historical Jesus, and the resurrection of Jesus. He has published articles in such journals as *Journal of Philosophy*, *American Philosophical Quarterly*, *Philosophical Studies*, *Philosophy*, *British Journal for the Philosophy of Science*, *Faith and Philosophy*, and *Philosophia Christi*. His authored books include *The Kalam Cosmological Argument* (1979), *The Cosmological Argument from Plato to Leibniz* (1980), *The Historical Argument for the Resurrection of Jesus* (1984), *The Only Wise God* (1987), *Assessing the New Testament Evidence for the Resurrection of Jesus* (1989), *Divine Foreknowledge and Human Freedom* (1990), *Theism, Atheism, and Big Bang Cosmology* (with Quentin Smith, 1993), *Reasonable Faith* (1994), *God, Time, and Eternity* (2001), *Philosophical Foundations of a Christian Worldview* (with J. P. Moreland, 2003), *God? A Debate between a Christian and an Atheist* (with

Walter Sinnott-Armstrong, 2003), and *Creation out of Nothing* (with Paul Copan, 2004).

Robert K. Garcia is a Ph.D. candidate in the philosophy department at the University of Notre Dame. His research interests include metaphysics, the philosophy of mind, ethics, and the philosophy of religion.

John Hare is Noah Porter Professor of Philosophical Theology at Yale University. His research interests include contemporary ethical theory, the philosophy of religion, ancient and medieval philosophy, Kant, Kierkegaard, medical ethics, and international relations. He has authored numerous articles for such journals as *Medieval Philosophy and Theology*, *Faith and Philosophy*, *Journal of Philosophical Research*, *Ancient Philosophy*, *International Journal of Applied Ethics*, and *Phronesis.* He has authored several books on the topic of religion and morality, including *Plato's Euthyphro* (1981), *God's Call* (2001), *Why Bother Being Good?* (2002), *The Moral Gap* (1996), and *God and Morality* (2007).

Donald C. Hubin is professor of philosophy at Ohio State University. His research interests span a broad range of topics in ethics, including the nature of justice (especially distributive justice), the relationship between rationality and morality, and familial rights. He has authored numerous articles for such journals as *Noûs*, *Journal of Philosophy*, *Philosophical Studies*, *Analysis*, *Philosophy and Public Affairs*, *Journal of Law and Family Studies*, *Law and Philosophy*, *Economics and Philosophy*, *Canadian Journal of Philosophy*, *Cornell Journal of Law and Philosophy*, and *Philosophical Forum.* He is associate editor of the journal *Ethics*, and is currently at work on a book entitled *Parsing Paternity: Legal and Philosophical Foundations of Fatherhood.*

Nathan L. King is a Ph.D. candidate in the philosophy department at the University of Notre Dame. His research interests include epistemology, ethical theory, and the philosophy of religion.

Paul Kurtz is professor emeritus of philosophy at the State University of New York at Buffalo, founder and chairman of the Committee for the Scientific Investigation of Claims of the Paranormal, the Council for Secular Humanism, and Prometheus Books, and editor-in-chief of *Free Inquiry* magazine. He is a former copresident of the International Humanist and Ethical Union. He is a Fellow of the American Association for the Advancement of Science, and Humanist Laureate and president of the International Academy of Humanism. He has written numerous journal articles and is author or editor of many books, including *Forbidden Fruit: The Ethics of Humanism* (1987), *Living without Religion: Eupraxophy* (1994), *Toward a New Enlightenment: The Philosophy of Paul Kurtz* (1994), *Challenges to the Enlightenment* (edited with Timothy J. Madigan, 1994), *The Courage to Become: The Virtues of Humanism* (1997), *Skepticism and Humanism: The New Paradigm* (2000), *Embracing the Power of Humanism* (2000), *Humanist Manifesto 2000* (2000), *Skeptical Odysseys* (2001), *Skepticism and Humanism: The New Paradigm* (2001), *Science and Religion: Are They Compatible?* (2003), and *Science and Ethics* (edited, 2007).

C. Stephen Layman is professor of philosophy at Seattle Pacific University. His research interests include ethics and the philosophy of religion. He has published numerous articles in such journals as *Faith and Philosophy*, *International Journal for the Philosophy of Religion*, and *History of Philosophy Quarterly*. In addition, he is author of the following books: *The Shape of the Good: Christian Reflections on the Foundation of Ethics* (1991), *The Power of Logic* (1999, third edition 2005), and *Letters to Doubting Thomas: A Case for the Existence of God* (2007).

Mark C. Murphy is Fr. Joseph T. Durkin Professor of Philosophy at Georgetown University. His research interests include moral, political, and legal philosophy and the history of early modern philosophy. Murphy has published articles in *Noûs*, *Ethics*, *The Thomist*, *Philosophy and Public Affairs*, *American Philosophical Quarterly*, *Law and Philosophy*, *Archiv für Geschichte der Philosophie*, *Faith and Philosophy*, and elsewhere. He is coeditor (with Robert C. Solomon) of *What Is Justice?* (1990, second edition 1999), and editor of *Alasdair MacIntyre* (2003). His authored books include *Natural Law and Practical Rationality* (2001), *An Essay on Divine Authority* (2002), *Natural Law in Jurisprudence and Politics* (2006), and *Philosophy of Law: The Fundamentals* (2006).

Walter Sinnott-Armstrong is professor of philosophy and Hardy Professor of Legal Studies at Dartmouth College. His research interests include ethics, philosophy of law, epistemology, and informal logic. He has published numerous articles in such journals as *Philosophical Review*, *Analysis*, *Journal of Philosophy*, *Philosophy and Phenomenological Research*, *Australasian Journal of Philosophy*, *Philosophical Studies*, and *Journal of Cognitive Neuroscience*. He is editor of several books, including *Philosophy of Law: Classic and Contemporary Readings with Commentary* (with Frederick Schauer, 1996), *Moral Knowledge? New Readings in Moral Epistemology* (with Mark Timmons, 1996), *Rationality, Rules, and Ideals: Critical Essays on Bernard*

Gert's Moral Theory with Reply (with Robert Audi, 2002), *Pyrrhonian Skepticism* (2004), *Moral Psychology*, volumes 1–3 (2008), and *Interdisciplinary Core Philosophy: Ethics, Philosophical Issues* (with Ernest Sosa, 2008). He is author of *Moral Dilemmas* (1988), *God? A Debate between a Christian and an Atheist* (coauthored with William Lane Craig, 2003), *Understanding Arguments: An Introduction to Informal Logic* (coauthored with Robert J. Fogelin, seventh edition, 2005), and *Moral Skepticisms* (2006).

Richard Swinburne is emeritus Nolloth Professor of the Philosophy of the Christian Religion, University of Oxford; emeritus Fellow of Oriel College, Oxford; and a Fellow of the British Academy. His interests include all the central questions of philosophy, and the meaning and justification of the central claims of Christianity. His authored books include *The Coherence of Theism* (1977, revised edition 1993), *The Existence of God* (1979, second edition 2004), *Faith and Reason* (1981, second edition 2005), *The Evolution of the Soul* (1986, revised edition 1997), *Responsibility and Atonement* (1989), *Revelation* (1991, second edition 2007), *The Christian God* (1994), *Providence and the Problem of Evil* (1998), *Epistemic Justification* (2001), and *The Resurrection of God Incarnate* (2003). He is also the author of a shorter book summarizing his arguments for the existence of God, *Is There a God?* (1996), and a shorter book summarizing his arguments for Christianity, *Was Jesus God?* (2008).